Family, Labour and Trade in Western Kenya

Publications from the Centre for Development Research, Copenhagen

Family, Labour and Trade in Western Kenya

Per Kongstad
Mette Mönsted

Published by
Scandinavian Institute of African Studies, Uppsala 1980

Publications from the Centre for Development Research, Copenhagen

No. 1. Bukh, Jette, *The Village Woman in Ghana.* 118 pp. Uppsala: Scandinavian Institute of African Studies 1979.

No. 2. Boesen, Jannik & Mohele, A.T., *The "Success Story" of Peasant Tobacco Production in Tanzania.* 169 pp. Uppsala: Scandinavian Institute of African Studies 1979.

No. 3. Kongstad, Per & Mönsted, Mette, *Family, Labour and Trade in Western Kenya.* 186 pp. Uppsala: Scandinavian Institute of African Studies 1980.

This series contains books written by researchers at the Centre for Development Research, Copenhagen. It is published by the Scandinavian Institute of African Studies, Uppsala, in co-operation with the Centre for Development Research with support from the Danish International Development Agency (Danida).

Cover photograph: Woman trader piling potatoes for resale at Karatina Market (Gunvor Jörgsholm)

© Per Kongstad and Mette Mönsted 1980
ISBN 91-7106-164-9
ISSN 0348-5676

Printed in Sweden by
Offsetcenter ab, Uppsala 1980

Acknowledgements

This manuscript is based on field research in Western Kenya in 1975–77. The research work was initiated while Per Kongstad was working for the Institute for Development Research, Copenhagen in collaboration with Danida and the Ministry of Finance and Planning, Kenya, and while Mette Mönsted was a lecturer in demography at Department of Sociology, Nairobi University.

We are most grateful for the support received from Professor Philip Mbithi, chairman of the Department of Sociology, Nairobi University and from the Chief Economist in Ministry of Finance and Planning, Mr. Y.F.O. Masakhalia, whose support made our research undertaking possible.

We have greatly benefitted from comments and critiques of the research outline and early chapters of the manuscript by members of staff of Department of Sociology, especially Drs. Diane Kayongo-Male and Tarsis Kabwegyere made essential comments on drafts and outlines.

Without the generous financial backing from Danida and the Faculty of Arts, University of Nairobi, we would certainly not have been able to carry out the extensive field work embodied in our study. We also gratefully acknowledge the assistance received from the Centre for Development Research, Copenhagen, where both of us were employed, while the essential work on the manuscript was done. Per Kongstad also enjoyed the privilege of research leaves from Roskilde University Center, Roskilde.

The considerable volume of data has made the phase of analysis extensive, and we are particularly grateful for the financial support received from the Danish Council for Development Research, which contributed to the completion of our work. The publication of our manuscript was made possible by a joint arrangement between the Scandinavian Institute of African Studies, Uppsala and the Centre for Development Research, Copenhagen.

We wish to acknowledge our indebtedness to the students of the University of Nairobi, who did the bulk of the field work carried out. Without their competent assistance we would not have been able to grasp the processes of social transformation in Western Kenya. We owe particular gratitude to Mr. J.W. Muthiru and Mr. E. Ndegwa. Their efforts to clarify our views on the socio-economic structure of the rural community gave our study a perspective we would not have reached otherwise.

Finally we certainly wish to record our thanks to Mr. Michael Maina, our research assistent, who did all the field work of the pilot studies at market places and also made the essential information on the conditions of market trade available to us.

Copenhagen, November 1979
Per Kongstad & Mette Mönsted

Contents

Chapter I
Introduction
    1. The scope of this book 9
    2. Labour and the household economy 11
    3. The method of the study and its data 13

Chapter II
Family and Labour 20
    1. The family economy 20
    2. Labour processes 24
    3. Family labour 43
    4. Hired labour within agriculture 73

Chapter III
The Family and Exchange 86
    1. The extension of the market 86
    2. Non-farm activities 94
    3. Trading centres and markets 97
    4. Markets and market trade in Western Kenya 99

Chapter IV
Women Traders 107
    1. Introduction 107
    2. The trade of women 109
    3. Agriculture and trade 111
    4. Regional variations 118
    5. The scale of women's trade 121
    6. Trade and family subsistence 129

Chapter V
Shopkeepers 133
    1. Introduction 133
    2. Shopkeeping and rural economic activity 134
    3. Shopkeeping and agriculture 142
    4. Labour and shopkeeping 146
    5. Scale of business and farming 149
    6. Three illustrative cases 153

Chapter VI
The Social Consequences of Transformation. An Interpretation at the Household Level. 159
 1. The nature and forms of internal dynamics 159
 2. The social consequences of changing labour processes 164
 3. The social consequences of the changing role of the household 168
 4. The expansion of the internal market and its social consequences 172
 5. On the social consequences in a wider perspective 177

References 183

CHAPTER I

Introduction

1. The scope of this book

This book is a result of a mainly empirical study carried out in Western Kenya from 1975 to 1977. Its principal objective is to present the evidence we have obtained of the reproduction of labour in selected rural communities of Nyanza, Western and Rift Valley Provinces.

By reproduction of labour we have in mind the whole process of production in typical rural households in Western Kenya, and the changing conditions under which men, women and children work and live there. During the work in Kenya some elementary questions began to be persistent about the direction in which this genuine agricultural society would move. Basically apprehended as some kind of a capitalist social formation, what is then the likely future of the many households who will have to remain rural and also pave the way for their children's survival as peasants, traders and labourers in the agricultural community? Has capitalism in its Kenyan appearance or form provided a basis of progressing material welfare for the majority? Or has it already blocked its own way of expansion, and by that impoverished those being gradually subsumed under it?

Capitalism whatever it does to mankind provides markets. With its establishment the market as an abstract principle becomes its *raison d'être*, and in more concrete ways its regulating mechanism. A study of the market in its more concrete forms, whether social or physical, therefore seemed to us one natural alley to grasp the transformation of rural communities and its social consequences.

But the roots of a social formation cannot be comprehended at the exchange level, as little as "statistics" may tell us about the dynamics of the basic social relations determining its nature. We therefore thought it necessary to begin with the production process itself, its labour process and relations and those factors at the household level, which seemed to command its changes.

To manage a field study one has to reduce the original visions of the study in many ways. In the following sections of this chapter, it is somehow spelled out how we came down to the final construction of our own study. Here it is sufficient to elaborate on the principal choices made, which certainly limit the validity, if not necessarily the scope of the study. Firstly being an empirical study it deals with a segment of social life, at a level of oral communication between individuals and of observations made by the field workers. To relate this segment and level to the abstractions at which the nature of the society may be understood and mediated is of course an impossible task. Here our theoretical problem comes in. As a more or less axiomatic statement we do not think that the forms in which capitalism dresses in social formations like Kenya, may be derived from European history or from the theories of imperialism. But we think that studies of the concrete process of transformation as capitalism becomes dominant, are nevertheless extremely useful in order to widen the perception of its nature in an international and contemporary context.

It is tempting here to quote Anne Philips in her critique of "under-development theory" when she says that the task is not to prove the inability of capitalism to solve the problems of mankind, but to analyze what is occurring (Anne Philips, 1977, p. 19) and that demand does necessarily have to be complied with at a concrete level.

Secondly, as we do not either think that the at least temporary consequences of the establishment of the market in a concrete social formation can be deducted from general theory at the world market level, the question of the importance of internally generated forces of change arises. A lot of the theoretical dispute here has been on whether a national capitalist process of accumulation will be established, or not. Now here the limitations of our choice of a unit of analysis must be admitted. We have had in mind, not the reproduction of local capital, or for that matter international capital, but exactly the reproduction of labour. At a more abstract level than ours, the reproduction of capital and labour must be seen of course under one umbrella, that of the mode of production. We shall not deny this relationship, but only point out that at our perception of the process transforming the Kenyan social formation, we have found it more relevant for the fulfilment of our objectives to follow the ideas of Bernstein. He focuses the decomposition of the "domestic communities into individual households", a process which "leaves its individual cells, the peasant households to confront capital in a direct relation" (Bernstein 1976, p. 17).

It is exactly the level from where we think we begin to get answers to our questions, which we may also begin to put into some meaningful context i.e. at the level of social relations of production and reproduction.

Thirdly, our empirical evidence of reproduction is not only restricted to the household level, it is also limited to certain strata of the social ensemble of Western Kenya, namely households which act in some capacity as agents or traders at rural market places. This restriction has to do with our original approach mentioned above, but it is also a result of the concrete working conditions we encountered, which made it impossible to choose a more "representative sample" of rural households. However, as it will be seen from the following chapters we have tried to compensate for this shortcoming by the use of secondary sources of information and supplementary field-work.

2. Labour and the household economy

The labour relations are perceived as the most important analytical factor determining the social processes in the communities. Especially as in the traditional and early colonial society the open land-frontier and abundance of land made labour the limiting factor. Some of the features totally changing in the communities are that the purpose of labour from not going beyond the scope of reproducing labour, even with an extensive exchange of labour, also begin to be involved in profitmaking and exploitative relationships. Thus giving basis for and being part of a social polarization process. The change also implies the perception of labour from that of a scarcity factor limiting the production of the society, to becoming a commodity of apparently abundant supply.

In an effort to show how the role of subsistence and the work of women and children has been part and parcel of the social transformation, examples of labour and exchange relations are analysed within their historical framework and for the new data we are presenting, specifically within the differential conditions of different social strata. The many examples of concrete labour relations and conditions of exchange seem to maintain that the purpose of production is still reproduction of labour, but now in exchange with the market and not only by subsistence farming.

The focus of the analysis is on labour relations as an important analytical concept and as a major agent of change in rural communities. The extent to which labour has become a commodity will give us evidence of the nature of and the relative dominance of market relations. When labour is being converted to a commodity, this will in itself imply that the population is forced to buy necessities in order to reproduce labour and thus contribute to the expansion of the internal market.

The analysis tends to concentrate around different farm activities, because all the activities in rural areas, also non-farm activities, are closely related to farming in the basically agricultural societies, where nearly all have close ties to agriculture. Trade and artisan production thus has to be analysed closely in relation to agriculture because of widespread overlap of persons engaged in them. The shops and workshops in rural areas are not only tied to the agricultural development through the market conditions and the seasonal fluctuations in purchasing power, but also through the economic conditions of the owners as farmers themselves. There is a flow of resources, cash and labour to and/or from agriculture depending on the seasons and the size or type of business.

The focus on labour relations, including the labour relations within the family, has produced a variety of problems in the analysis in relation to the exchange of labour and the control of the surplus. If family labour relations are not included, the feature of the labour market will be more clearly those of a capitalist labour market, where a surplus is appropriated. The labour relations within a family maintain many of the same features with the husband as the owner of the means of production. Women are working in the food production mainly for subsistence and may control a possible surplus, but they also work in the cash crops, which may be disposed of by the husband alone. These labour relations within a family raise the question of whether the contribution of the men to the household mainly based on the surplus from cash crops equalizes the value of family labour, or whether the husband rather appropriates a surplus derived from the labour of women and children. If the latter is the case it appears as if men are exploiting the work of women in the cash crops, while they still leave the basic costs of reproduction of labour through subsistence production and other activities to the women. The study of labour relations including the intrafamily labour relations naturally leads to the analysis of the special work conditions of women and the double exploitation of peasant women relative to peasant men, but it also introduces a variety of difficult methodological problems of analysis.

As labour processes are mainly organized at the household level, and as the exchange of commodities also normally takes place in relation to the household, we have also for these reasons chosen the family or household as our unit of analysis in the study. In the traditional society the community may have been the unit of simple reproduction, but the decomposition or atomization of the community to individual households due to the changing conditions of existence is an ongoing process. This is noted by Bernstein, who continues:

> "In this way the *relations of production* of the domestic mode are destroyed, leaving its individual cells, the peasant households, to confront capital in a direct relation. The tendency of the search for cash incomes to meet the needs of simple reproduction is precisely to *individualise* the basis of simple reproduction to substitute the household for the community" (Bernstein 1976, p. 17)

Later in the book we raise however the question of whether this unity of the household holds in relation to reproduction as we have indicated above.

What is in fact the stable unit of reproduction when the work load, authority and responsibilities of men, women and children are scrutinized for analysis.

3. The method of the study and its data

The study may in some respects be characterized as a series of community studies. The purpose of the study however has not been to characterize local communities or regions, but to analyse the social processes related to the transformation of society. The data on the other hand are related to different geographical areas and therefore include variations with respect to historical and economic conditions and to population composition.

The population of the communities is of different tribal background, such as Kikuyu (mainly in the Uasin Gishu and Trans Nzoia Districts), Luo (mainly in Kisumu and South Nyanza District), Abaluyia (mainly in Bungoma and Kakamega Districts and a few in Trans Nzoia), Kalenjin speaking Nandi (mainly in Nandi District), Kipsigis (mainly in Kericho District) and Gusii in the Kisii District. The study, however does not make any effort to characterize the specific tribal groups or explain the different conditions by their tribal background. The framework of the analysis is that the material basis for the population determines the life conditions and that different ethnic or personal characteristics play no or only a marginal role. The areas studied should therefore yield a basis for some more general characteristics of the living conditions for the different ethnic groups living in the areas.

The areas included in the analysis show some differences with respect to population density and climate (rainfall and altitude), and population composition. The difference in population density and in other social variables seems to reflect the colonial administrative areas, and thus the main differences are found between the earlier 'Reserves for the Native population' and the 'White Highlands'. The African farms in the Rift Valley are much larger, both the average and the typical farms, than those in the 'Reserve' areas. This is valid for farms in the Rift Valley, whether in settlement schemes, cooperatives or other purchasing societies. The type of market involvement and the access to land show therefore, as expected, differences as well. One of the socially most dominant differences is the presence of many landless farm labourer families living in the Rift Valley, under life conditions which are crude and deteriorating due to the change to more emphasis on casual rather than permanent labour on large farms. On the other hand the families with less than 1/4 acre in the 'Reserves' are also forced to seek most of their reproduction from labour contracts. The high dependence on family labour in the small farm areas makes availability of jobs in farming meagre, other incomes may be just as poor due to heavy competition for incomes.

Map of Western Kenya.

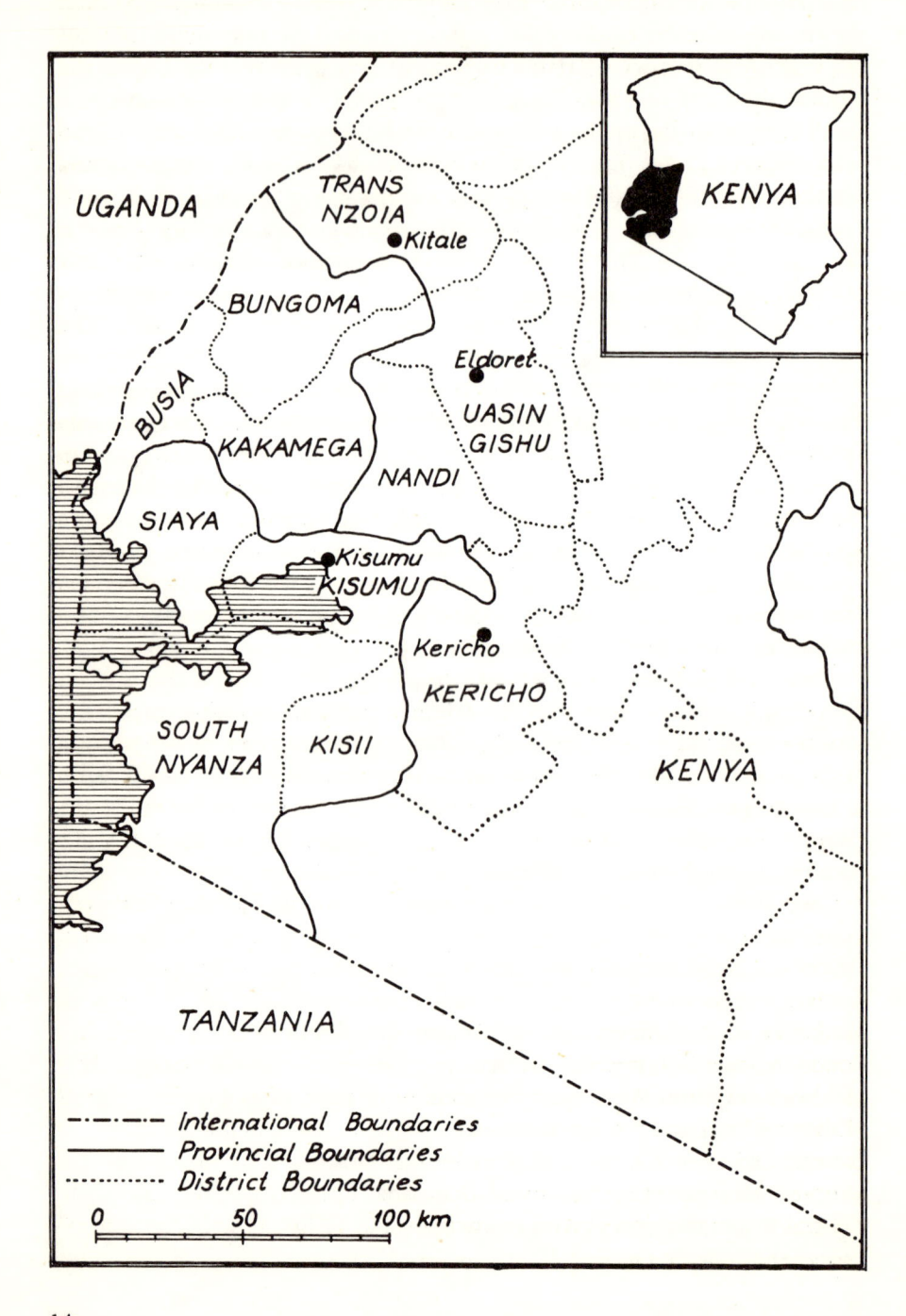

The differences in the average size of holding give a basis for different crop patterns, with more food – especially maize – in the small-holdings. Also the climatic differences affect the crop pattern and the number of harvests per year. With respect to rainfall the general pattern is that the higher the altitude the more rain and the higher the reliability of rain.

All the study areas are located within the high potential agricultural land with respect to rain. The Northern areas of Trans Nzoia, Bungoma and Northern parts of Nandi Districts have a long rainy season with maximum rainfall in April–May and in Trans Nzoia also in August. The dry season is December–January. This pattern implies that even in the lower areas only one crop of maize will be grown per year.

The Southern areas have rain in two relatively distinct rain seasons. The long rains in March–July and the short rains in October–November. Kakamega district however has a relatively even distribution and has rain also outside the seasons, but rarely in December–January, whereas Kisumu District and the lower parts of South Nyanza and Kisii are very dry outside the rainy seasons. The lower parts of Kisii and South Nyanza may have two maize harvests per year with the short maturing varieties, and Kakamega and the study areas of Kisumu may well reach two crops of maize. In all the areas there are possibilities of harvesting at least two crops of beans and vegetables, and in some areas of South Nyanza and Kisii fingermillet is exchanged with maize in the rotation.

The export industrial crops cultivated in the areas are: in the highest altitudes, pyrethrum, tea and wattle trees; in medium altitudes, tea, coffee, sunflower and sugar-cane, and in low areas, sugar-cane and cotton. Only one of the areas studied is a mono-cultural cash crop area, the sugar-cane scheme in Kisumu District, and one area of Kericho is just at the border of the tea estate areas. All the other areas are characterized by mixed farming and a combination of food-crops and cash-crops.

Case studies are collected from sublocations within the following locations[1]:
Saboti and Nzoia location of Trans Nzoia District
Kabiyet and Kaptumo locations of Nandi District
Metkei location of Elgeyo Marakwet (only shop-keepers)
Bokoli location of Bungoma district
Idakho, Isukha and West Bunyore locations of Kakamega District
Muhoroni location of Kisumu District
Londiani and Buret location of Kericho District
Kabondo location of South Nyanza District
Central Kitutu location of Kisii District

[1] See appendix on sublocations and trading centres.

Markets and Trading Centres Studied 1975–77 in Western Kenya.

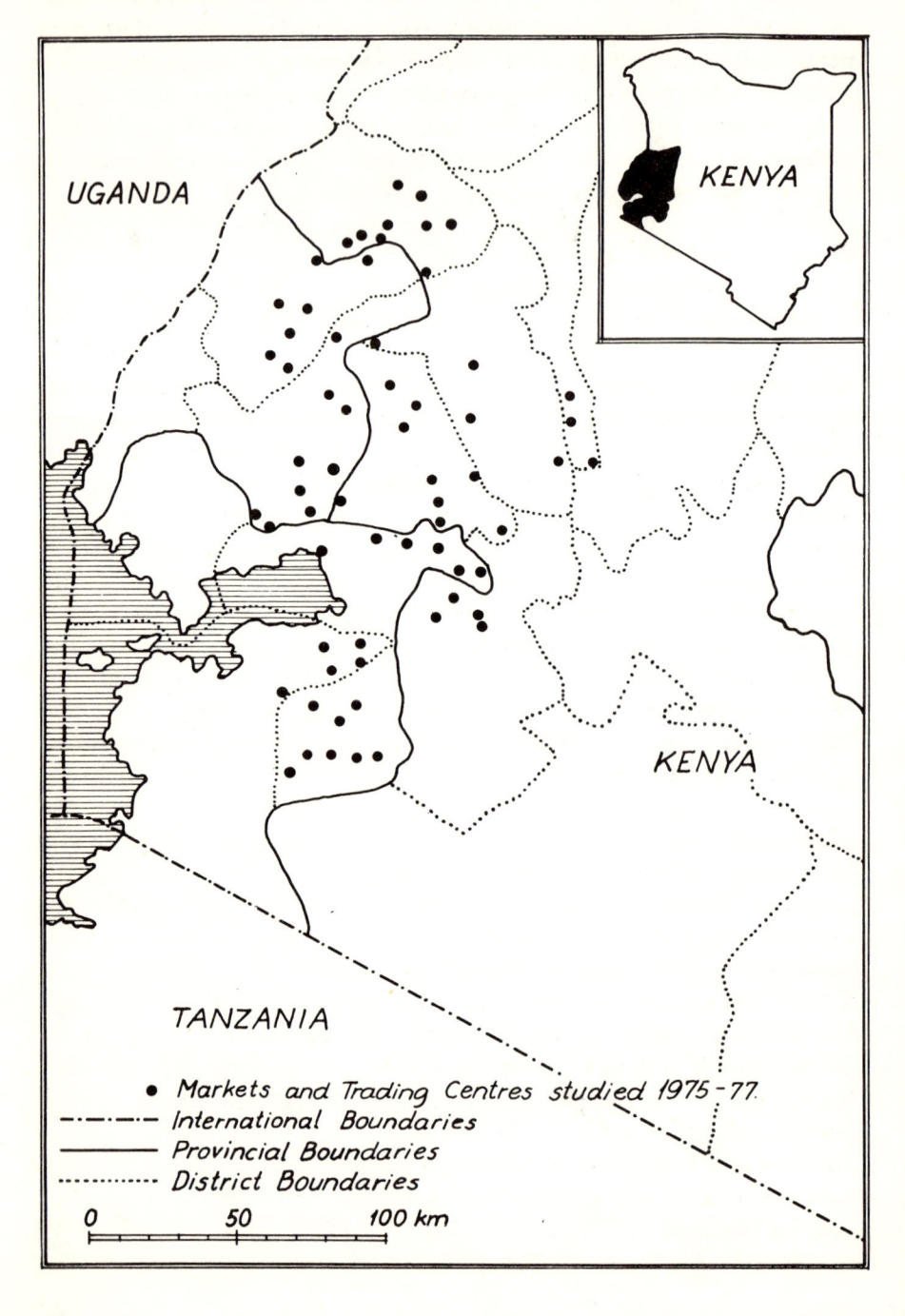

The method of the study is closely tied to the application of case studies, which were done not as a statistically representative survey, but as an attempt to cover a variety of conditions of reproduction of labour in the rural areas. On the basis of literature and key interviews the type of cases to be included were decided. Students were used as interviewers collecting the cases from their own home areas, thus representing by themselves key persons for information. Other local key persons were interviewed, representing the local administration, large farms, cooperative farm managements and old businessmen, providing information on the history of trading centres.

The study, carried out in 1975–77, consists of different types of case studies, covering different social groups such as; shopkeepers and artisans at trading centres (271 cases), women traders at open market-places (212 cases), and women interviewed in a series of case studies in the households, representing different social strata and age groups in the sublocation (191 cases). The data show different conditions of reproduction of labour for the important social groups of the rural community, but they may not by themselves be used as a descriptive statistic representative of an area. They have to be seen as a part of an analytical study giving evidence for some of the conditions of living and of the reproduction of labour. The scope of the analysis and use of data is clearly beyond that of the limited empirical data, also as related to the analysis of the social processes and theoretical interpretation of the reproduction of labour, and economic conditions of households in the commercialization of the rural communities. Other sources of information were drawn into the analysis in order to give evidence of the complexity of the community as such, especially the statistical surveys of the Central Bureau of Statistics. Some of these surveys supplement information for the provinces for nearly the same period of study, namely 1974–75, and may supplement data for the exchange relations of the rural households.

The district data are not of equal quality, especially the areas of Trans Nzoia, Uasin Gishu, Nandi and Kericho Districts are very poorly covered statistically. In the surveys including Nandi and Kericho, only small-holdings are included, and no recent statistical information is gathered in the settlements or large-scale farming areas covering a major part of the district. The implication is that the information on these areas may have some relevance for the households involved also in our data, but has no relevance for a generalization beyond this type of households, or to the general conditions of the population in the Districts set by the social structure of large-scale farming.

As mentioned previously the unit of analysis is the family, interpreted as the nuclear family. In most of the families this will be equivalent to the household, and the organizing unit for production and reproduction. Thus the household contains the main features of the social and economic conditions for the production, and may be the most theoretically relevant unit. But as the economic and social relations between spouses are important also for the families where the husband is a migrant worker, the family is chosen as the basic unit in order to include these cases.

In the Central Bureau of Statistics' survey on rural households, the unit of analysis is the rural small-holder household defined as "A person or group of persons living together under one roof or several roofs within the same compound or homestead area and sharing a community of life by their dependence on a common holding as a source of income and food, which usually but not necessarily involves them in eating from a 'common pot' (Integrated Rural Survey 1974–75, p. 20). This type of definition covers well also the majority of our cases who own land themselves, but not the landless farm labourer families, and not the families depending partly on land and partly on other incomes, nor households where the husband is a migrant worker. In relation to the ties between the members of the nuclear family and other family members, they are not included in our cases, except for possible labour relations.

With the focus on the labour relation in the family and the probing into who is contributing labour, the definition of labour force does not in itself tend to make any restrictions of the groups of persons involved. Children are included as a specifically important group and the work of relatives and hired labour relations are included in the labour relations and the labour profiles.

Another concept of importance here is division of labour. The concept of division of labour within the family refers to the sexual division of labour with respect to allocation of tasks as well as to the distribution of work and obligations between husband, wife, children and possible other members of the household. The most important relation is the sexual division of labour, tied to the contributions of husband and wife to the reproduction of labour, thus covering both work contributions and cash contributions. The concept is therefore mostly limited to the family relations, but indirectly to the social division of labour in the society, via the labour relations between different social categories of the rural community, and the change in the organization of work and work processes.

The data collected and the statistical data together include information from a short period of time. Basically however the study is a one-point-in-time study, leaving us with major difficulties of interpreting the data in relation to change processes. Historical data are included and the commercial features of the labour relations and other exchange relations of the households are related to the commercialization and the transformation of the rural community. In this way the interpretation of the data is linked to the processes and indicators of change in the rural communities.

Because of the variety of information and the number of cases, the data on labour are more qualitative than quantitative. Labour relations in a hired labour context are relatively easy to observe and measure, but in terms of family labour, the only method for measuring is a time budget survey for each of the family members, and covering different seasons of work. This is an extremely time-consuming exercise especially if many families from different social strata and areas are included. Such a survey must include all family members over 8 years of age. The work conditions of the authors did not allow this method to be applied, and the data are therefore limited to the one major interview and to an evaluation of the labour contribution of family members. The data therefore say more about the existence vs. non-existence of certain labour relations than about the relative importance and number of days or hours involved.

The structure of the book reflects the different aspects and subsurveys that had to be carried out in our work situation during the field-work.

Chapters II–V all illustrate different aspects of how the family is involved in exchange relations with the market. Chapter II tries to cover the background for the present labour relations, and the variety of labour relations between families and within the family. The work of men, women and children is analysed in relation to agricultural work and to other necessary work in the household. Chapter III provides evidence for declining subsistence farming relative to an increasing food market. The chapter presents data for how closely the majority of peasant families are drawn into market relations, and what role the local trading centres and market-places play for the items sold and purchased.

Chapters IV and V describe groups of traders, namely the women traders mainly selling foodcrops at the open market-places, and shopkeepers who are predominantly men at the rural trading centres. The trade is analysed in relation to agriculture and the family obligations, and in relation to the possibilities for income earning or accumulation.

Finally in chapter VI we have tried to relate our findings to a more general level of social analysis of rural Kenya.

CHAPTER II

Family and Labour

1. The family economy

To those who are in some way familiar with the social and economic life of the rural majority in Kenya, it is quite obvious that the family is the basic institution.

In this chapter an attempt is made to analyse the family as an economic institution through which labour is allocated and organized as the basic input of the reproduction process.

In line with our fundamental views we shall not restrict the presentation to deal with pure technicalities – the labour process – but try to see the family as an economic institution in a historical perspective, and thus relate it to the changing social conditions to which it has had to adapt itself over the past 20 years. Here, of course, the internalization of capitalist commodity circuits in its cycle of reproduction, to quote Bernstein (Bernstein 1976, p. 24), is a central theme. But it has not been our aim to participate in the debate on the articulation of modes of production at a general level beyond the scope of this book.

The first section of this chapter therefore deals only briefly with the conceptional framework of "family economy", while the next two sections represent an attempt to see how the labour processes and family labour vary according to the position of families in the ongoing process of social differentiation characterizing rural Kenya, and at the same time to demonstrate the complexity and heterogeneity of labour relations vis-à-vis such phenomena as the socially determined division of labour and technological change. In these two sections we are drawing heavily on our own field data which again means that the validity of the presentation is limited to the social strata and geographical areas of Western Kenya included in our study.

The fourth and final section in fact will demonstrate our view that even if essential to most people in rural Kenya, the family economy as a mode of reproduction does not describe any longer the labour relations of the rapidly increasing number of landless families. The section is focussing the commercialization of labour exchange and the exchange conditions for hired labourer families.

Overall, this section deals with the increasing intensity of relationships between direct producers and the market circuits as a logical outcome of the capitalist dominance of exchange and production.

Chapter II as a whole should be seen as an attempt to demonstrate and underline the transitional character of the family as a form or mode of reproduction rather than an attempt to describe its pecularities as an economic unit. As such chapter II establishes a framework for the discussion of exchange relations in chapter III and the subsequent presentation and analysis of our findings related to the study of shop-keepers and women traders in chapters IV and V.

As our whole study was geared to the analysis of the labour conditions and exchange relations for families of the particular social stratum trading at market places in Western Kenya, the family or household naturally became our unit of analysis. We will argue however that in general the rural family in Kenya also constitutes a social category of production and exchange and that its purpose and organization reflects the needs of simple reproduction more than the needs of capital to produce surplus value. We are well aware however that the internalization of capitalist exchange relations in the cycle of reproduction has already become a feature characterizing the economies of practically all peasant families in Kenya.

Most peasant families depend on the purchase of some inputs as seeds, fertilizers and tools and therefore also need to sell either produce or labour for cash. But cash has also become necessary to meet the increasing costs of reproduction. School fees have to be paid for children continuing after standard 4, and salt, sugar, kerosene, cooking fat etc. have to be bought in shops at market places. But families also increasingly have to buy food in addition to their own subsistence production either because they are short of land on which to grow their food or because they have to sell necessary food crops to provide cash and therefore have to buy food at a later stage.

As capital deepens its interference in the reproduction cycle, whether through the extension and intensification of commodity circuits or through coercion by state regulations of production and exchange, the family economy will be further changing. Its purpose or economic "raison d'être" will be more and more to satisfy the needs of capital for surplus value originating in agricultural cash crop production and less to satisfy the family subsistence needs. Its organization will also change accordingly i.e. the allocation of work to different tasks and the labour process will be more and more scheduled to the technical conditions of cash cropping etc.

The family economy will also be deeply affected by the progressing polarization of the ownership of land. While it is a question for discussion how far capitalist labour relations, i.e. wage labour, have penetrated Kenyan agriculture, it seems quite clear that land has already been converted to a commodity practically everywhere. Not only do large-scale farms occupy a disproportionately large share of fertile land, but in the traditional peasant areas of Western Kenya, transactions in the land market for example by land purchase by rich peasants, school teachers, shop-keepers etc. leave an increasing number of families without land and therefore deprived of their own means of production. This process means of course that the economy of landless families will depend totally on the pay its members can obtain for selling their labour force to other peasants.

At present we would argue that a total commercialization of labour relations has not however been reached in Western Kenya in general, and the family more or less defined as the conventional nuclear family or household typically provides the social basis of subsistence production and the organizational framework for the allocation of labour, the division of labour and the labour process.

In physical terms production takes place in the homestead of the rural family. The household typically lives in an individual farmstead surrounded by its land or, "shamba" which then is the locus standi of its economic activity. The agricultural landscape of Western Kenya therefore is more characterized by scattered habitations than by a village pattern of settlement.

In many ways of course the actual mode of reproduction reflects the past. The family as the basis of agricultural work, and the cultivation of the shamba, is rooted in the pre-colonial social organization, and the scattered settlement pattern with families living in the middle of their shamba land also represents a modified continuation of traditional land tenure systems.

We would not argue however that these features of the past would justify that typical households when aggregated should be characterized as a particular mode of production. Essential features of the pre-colonial social and economic system were lost in the epoch of colonialism and the early days of "Uhuru" (independence). Without digression into the description of the profound changes of the conditions of livelihood during the past 70 years, it should be noted here that the open land frontier has been more or less closed. Land has been adjudicated into individual property and land use as a consequence changed. Communal grazing is disappearing as "enclosures" advance and shifting cultivation has had to be abandoned with increasing land shortage in agricultural areas. Also the social relations of labour have changed profoundly with the increasing compulsion to earn cash in addition to the subsistence agriculture. Communal labour as a general practice of the communities including socially related families in a location has therefore vanished except in some rudimentary form as low paid women's labour.

We therefore in many ways tend to agree with Bernstein when he says that the destruction of the domestic mode of production historically has led to the degradation of the conditions of existence for domestic communities and their decomposition into individual households as the basic units of simple reproduction. Referring to Meillasoux he argues that "the tendency of the search for cash income to meet the needs of simple reproduction is precisely to individualize the basis of simple reproduction... and to substitute the household for the community" (Bernstein 1976, p. 17).

We may also refer here to our own studies which strongly reflect this tendency for individualization. Only 15 % of our case studies showed evidence of reliance on support from relatives etc. Most respondents also directly expressed that the material welfare of their families was a matter of the household's own efforts. The following sections of this chapter will deal with the more precise ways in which the rural household functions as an economic unit.

Here it should however be pointed out that the general characteristics of the process which have led to an individualization of the household economy, also mean that the nature and forms of the family units' liaisons with the market or the capitalist circuits of exchange take place in a complex pattern of relationships.

These first of all depend on the position of the families in the emerging structure of social differentiation, but secondly also vary significantly between geographical areas and even from location to location within the same region.

Thirdly however the division of the family unit into male and female spheres of reproduction, as it will be seen from the two next sections, seems to indicate that the individual members of a family unit held together by its patriarchal organization, are increasingly being exposed to quite different relations with the market.

Drawing on our own field-data we would tend to argue that a flux of social and class relations co-exist in the different subsocieties and with the individual households for the time being. Heterogeneity rather than homogeneity therefore overrides the general pattern described above.

Just to illustrate this point here, our cases include examples of households, where the husband manages his own farm producing cash crops along with a large shop and other business ventures, while his wife or wives work in their small shambas together with their children and in addition work on the farm as unpaid family labour controlling the work of labourers employed in capitalist wage-labour relations by the husband.

At the other end of this "scale" we find cases where husband, wife and grown-up children mainly exist as a household whose reproduction is for the most based on the role of their labour force to other peasant families. The relative autonomy of these extremes to decide the ways to meet the needs of reproduction is of course fundamentally different. But moreover the relative autonomy of the household to decide on its economic activity is both a question of its linkages with capital and its cohesion as a social unit.

Capitalist farmers and shopkeepers necessarily operate under the conditions set by the laws of motion characterizing the expansion of capital in Kenya – as capitalist farmers; they in principle at least, may choose to return to subsistence production as their main objective. Wives and children in the household may be sharing in the husband's profit-making from cash cropping or trade – but may also be left on their own meagre basis of reproduction searching for cash through petty trade on the local market-place or even by working for neighbours, etc.

The flux characterizing the social relations of labour and exchange in which the family unit has so far survived, may thus be seen as an expression of stages of transition in which the rural social formations of Kenya certainly are developing.

2. Labour processes

In relation to the analysis of labour processes we have to make clear what kind of labour is involved, and how it is related to the traditional labour structure and to the present pattern of social differentiation.

In general peasant households are characterized by a fusion of farming (the enterprise) and the domestic economy of the family household in much the same way as described by Galeski (Galeski 1972, p. 11). The work processes are not standardized or characterized by a high level of specialization, but rather by a variety of work tasks, many of which change according to time of the day, days in the week and mainly according to season. An analysis of labour processes has to be related to the development of the labour processes and the division of labour in different historical periods, and any discussion and analysis of the work and labour processes should be related to the present social differentiation in the rural areas and other social and economic conditions for the work in agriculture and household.

The traditional division of labour in the subsistence agriculture has some consequences for how the allocation of labour and responsibilities have developed, but does not exist any more in its pure form anywhere, as the conditions for it are eroded.

In the traditional societies work was allocated mainly according to age and sex groups in the community. Also the relations between relatives were determined to a high extent by age and stage in life of a nuclear family unit.

There are still some of these features existing, but age as a determinant for distribution of work responsibilities within the adult group seems to have declining importance, due to the increasing importance of non-farm employment and incomes, and increasing emphasis on qualifications rather than age in the society as such. The sexual division of labour, however, still seems to present an important variable for the explanation of the division of labour in the rural community, and for the complex economic household structures.

The traditional anthropological theories dealing with the division of labour according to sex have tended to refer to the biological differences between the sexes, thus explaining the allocation of work for the husband and wife by their different biological capacity to do the tasks, and to the necessity for women to be engaged in the production just around the house because of child care.

Murdock in 1949 phrases it like this:

> "Man, with his superior physical strength, can better undertake the more strenuous tasks, such as lumbering, mining, quarrying, land clearance, and housebuilding. Not handicapped, as is woman by the physiological burdens of pregnancy and nursing, he can range farther afield to hunt, to fish, to herd, and to trade. Woman is at no disadvantage, however, in lighter tasks which can be performed in or near the home, e.g. the gathering of vegetable products, the fetching of water, the preparation of food, and the manufacture of clothing and utensils. All known human societies have developed specialization and co-operation between the sexes along this biologically determined line of cleavage." (Murdock, 1949, p. 7).

The biologically based explanations can explain certain aspects of what Marx calls the "Natural division of labour", but they lack all explanations for the changes in the division of labour over time, when the simple production relations are no longer existing, and they lack explanatory value for the regional differences. Such as, e.g. the heavy carrying, done by females in the Kikuyu society, or the traditional food trade of women in East Africa.

Just as the division of labour in society is based on the economic production relations, the division of labour within the family is closely related to the production and organization of the production in the family, and through this to the division of labour and specialization in the society.

The pattern of division of labour in the traditional societies living in Western Kenya today, shows some regional variations, but the general pattern is very much the same. The main differences seem to be related to the importance of cattle relative to crop cultivation, which is related to the pattern found in most of the communities, namely that the men were responsible for animal production, the cattle, and women were the daily workers on the crops cultivated. The general pattern showed the following features:

Men were responsible for the kind of work in agriculture involving physical strength in short peak periods. They were clearing the land in the shifting cultivation, building houses, taking care of the livestock and hunting. Through hunting and animal production, men were responsible for most of the protein supply for the family. Men were also responsible for training their sons in their work tasks. Certain age-groups, usually the younger men, were responsible for the defence of the local community or homestead as warriors, and for cattle raiding within some of the tribal communities. The political decisions were taken by the elder men in the community. Men's work in agriculture was usually limited to the peak seasons, mainly the hard work of clearing land. The remaining work was mostly done by women and children. In some areas, however, men were more involved in some of the regular cultivation, for example, tending the bananas, whereas in other areas they did nothing except the clearing of land. The normal pattern seemed to be that the daily work in agriculture was the responsibility and work of women.

Women were thus the cultivators, once the new land was cleared and dug. They did the planting, weeding and harvesting, and they had the main responsibility for supporting the family with food from their cultivation. Women were also responsible for fetching firewood, preparing crops, cooking, washing, and taking care of the house and the children, and training the daughters.

The sexual division of labour was quite distinct, and determined the work of boys and girls from around the age of 12–13 years. Before that time, they assisted with very much the same work, even if boys did more herding, and girls assisted more with fetching water and cooking. But both girls and boys assisted with child care, fetched fire-wood and worked in agriculture.

The division of labour in the family and the possibility to carry out the work varied in different stages of life, and the dependency on help from relatives also showed major variations according to age and stages in life.

A newly married couple often did not have any land, but were supposed to live with the husband's family for some time. They would often start to cultivate a new piece of land close to the husband's home or a part of the father's land, but until they had harvested the first crop, they were totally dependent on the assistance from the husband's parents. In this stage of life, the young wife assisted her mother-in-law with her cultivation and got food from her, and the mother-in-law may also have helped with the farmwork in the newly cultivated land. In principle the wife was allocated a piece of land at marriage, and from this she was responsible for feeding the family. During the first years of marriage, when the young wife had problems with managing all the work, while she was pregnant and had only small children, she could not fulfil this obligation of feeding the family from the land. In this period she had to rely on assistance from her husband in farmwork, which he was normally not responsible for, and assistance was also required from other relatives. Later when the oldest children were old enough to start helping in the house and taking care of younger siblings, and when they at the age of around 8 years began to assist in farming, the dependency on work from relatives declined, and assistance was withdrawn or limited except for certain periods of sickness and just after childbirth. When the family reached this stage, where they could more or less manage with their own family labour, they were also involved in work for other relatives in mutual assistance arrangements.

In some cases the mutual assistance had more the character of communal labour, where a group of neighbours or relatives worked together. Such cases could be found in work for clearing new land, building houses, digging water furrows or hunting. But groups of women could also go together to do manual work on the land such as digging the land of the group members in turns.

All of this work, both the family labour, the work of relatives and communal labour, was related to the simple reproduction, and not to accumulation for any of the members. Even if the pattern was not an equal distribution of labour between families, the work was mutual in character, and catered for the simple survival of the family; and, with respect to the communal labour and mutual arrangement, to the survival of the clan or extended family living in the scattered homesteads of the area. At this stage a surplus had to be produced only to last in the granary until the next harvest. The surplus was consumed, or could be converted to cattle, or redistributed within the clan system, but there was no way of investing it in economic ventures. Young girls were married outside the clan and relations between the clans were therefore established which, in cases of deficiency of food in one area, gave basis for a system of redistribution of the surplus produced in other areas. These arrangements, however, were governed by the need for survival and not for profit, as the conditions were that of relatively homogeneous societies, with an open land frontier and therefore relative abundance of land, and differences mainly reflected age groups and political influences and not so much economic differences or social differentiation with respect to economic potential.

Examples of social differences were reflected in the chiefdoms and mainly in the kingdoms of Western Kenya and Buganda. Chiefs were generally more powerful, but the power was mostly related to wars, and they did not necessarily have to be more wealthy. In the traditional kingdoms in East Africa tributes in kind were paid and gifts presented to the king. Livestock and young women could be some of the more important gifts presented. The kings and in some cases the chiefs thus may have had larger herds and more wives than other peasants. More wives also implied that in the traditional land tenure they had more land, as they could cultivate more with the larger labour force of wives and children.

The surplus in such families, however, could not be invested or used economically, but could provide a higher level of consumption.

Throughout the colonial and post-colonial period, the relations of production and exchange characterizing the pre-colonial society however were more or less destroyed by a variety of internal and external factors influencing the economic and the legal system.

Already at the time of the building of the railway, the imported labour force of Indian coolies gave a basis for a foodmarket for the labourers along the railway and in Nairobi, which expanded rapidly in the period just after 1900. Some of the tribal groups were involved in the production of food, mainly maize and vegetables for the labourers, and sold the crops to the colonial government. The Kikuyus and the Kipsigis were active in this trade, which immediately changed the conditions for food crop production, directing it to the market instead of to subsistence only. The expansion of the cultivation at that time, however, was based on access to sufficient land and labour. Labour relations were still based mainly on family labour, and those with the largest families – the most wives – could expand the area cultivated to sell food crops. Kitching describes how the Kikuyus of Kiambu around 1905–10 begin producing and selling food for the Nairobi market (Kitching 1975, p. 28).

With the immigration of the white settlers from Europe, the fertile plains of the Rift Valley were alienated land reserved for European settlement engaged in large-scale farming. The African population was left with the "Native Reserves", some of which, especially in the Central Province, were already pretty densely populated.

In order to secure labour for the European farms, Africans were first recruited as forced labour on the farms, and as this did not provide the needed labour power, poll tax and hut tax were introduced in order to force the African males to work as farm labourers on the European farms to pay the tax in cash. The tax could not be paid in kind, and to avoid that money was generated from their farm produce, restrictions were put on Africans growing export crops. Prices for food crops also discriminated against African producers.

"By the mid-1920s more than half the able-bodied men in the two largest agricultural tribes (the Kikuyu and Luo) were estimated to be working for Europeans" (Leys 1975, p. 31). The recruitment of African males for the labour force on the large farms, implied that they left their own farmsteads for longer periods than before, and more of the work was left for women, children and old people at the homesteads. This process may in some of the areas not have had major impact on the agricultural production, as the men's work was so clearly seasonal. Only if the seasons of employment and the seasons of homestead work were overlapping, may production have declined. The work demand changed a lot over the year in the farmsteads, and in some periods only the women and a few of the older girls were working in agriculture, whereas in other periods of the year, the labour force involved everyone who could possibly work in the fields. Young children and old people, i.e. the fringe groups of the labour force, were involved in the work. When the men were away, some of these fringe groups may have been more involved in the work again, also in other seasons, to fulfil the work obligations and make it possible for the family to survive.

It appeared as if the employment was most often seasonal, and that the permanent workers employed on the European farms were tempted to stay there by the access to more land of their own to cultivate at the European farms than they had at home. In the densely populated Kikuyuland, many left their small plots to their family and left for the European farms as squatters, for whom part of the salary was a plot of land to cultivate. Already at this time there must have been some social differentiation in the Central Province, as the unequal distribution of land determined who left the "Reserves" and who stayed and produced enough for the family support and maybe even for selling crops to the developing food market.

The recruitment of African soldiers during the world wars had the same effect as the labour migration, of withdrawing men's labour from the homestead. This was for longer periods, and the men could not be expected to be home during the peak agricultural seasons. This may have implied lower output in certain areas, where new land was difficult to clear without the work of the men, and it was more difficult to replace many men in the community with fringe age-groups for longer periods. Around and after the First World War an increasing food market developed, and more people were involved in production of food for the market.

By the introduction of money as the regulating device in transactions between individuals, families and clans and by the gradual extension of market relations, a process of polarization or social differentiation, already embedded in the precolonial social formations, gained momentum.

Those families who already had more land at their disposal by customary tenure agreements than was necessary to reproduce themselves, went into production for the market and often established trade in cattle, grains etc, as well. The male heads and sons of families already influential in the pre-colonial epoch had easier access to the colonial machinery than the majority of peasant families and thus became more firmly established in their claims on land than those who eventually were forced to accept a status of tenancy by colonial court decisions etc.

The unequal access to education in the missionary schools, probably regulated by the standing and degree of "civilization" of some families during the first colonial years, implied that employment in the colonial establishment became possible. Chiefs, headmen, artisans, mission boys and other more educated employees in the early colonial government were paid high enough wages to yield a revenue with which to cement their social position, acquire more land for market production or engage in trade with food crops or livestock.

Some of the influential employees went into shopkeeping from just before 1920, maize mills were built and African landlords acquired houses for rent in the African living quarters in Nairobi.

The colonial restrictions were mainly related to the protection of the settler economy and to long-distance trade of certain goods where the colonial government saw a source of revenue by monopolizing it. The African social strata which already held powerful positions still had many sources of incomes and investments to expand their economic powers, and trade increased rapidly especially in the 1930s. The majority of the peasants could not exploit the economic possibilities arising, and had to stay in the subsistence economy or the near tenant status.

The squatters who in the early 20th century had relatively fair conditions of reproduction, with good land for their own agriculture and livestock, were gradually becoming more affected by the economic pressures from the settlers. The tendency was to tighten work conditions by increasing the number of days which they had to work at the settlers' farms, and by wage stagnation and control of access to grazing land and agricultural land. During the economic crisis in the 1930s many squatters were evicted from their land, and others were subject to further cuts in their salaries.

In the early fifties the colonial government reacted to the costly and often unqualified settler production of the export crops. A small peasant production of food crops had already proved competitive, and instead of restricting the African small-scale production further and protecting the settler farms, the government saw its benefit in the opening for and encouragement of small peasant production of export crops, such as tea and coffee.

The small peasant production of export crops and food crops for the market increased during the 1950s to be approx. 50 percent of the total marketed agricultural production. The relative importance of peasant farming for marketed crops has since been stable at this level.

With the introduction of an export crop production among the African middle-peasantry the family land, which had hitherto only been serving the purpose of subsistence and in some areas a little food production for the market, became gradually subdivided into two parts, one for food crops for the family, which the wife was still responsible for and which was the basis for the reproduction of labour, the other for cash crops, which the husband, who had been the income earner and had been working in the European export crops, became responsible for, and which was the basis for a profit directed agricultural production.

This division of the land into two parts changed the labour relations in the family, as the wife also became involved in some the work on the export crops, which was done in addition to the work previously done for the reproduction of the labour in the family in the subsistence agriculture.

In this process not only did the work burden of women increase but unpaid family labour relations were also involved directly in work processes with a definite value on the market. Subsistence agriculture maintained the function of reproducing labour at very low costs for the developing cash crop market. Labour costs could be held at a minimum because the basic costs of family survival were covered already by the work of women and children.

Within the same period, when the labour market developed in relation to the European farms and the employment in colonial administration, the combination of (1) the increasing population, (2) the unequal distribution of the population on the land and (3) the adjudication and consolidation of land, implied that land gradually became a scarce commodity. Shifting cultivation was in many areas replaced by a need for manure or fertilizer to maintain the fertility of the soil, but in the 1940s the land fertility, however, seemed to be declining and needed investments to restore fertility (Leys 1975, p. 67). With the pressure on land and the expansion of the market economy in the 1930s, a land market developed where the social strata earning a cash income began to buy land, which was considered the only reliable security to maintain economic power and social prestige. From this time land not only had use value, but also became an object for economic investments by some social strata.

Other legal constraints affected the division of labour in the bulk of the peasant families, namely the laws against cattle raiding, tribal wars, and especially hunting. The latter prohibited the traditional access to meat, and the proteins for the family, earlier derived from the men's hunting, now had to be substituted by cash incomes to buy these products.

All the changes in the peasant production mainly restricted the traditional duties of the men, such as clearing new land, hunting, warfare, cattle raiding. The traditional duties vanished, and were partly replaced by the need for cash incomes. In the agricultural production it was easier to do without the men for a part of the year than to do without the women, and besides, men had much easier access to engage themselves in employment or business outside agriculture.

The type of women's work did not change much, but the work load may have changed depending on the crop pattern developing. First of all the increasing emphasis of cultivation relative to livestock increased the work burden of women. Secondly, export crops and cash crop production increased the work load of women, as women still had to supply the food crops necessary for the family survival. Some of the new crops such as hybrid maize clearly gave higher yields, but also demanded higher labour input in the weeding periods, which were already the busiest of all seasons.

The men's work of breaking new land in shifting cultivation was replaced by the use of manure and fertilizer. It appears that this shifted work from men to women. In a study of hybrid maize production in Arusha and Morogoro in Tanzania, it was revealed that women alone spread fertilizer in 80 percent of the cases and assisted in this process in all cases (Fortman 1976, p. 6).

There seems to be two well defined trends in the development of the division of labour in the family, the one being a change of allocation of work in the household and agriculture from men to women, as women take over more and more of the work and responsibilities of agriculture. Work previously done by one sex, which changes to be done by the other sex is always from men to women and not vice versa. This is shown in the present study and by Jane Wills in her study in Embu (Wills 1967).

Given the work load in peasant households, work is not only shifting from men to women, but processes which are subject to an improved technology and a commercialization often shift from women to men or remain with the men. Examples are that of ploughing, which is often bought as a service with tractor or ox-driven ploughs, or maize milling, where the tedious and labour consuming work of grinding maize is replaced by the transport of maize and need for cash to pay for the grinding at the maize mill.

The technological changes in agricultural production, however, are closely related to the social differentiation of the rural community, therefore the relationship between labour processes and social strata will be analysed first.

The relationship between labour process and the process of social differentiation presents a problem. Neither the orthodox Marxist theory of class formation or any other clearcut classification of social strata fits the complex pattern of reproduction in which the labour process is imbedded. As some kind of classification is necessary in order to describe the labour processes we have decided to operate with three main social strata, namely rich peasants, middle peasants and poor peasants/landless labourers. We use these strata in much the same way as Galeski does in his classification of Polish peasants.

In the preliminary categorization used, the general features of the three classes are: (1) The rich peasants have land enough to produce for subsistence and to produce a surplus, they use family labour, but also supplement by buying labour in peak seasons or in longer periods. (2) The middle peasants generally produce just enough from their farm to balance at subsistence. They have no real surplus and no deficit. The middle peasantry mainly rely on family labour. (3) The poor peasants produce too little from the farm to cover subsistence. On the farm they rely on family labour, but because of the insufficient production they are dependent on selling their labour for their survival.

These standard descriptions are in line with the categorization made on the European peasantry (Galeski), but the problems arise when the actual activities and mode of reproduction are described in the Kenyan rural context, where most of the households are engaged much more in the market economy both through the food market and the labour market. The problems of the complex labour relations of these social strata are therefore presented.

The actual labour exchanges in the rich peasantry show that the larger the farm, or higher the incomes, the less the husband is involved in the daily work on the farm. He may be the manager, and he controls the crop pattern, the technology and labour recruitment. But often he leaves the work and daily supervision to the wife. The manual labour on the farm may also depend to some extent on family labour, supplemented by hired labour in the peak season, or with permanent hired labour. In certain peak periods children and the wife work long hours in the field, e.g. in the weeding of maize at a time when the demand for labour is very urgent. The reliance of commercial rich peasants on family labour is also found in other studies, e.g. in Buganda in the mid-1960s (Richards et al. 1973, p. 184). Rich peasants clearly do buy labour in any case and none of the family members are selling their labour as farm labourers in this strata. But within this group incomes from government employment, e.g. teaching or different kinds of business are widespread.

The labour relations of middle peasant families are much more complex than the theoretical ideal of the sole dependency on family labour. Most often labour is both sold and bought, and in some cases *farm labour* is both bought and sold. Within this group many of the men have some supplementary incomes, some from small shops, some from employment. Men may be permanent farm labourers or do casual farm labour in certain seasons, while in other periods they employ casual labour for their own cash crops. Women often supplement their farming with the trading of their food crops or other food, or brewing, or they work as casual labourers for other farmers to earn enough for the purchase of food. The labour relations of the middle stratum show some apparent contradictions in both selling and buying farm labour. This may be explained by several factors, some of which are the season of work and the type of work done, e.g. tea and coffee plucking and weeding is often done as casual labour by women, whereas a service such as tractor ploughing is often bought even if cash for this has to be generated by casual farm labour on other farms. Some explanation may also be found in differential prices of labour. A husband may, for example sell his labour for digging, weeding, pruning coffee or tea or other work for around 5 shs. per day, and may buy the labour of women for weeding for 2–3 shs. per day and thus make a profit from the labour exchange. Some of the landless labourers may also be underpaid due to lack of bargaining power. Work groups of women, youngsters or children to do piece-work in farming are also more often bought at a lower price than individual casual labourers. Thus the same person may at different seasons buy and sell the same type of labour, and may do so with a profit.

A more complex pattern however arises when the husband employs farm labour for his cash crops, and at the same time the wife has to sell her labour as casual labour to get money for food or household expenses. This contradiction within the household and family economy may be related to the subdivision of the family economy where responsibilities have been divided with the wife responsible for the supply of food and daily necessities, whereas the husband may work free from the obligations of reproducing labour and be free to direct his concern and attention to the business of the cash crops.

The group of poor peasants and landless labourer families is the group mainly dependent on selling their labour. With the increasing pressure on land, this group in the rural community is increasing rapidly and becoming increasingly dependent on selling their labour throughout the year. Until recently, it was often possible to borrow unused land for cultivation from relatives. This option is becoming more and more limited, and only the possibility of renting a piece of land remains. For most of the young people in the densely populated areas, e.g. in Kisii and Kakamega Districts, the hope of getting land of their own seems to disappear. Land is already fragmentized to very small plots, and land has to be bought from incomes

Most farm work done by women is with the hoe. (Gunvor Jørgsholm)

earned in employment which they will not get either. The number of landless non-educated people is increasing and therefore the competition for the same farm labour jobs is also increasing. Besides, there is a tendency for the farm labour market to replace permanent farm labour by casual labour only employed in peak seasons (Kenya Statistical Digest, March 1972,

35

p. 7). This group of poor peasants therefore is being increasingly proletarianized even if some still try to rely on their family and relatives for support.

Returning to the labour processes in agriculture, the conditions for buying and selling labour and for benefitting from mechanization or improved technology is determined not only by land distribution, but also by the crop pattern and ecological conditions which together provide the framework for the labour profile for different areas. In areas where the crop pattern is highly diversified the aggregate labour profile will tend to be flat, reflecting the fact that the different peak seasons of the crops smoothen the labour profile. A flat profile will give a basis for relying more on family labour and less on seasonal buying and selling of casual labour.

On the other hand, in areas with a low crop diversity, the labour profile will tend to reflect the peaks of labour in maize production. The labour profile will show major variations and thus be a basis for exchange of labour in certain agricultural seasons.

Data on labour profiles are available as aggregate labour profiles from districts and provinces (Gwyer 1972, and Integrated Rural Survey 1974–75), but not for the locations and sublocations from where case studies are selected. The aggregate pattern for the whole district may well be different from that of the location studied, for instance within Kisumu District, the sugar belt has a much more flat labour profile than the one revealed for the district, and the Bokoli location of Bungoma District has a profile reflecting more the domination of maize production. Labour profiles are not available for Trans Nzoia and Uasin Gishu Districts, but apparently they may be close to the ones from Kericho and Nandi District. Background data from the two districts are in all cases very poor, as no recent research or public statistics are available from these parts of the Rift Valley. In the graph, the districts of Kisumu, South Nyanza and Kakamega show most seasonal variations in the labour profile, determined by the peaks for maize cultivation. Bungoma and Kisii show a medium variation, but still with emphasis on the work during the rainy season (around April). The Nandi and Kericho District profile is very smooth throughout the year, even if labour input in livestock, which is an important part of the farm work in these areas, is not included.

The main impact of technological changes in agriculture is the changing crop pattern, i.e. the new crops introduced and the upgrading of cultivation relative to animal production.

Especially maize production is increasing in the previously cattle dominated areas, giving a higher output and better utilization of family labour. The new crops such as the export crops of coffee, tea, pyrethrum etc. are quite clearly expanding the labour input needed in agriculture, as few

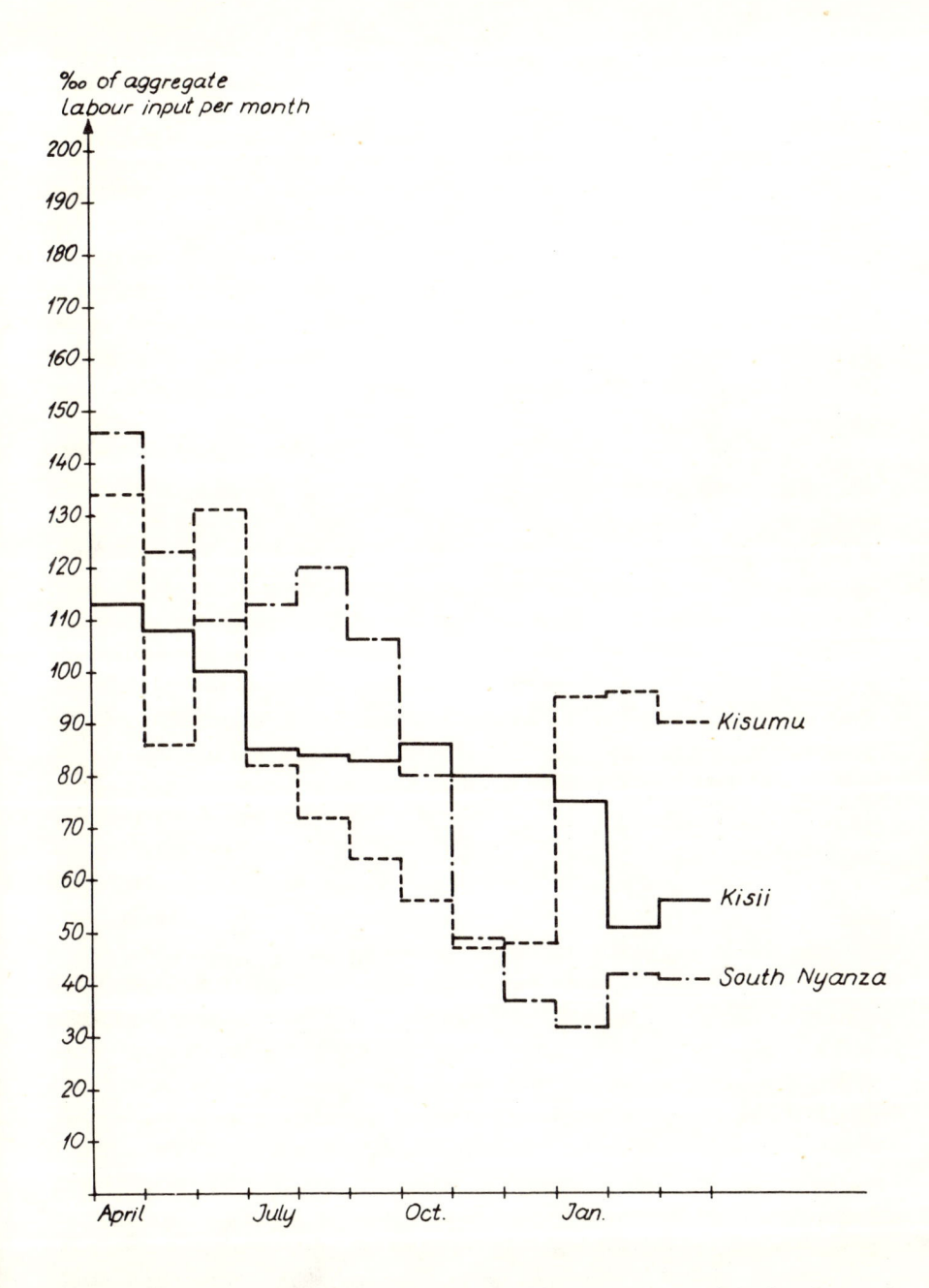

Figure 2.1. *Relative labour profile on basis of aggregate labour input per month for three districts of Nyanza Province.*

Source: Gwyer 1972, table 24.

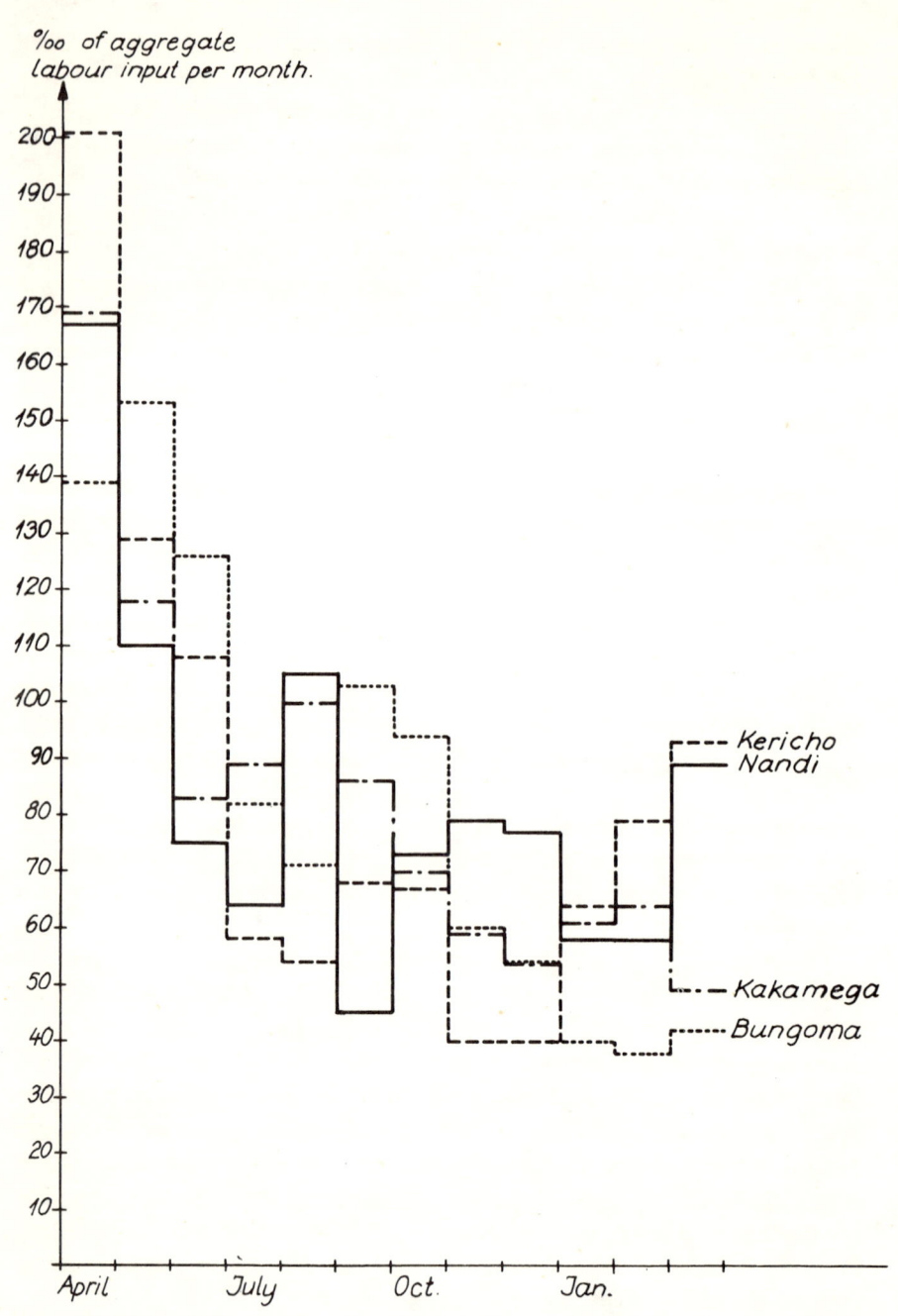

Figure 2.2. *Relative labour profile on basis of aggegate labour input per month for districts of Western and Rift Valley Provinces.*

Source: Gwyer 1972, table 24.

processes are mechanized. The availability of cheap labour thus determines the output of the farm. The hybrid maize cultivated with fertilizer has increased the work burden of spreading fertilizer and especially weeding, but without mechanizing any labour processes. The higher technology and increased productivity of the land has implied an increased labour input, most of which is done by more intensive work by family labour, and some by casual labour in the peak seasons.

Technological changes in the form of mechanization of work processes have been very limited and are mostly tractor ploughing for preparing the soil. Only for crops such as wheat and sisal are some work processes mechanized to save labour in areas where availability of seasonal casual labourers is scarce.

A change of crops in order to save labour has been introduced for some large-scale farms in the Rift Valley, where the labour supply is scarce. Within the high altitude areas of Uasin Gishu and Trans Nzoia wheat production has expanded at the expense of maize. Wheat production has always been highly mechanized. Also in the grassland of Narok District the supply of labour is poor due to very low population density, and wheat production has been introduced in the earlier grazing land.

Within areas of Bungoma, Uasin Gishu and Trans Nzoia, maize has replaced coffee production to save labour input, and many large-scale farms also expand grade cattle, where a few permanent labourers can manage the work, in order to avoid the problems of getting sufficient casual labourers at the peak seasons. Labourers for maize weeding are used only for a short period and the labourers in the areas of, e.g. Uasin Gishu are not sufficient. Labourers are brought in and migrate from surrounding areas for this season.

The improved technology within the sugar schemes has changed the labour relations, but more because of changed organizational structure than because of mechanization. In these schemes the peasants have little or no autonomy, they are restricted to follow a certain production pattern, and family labour plays practically no role in the production of this cash crop. The contracts with the sugar companies make the peasants the formal owners of land, but without any rights to dispose of the land. Even the organization of labour and the supply of labour is at contract with the sugar company. The company in turn hires a pool of labourers, who do the labour on the different fields to secure a standardized and correct cultivation, and secure a continuous supply of sugar to the factory.

In relation to the technological level in Kenyan agriculture, tables 2.1 and 2.2 from the Integrated Rural Survey 1974–75 of small-holders in Kenya provide some evidence for, on the one hand the limited machinery owned

Table 2.1. *Mean value of assets[1] per holding by Province[2] (Value in K.shs.)*

	Central	Coast	Eastern	Nyanza	Rift Valley	Western	Total
Land	4,395	1,887	1,193	682	1,569	1,155	1,820
Buildings	2,774	2,871	1,812	1,023	1,803	1,384	1,796
Farm Equipment	182	86	177	68	422	94	146
Transport Equipment	534	90	163	99	400	126	234
Livestock	2,806	2,242	2,673	2,066	5,457	1,331	2,462
Crops in Store	245	138	250	301	287	247	259
Planted Crops	273	81	153	109	375	129	174
Inputs in Store	24	2	17	9	14	5	14
Total Assets	11,233	7,397	6,438	4,357	10,327	4,471	6,905

[1] Excluding domestic household assets.
[2] Excludes pastoral and large farm areas.
Source: Integrated Rural Survey 1974–75. Central Bureau of Statistics, Nbi. 1977, p. 48.

by peasants and on the other hand the limited annual costs of farm inputs particularly for mechanization, especially in Western Province. The total amount used as input in farming is low in both Nyanza and Western Province, while the farm input is much higher in the Rift Valley areas, even if the large farms and Uasin Gishu and Trans Nzoia District are not included.

In conclusion, the impact of technological innovations on agriculture seems to be that they have emphasized a change of crops and the introduction of fertilizer to increase the productivity of the land. But the need to invest in mechanization has been limited due to several reasons. The relative cost of labour to machinery seems to make the machinery more costly, mainly because the investment in machinery is not sufficient, the transport and especially the maintenance is very costly and complicated in rural areas. Also the supply of cheap labour is sufficient for the existing production in most of the areas. Here the supply of family labour is the most important factor for most of the farmers, but even the large-scale farmers may, with a changing cultivation pattern, e.g. a change to livestock, have enough cheap labourers to maintain many of the work processes.

The family labour relations still play a major role in agricultural production in rural Kenya, though under different conditions than in the traditional society. The other labour relations such as mutual assistance between relatives and communal work seems to be much more affected by the commercialization of the labour market. However, some forms of labour assistance from relatives and communal labour still exist, even if the conditions for the non-exploitative mutual labour relations have been eroded. The forms also show that these new relations are adjusted to some of the traits of a capitalist economy.

The study in 1975 revealed examples of young girls from poor families helping richer relatives with housework and agriculture. This relationship is seen as an extension of earlier mutual assistance relations, where the richer relatives pay food and clothing for the girl and often help to pay school-fees for her siblings – usually brothers. The "employed" girl does not take up food from other siblings and richer relatives often use this system to get very cheap labour through these relations.

This study emphasizes more the complex family relations, than the earlier study done by Marris & Somerset, who emphasized only in relation to the

Table 2.2. *Percentage distribution of farm inputs per holding by Province*[1].

	Central	Coast	Eastern	Nyanza	Rift Valley	Western	Total
Purchased Seed	7.46	4.59	15.97	8.92	8.84	12.54	10.19
Machinery Contract	1.47	2.30	5.21	12.42	12.21	5.37	5.35
Fertilizers	8.34	0.51	7.12	3.18	13.16	5.07	7.25
Sprays	2.36	0.00	3.13	0.00	0.32	0.00	1.73
Other Purchased Crop Inputs	6.97	0.26	3.65	19.11	6.53	5.37	7.43
Total Purchased Crop Inputs	*26.59*	*7.91*	*35.07*	*43.63*	*41.16*	*28.66*	*31.95*
Purchased Feed	9.22	0.26	1.22	0.00	2.32	1.49	4.32
Other Livestock Expenses	5.99	0.26	4.69	0.96	14.74	3.58	5.35
Total Livestock Expenses	*15.31*	*0.51*	*5.90*	*0.96*	*17.05*	*4.78*	*9.67*
Wages to Regular Labour	7.07	37.76	15.45	11.46	15.68	8.36	11.57
Wages to Casual Labour	15.21	23.98	10.42	20.06	14.11	27.16	16.06
Total Wages to Labour	*22.28*	*61.73*	*25.87*	*31.53*	*29.89*	*35.52*	*27.81*
Own Produce Used as Seed	2.85	3.06	14.06	4.78	0.42	1.49	5.35
Own Produce Fed to Stock	9.91	6.12	2.26	3.82	5.79	4.48	6.04
Own Produce Given to Labour	1.86	4.34	3.65	4.14	2.74	4.78	3.11
Total Own Produced Inputs	*14.62*	*13.52*	*19.97*	*12.74*	*8.95*	*10.75*	*14.51*
Farm Repairs	21.30	16.33	13.37	11.15	2.95	20.60	15.89
Total Farm Costs	100.00	100.00	100.00	100.00	100.00	100.00	100.00
Total Value of Farm Costs (K.shs.)	1,019	392	576	314	950	335	579

[1] Excludes pastoral and large farm areas.

Source: Integrated Rural Survey 1974–75, p. 72.

shopkeepers, that the family and relatives ruined the shops of the businessmen, by demanding assistance for school-fees and free goods from the shop. That is, they saw the system of relatives as an obstacle to the rising class of entrepreneurs (Marris & Somerset 1971, p. 132).

Other patterns of mutual assistance have their present forms of derivatives in the economy. Women, mainly in the traditional peasant farm areas go together in women's groups, which help each other and thus formalize a kind of social security system. Some of the women's groups also form work teams, which do agricultural work on each others land in turns, and receive only food. They also work for others on a piece-rate basis, and at a lower price than individual casual labourers. These work groups, which may also include young girls, play an important role in the agricultural labour market in Kakamega District, but are also found in other areas such as Kisii. The earlier scheduled areas of the Rift Valley have been much more penetrated by the capitalist labour relations, and work groups are not formed in these areas.

Communal work has also found new expressions mainly in the Harambee (self-help) projects. The purpose of the self-help projects is to build infrastructures relying on the local resources of funds and labour. Some projects such as providing water, health centres, schools etc. are definitely beneficial to the local community. The social and political pressure to contribute to these projects is very strong, and women who have little access to money form the bulk of the labour force on these projects. The structure of these projects provides a good opportunity for the central government to decentralize development expenditure, and extract an extra surplus from poor peasant families. The interpretation of the self-help system depends on the character of the project, and may vary from being a very important local improvement, e.g. better water supply, to the extreme of a new type of taxes and forced labour imposed by local politicians or the local elite, e.g. building teachers' or chiefs' houses.

The description of the labour processes in this chapter shows how the market is internalized in the peasant economy as an organization. Peasant families are subsumed to the market economy either through the selling of farm produce and/or by selling their labour.

The process of change has eroded the basis for a system of mutual and non-exploitative labour relations within groups of relatives and neighbours, where the purpose of production was reproduction of labour, and not for investment. Now labour may also be used for accumulation of capital, which may be invested in business ventures beyond the consumption of the family and clan. The purpose of production and labour thus becomes geared to profit and subsumed to the needs of capital. In this system some may accumulate, but the majority will have to produce a profit, which is only covering the simple reproduction of labour.

The exchange relations between the peasant family and the capitalist market exploit the labour and underpay the agricultural produce. The family unit as a stable economic unit has difficulties to be maintained when it is constantly drained of resources. The division of labour and problems of a possible subdivision of the economy into a male and a female system may be seen in this context.

3. Family labour

In the previous section a generalized pattern of the development of the family economy and the division of labour was related to the general economic development in the non-scheduled areas of Kenya. But even if these general traits may well cover the majority of the rural population, there are regional variations based on different traditions, history and relations to the colonial power, and to different ecological and economic potential. All the areas studied are within the agricultural zone, and no pastoral or nomadic population is included.

However, some of the tribal groups have a longer tradition for crop cultivation relative to the livestock dominated economies, and these differences provide a basis for differences in the relative dependency on male vs. female labour. Especially among the Nandis the cultivation of vegetables was traditionally seen only as a supplement to the basic animal products such as meat, blood and milk. Thus provision of the main food products was the responsibility of the men, and the work burden of women in agriculture was much less than in the other communities.

The present structure of the division of labour retains some of the traditional features. Even if Nandi women are actively working in agriculture providing maize and vegetables for the household consumption, the proportion of land cultivated is less than in other areas leaving more land for grazing, and Nandi women are not considered responsible for providing food. In the 1975 study, Nandi men were providing supplementary food, and buying goods for the household. The women were rarely involved in trading and in making purchases and had very limited access to money. The colonial impact on the Nandis was also different than the impact on many of the other tribes, where men were involved in farm labour. Nandi men fought against the British colonial government in the period 1895–1905 and after the defeat in 1905 they refused to work for the Europeans. The women were sent to work in cases of forced labour.

The colonial impact on the Abaluyia and Luo seems to have been the high emphasis on education, the many missionary schools, and the use of men

Family labour – packing tomatoes for sale. (Erik Betting)

from these areas for bureaucratic work. There is a very high out-migration of especially males from these areas, particularly from the densely populated Maragoli area in Kakamega District. The high emphasis on education and white collar jobs, seems to have withdrawn men from their own farm work more rapidly than in other areas.

In Kisii District the Gusii people had emphasized agricultural development with intensive cultivation since the land was scarce and the population is surrounded by other tribal lands, which leaves no possibilities for expansion. Education was emphasized relatively late in this area, and the men tend to join agricultural work much more frequently than is the case among the other surrounding tribal communities.

The general trend for all the groups and areas studied is the male control of land, i.e. men own the land, and land is inherited by male dependents. The man who owns land may dispose over land and the allocation of food crops vs. cash crops, as well as what type of cash crops are to be grown. Once the wife is allocated a shamba for food crops, she is able to decide what food crops are to be grown on it.

The decision making is however very restricted in many cases; e.g. many export crops, coffee, tea, pyrethrum and even sugar are dependent upon local collection and processing, which predetermines choices for large areas. Thus leaving only decisions to be made on the relative emphasis on cash crops vs. food crops. The distinction between cash crops and food crops is difficult to maintain in areas where maize is the main cash crop, such as in the study areas of Bokoli location (Bungoma District) and of Kabondo location (South Nyanza District). The vague distinction between the male and female crops implies that quarrels over who can dispose of the output is a characteristic feature of ture of the scarcity seasons (Storgaard et al., 1971, p. 15).

The different crop patterns play an important role for the division of labour in the family, for the need for family labour and pressure on labour in the different seasons. Table 2.3 records the area cultivated with the different types of crops, but only for small farms and settlement schemes, and Uasin Gishu and Trans Nzoia Districts are not included. The table shows the relative distribution and includes interplanted crops for 1969/70. Therefore the aggregate area of crops is larger than the total cultivated area. The most frequent interplanting is that of maize and beans, also shown in the later data on landuse for small-holders for each of the three provinces in 1974–75 (see table 2.4).

The most characteristic feature is the high percentage of the cultivated area used for maize production. In all the districts it is more than 60 % of the cultivated area, even in Kakamega, where bananas are also considered an important staple food crop.

The use of hybrid maize may have been higher in 1975, but still Nyanza Province has a relatively low use of hybrid maize and very often still has interplanting of maize and beans. Only Kisii District within Nyanza Province has introduced hybrid maize on a larger scale. The traditional crops of sorghum, millet, and cassava are still grown in relatively large areas of Nyanza and Western Provinces. The most important cash crops apart from maize are coffee, pyrethrum and tea in Kisii District and cotton in South Nyanza. The major sugar production of Kisumu and South Nandi District is not really included at this time in small-holder farms. The table indicates tea as the most important cash crop for Kakamega area, whereas cotton is to a limited extent introduced in Bungoma. The crop pattern is important as a background for the data on labour input and labour profiles in the districts and provinces.

The labour profiles in terms of mean number of people working on the

Table 2.3. Estimated crop areas and land use by Districts on small farms and settlement schemes, 1969/70 (in thousand hectares).

	Nyanza Province					Western Province						Rift Valley Province				
	Kisumu	Kisii	S. Nyanza	Siaya	Total	Kakamega	Bungoma	Busia	Total	Kericho	Nandi	E/Marakwet	Total
Cereals
Improved Maize	0.8	22.2	1.2	4.3	28.5	41.3	21.7	2.1	65.1	12.5	11.9	5.6	30.0
Unimproved Maize	32.9	26.9	62.5	40.0	162.3	34.9	17.1	17.4	69.4	24.1	10.0	8.5	42.6
Millet (different types)	0.2	8.7	5.5	0.3	14.7	5.4	5.6	7.2	18.2	2.7	0.8	2.1	5.6
Sorghum	23.6	1.5	28.4	23.6	77.1	9.5	4.5	7.8	21.8	0.2	–	0.4	0.6
Other Cereals	–	–	0.1	–	0.1	0.2	0.3	–	0.5	–	–	1.7	1.7
Pulses
Beans	9.1	4.2	14.3	12.4	40.0	10.8	4.6	5.0	20.4	0.2	1.2	7.9	9.3
Peas (different types)	3.1	–	2.6	2.2	7.9	0.8	–	0.1	0.9	0.3	–	0.7	1.0
Other Pulses	0.8	–	–	**	0.8	0.1	–	0.1	0.2	–	–	**	**
Temporary Industrial Crops
Cotton	0.8	–	12.3	3.9	17.0	0.4	3.3	10.5	14.2	–	–	–	–
Sugar cane	1.2	1.1	2.5	0.5	5.3	2.1	0.1	0.1	2.3	2.9	1.5	**	4.4
Pyrethrum	–	4.8	–	–	4.8	–	–	–	–	–	–	0.2	0.2
Groundnuts	1.2	0.2	4.0	1.1	6.5	0.9	0.5	0.3	1.7	–	–	–	–
Other Temporary Industrial Crops (oil seed)	0.3	–	0.1	0.9	1.3	0.2	0.7	0.3	1.2	–	–	0.1	0.1
Other Temporary Crops
Cassava	3.2	–	8.3	5.5	17.0	6.3	3.3	7.2	16.8	–	**	0.5	0.5
English Potatoes	0.2	0.4	0.2	–	0.8	**	–	–	**	1.1	–	0.6	1.7
Sweet Potatoes	1.9	2.1	1.2	0.2	5.4	0.9	1.3	0.8	3.0	0.1	**	0.3	0.4
Cabbages & Other Vegetables	0.1	0.2	0.2	**	0.5	2.2	–	**	2.2	0.1	**	0.1	0.2
Other Temporary Crops	0.1	0.7	**	3.4	4.2	0.3	0.2	**	0.5	–	**	0.1	0.1

Permanent Crops											
Coffee	**	9.4	1.0	**	10.4	3.3	0.9	—	4.2	0.2	0.1	—	0.3
Tea	—	3.8	—	—	3.8	4.2	—	—	4.2	2.7	1.2	—	3.9
Bananas	0.8	5.1	0.6	0.1	6.8	7.2	2.1	0.3	9.6	—	0.1	0.2	0.3
Other Fruit	—	0.2	0.1	**	0.3	0.1	0.1	**	0.2	**	**	—	**
Other Permanent Crops	0.2	0.3	0.2	0.1	0.8	—	—	—	—	—	—	—	**
Total Land Use												
Aggregate area of crops	80.5	91.8	145.3	98.7	416.3	131.1	66.3	59.2	256.6	47.1	26.8	29.0	102.9
Total cultivation	48.7	77.0	101.9	56.6	284.2	114.3	56.0	41.9	212.2	47.6	25.4	18.5	91.5
Paddocked grazing	0.2	2.2	—	0.1	2.5	0.4	0.2	—	0.6	0.2	—	0.2	0.4
Other Farm Land	162.5	127.7	469.4	168.9	928.5	223.1	194.2	121.0	538.3	235.4	171.8	175.0	582.2
All Farm Land	*211.4*	*206.9*	*571.3*	*225.6*	*1,215.2*	*337.8*	*250.4*	*162.9*	*751.1*	*283.2*	*197.2*	*193.7*	*674.1*

Source: Statistical Abstract 1976. Central Bureau of Statistics, Nbi., pp. 123–124.

Table 2.4. *Total area under crops October 1974–October 1975 by crop and province[1] [4] for small farming areas (in thousand hectares).*

Kenya Crops cultivated	Nyanza Pure	Mixed	Rift Valley Pure	Mixed	Western Pure	Mixed	Total, Kenya Pure	Mixed
Cereals								
Local Maize	85.4	205.3	21.6	2.6	10.7	63.6	224.6	970.0
Hybrid Maize[2]	31.7	19.7	87.3	13.8	94.6	84.8	258.2	242.6
Finger Millet	16.2	6.9	4.9	9.5	6.9	19.4	30.5	47.4
Sorghum	13.4	162.3	0.0	0.0	3.1	16.9	16.8	189.6
Other Cereals	0.0	0.3	0.1	0.0	3.5	6.6	18.5	93.4
Pulses and Nuts[3]								
Beans	3.5	70.1	0.9	6.1	11.5	136.9	49.9	713.6
Cow Peas	0.0	2.9	0.0	0.0	0.4	12.8	11.7	259.5
Pigeon Peas	0.0	0.0	0.0	0.0	0.0	0.0	0.1	115.2
Field Peas	0.0	0.0	0.0	0.0	0.4	4.1	12.3	
Groundnuts	0.6	11.4	0.0	0.0	2.9	2.7	3.5	14.3
Other	0.0	1.7	0.0	0.0	0.8	0.6	1.1	36.3
Root Crops								
English Potatoes	0.1	0.1	0.9	0.9	0.0	0.0	48.9	212.3
Sweet Potatoes	7.7	6.5	1.0	0.3	1.2	0.4	10.9	21.7
Cassava	19.4	7.5	0.7	0.4	21.0	13.7	41.2	28.7
Other	0.0	0.0	0.0	0.0	0.0	0.0	17.7	24.4
Fruit, Vegetables and Oils								
Bananas	3.1	7.1	0.0	0.1	7.4	6.6	19.6	110.8
Other Fruits	0.0	0.0	0.1	0.1	0.3	0.0	1.2	12.3
Vegetables	0.1	1.1	0.2	1.1	1.5	3.5	4.0	52.0
Oilseeds	0.0	0.0	0.0	0.0	12.3	7.1	13.0	11.5
Temporary Industrial Crops								
Sugarcane	41.3	0.2	0.9	0.0	6.5	0.8	55.0	8.7
Pyrethrum	9.5	0.4	2.6	0.6	0.0	0.0	22.4	4.7
Cotton	10.0	15.2	1.1	0.0	13.7	6.4	25.0	45.1
Other	0.0	0.0	0.2	0.2	0.4	0.0	2.6	3.4
Permanent Crops								
Coffee	9.7	4.1	0.1	0.0	1.1	0.1	92.0	19.3
Tea	5.4	0.1	3.5	0.2	1.8	0.1	59.0	5.8
Coconuts	0.0	0.0	0.0	0.0	0.0	0.0	2.0	49.3
Cashew Nuts	0.0	0.0	0.0	0.0	0.0	0.0	5.5	48.0
Other	0.4	0.1	0.0	0.0	1.7	0.0	23.1	10.5

[1] Includes areas planted in both long and short rain season where two crops are grown within one year.
[2] Includes yellow and synthetic maize.
[3] Excluding cashew nuts.
[4] Excludes pastoral and large farm areas.

Source: Integrated Rural Survey 1974–75, p. 79.

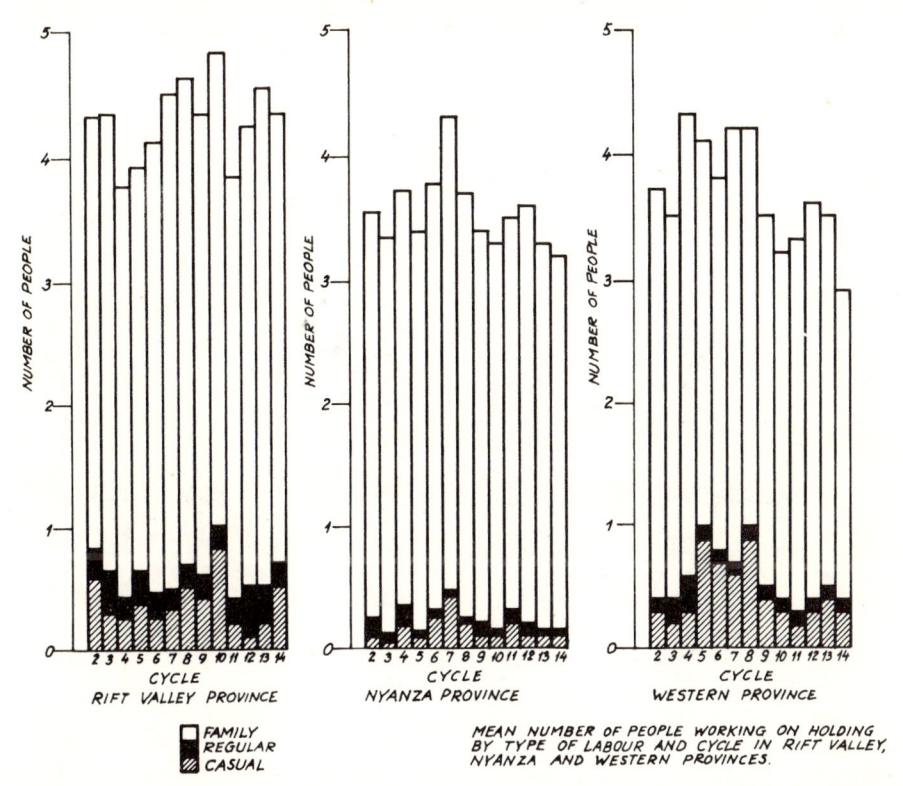

Figure 2.3. *Mean number of people working on holding by type of labour and cycle* in Nyanza, Western and Rift Valley Provinces.*

Note: *see explanations p. 52.
Source: Integrated Rural Survey 1974–75 pp. 91–92.

holdings of peasant farms show the very high emphasis on family labour in all the three provinces; approx. 3 members of the family were working in agriculture. The seasonal variations for family labour are relatively limited, though much more clear when the man-hours per holding are calculated (figs. 2.4–2.6). It is characteristic that hired labour only plays a limited role, smallest in Nyanza Province, but still represents only one person or less per holding in Western and the small-holder areas of Rift Valley (Nandi and Kericho District).

Among hired labour, casual labour caters for most of the work. The relative importance of family labour vs. hired labour is much more clear in the 3 graphs 2.4–2.6, showing the lowest use of hired labour for Nyanza Province with an average of 140 man-hours per annum, to 264 man-hours in Western and 475 man-hours on the holdings of Rift Valley. The family

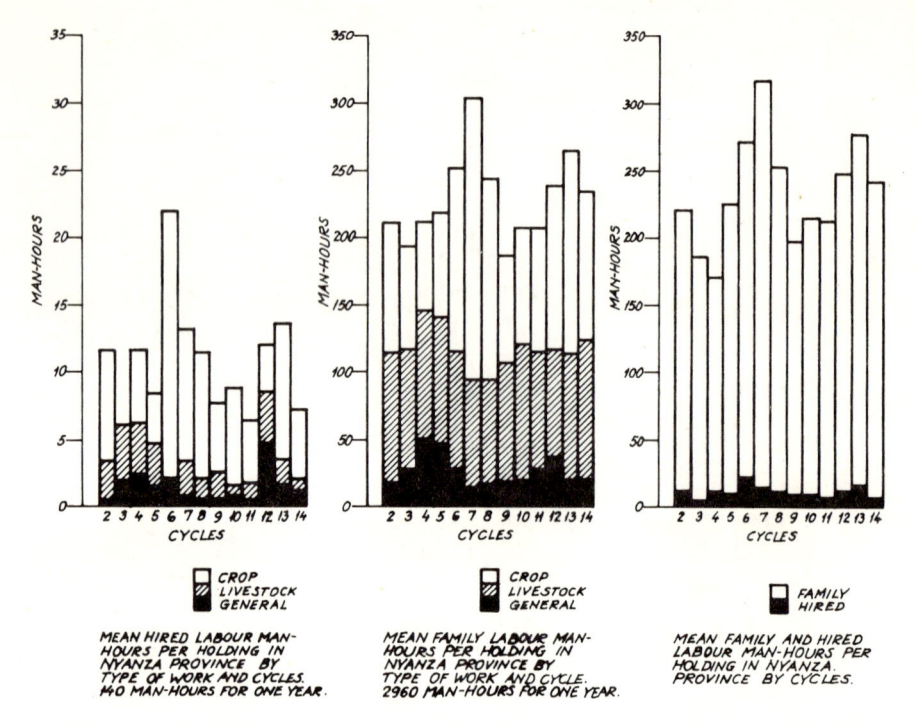

Figure 2.4. *Labour profiles for hired labour, family labour and types of work for holdings in Nyanza Province.*

Note: Explanations for cycles see p. 52.
Source: Integrated Rural Survey 1974–75 p. 96.

labour contribution is exceptionally uniform with 2960 man-hours per annum in both Nyanza and Rift Valley graphs and 2220 in Western. The latter smaller figure most likely reflects the many very small holdings in Western Province.

The relative importance of livestock is the most characteristic feature of the areas of Rift Valley, where 65 % of all family labour is used for the livestock and 61 % of the total input of man-hours. The comparable figures for Nyanza Province was 40 % of family labour and 39 % of total labour input, whereas Western Province used 38 % of family labour and 36 % of total labour on the livestock. Thus the role of livestock in the areas of Rift Valley is dominant relative to crop production, whereas crop production is dominant in the two other provinces.

The problem of evaluating the data at the provincial level is that there are major regional differences within the provinces in relation to distribution and pressure on land, crop pattern and whether one or two crops of maize

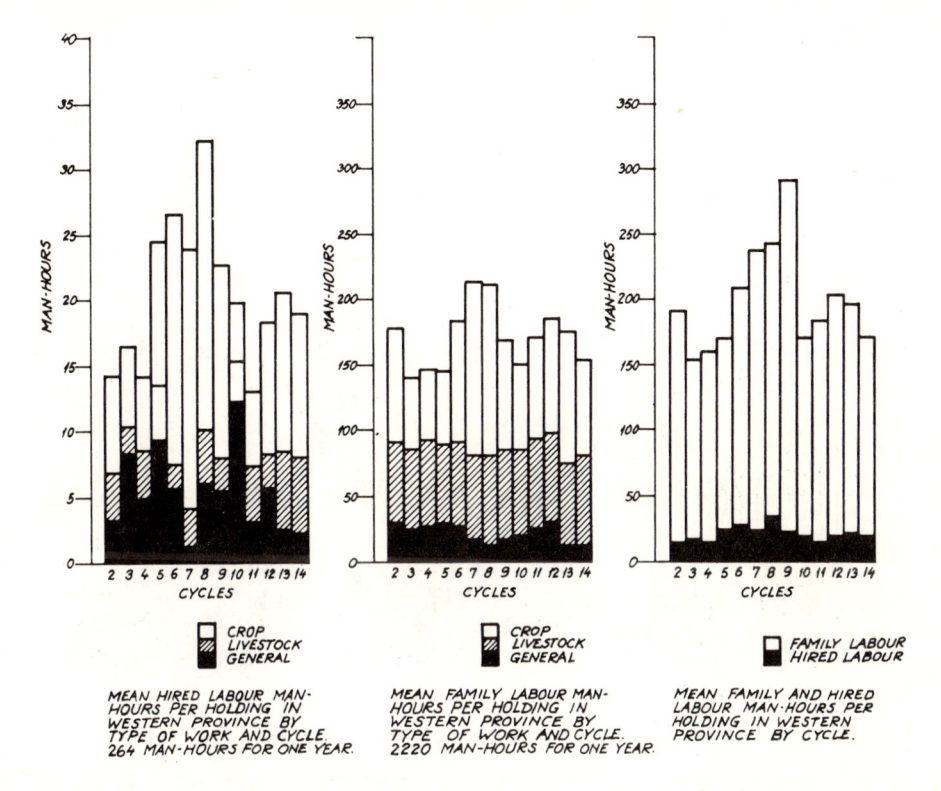

Figure 2.5. *Labour profiles for hired labour, family labour and types of work for holdings in Western Province.*

Note: Explanations of cycles p. 52.
Source: Integrated Rural Survey 1974–75, p. 98.

can be grown per year. The aggregated provincial data do not reveal as much differences as could be expected in relation to the study areas. As is shown in table 2.5, maize production dominates most of the cultivated area and the labour input for local and hybrid maize for some of the districts is thus provided in table 2.6.

The findings on labour input show not only that the labour input varies to a large extent, but also the surprising finding that local maize is more labour intensive than hybrid maize.

The major regional variations in labour input may reflect climatic variations, mainly the distribution of rainfall and altitude, influencing whether one or two crops of maize can be grown per year; Kisii has two crops while Bungoma because of the rainfall has one crop. There may be marked variations with respect to interplanting of maize, and maize interplanted

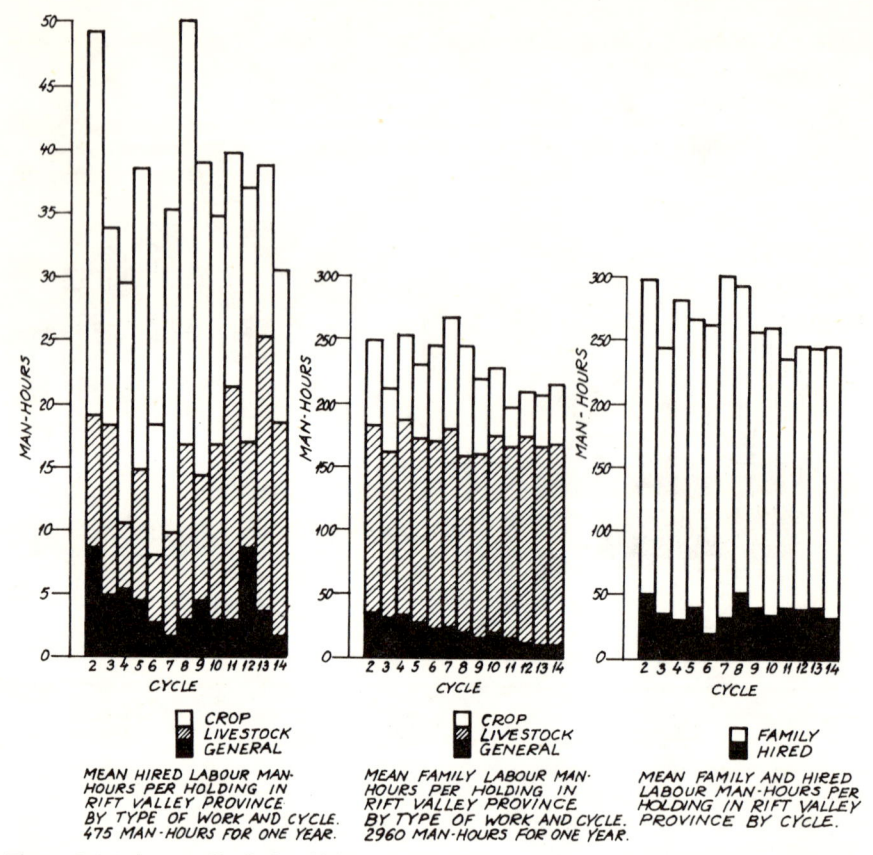

Figure 2.6. *Labour profiles for hired labour, family labour and types of work for holdings in Rift Valley Province.*

Source: Integrated Rural Survey 1974–75, p. 97.

Note: Explanations of cycles in figures 2.3–2.6.

Labour data was collected from the household for one week in every four and as noted earlier, during the course of the "Enumeration Week", a household was visited twice by the enumerator. In detailing the data on labour inputs in this chapter the totals for an enumeration week were multiplied by four to obtain the total for a cycle. The following key detailing the dates of each cycle will assist the reader in converting cycles to months.

Cycle 2	– Dec. 1st	– Dec. 28th 1974	Cycle 9	– Jun. 16th	– Jul. 13th 1975
Cycle 3	– Dec. 29th	– Jan. 25th 1974/5	Cycle 10	– Jul. 14th	– Aug. 10th 1975
Cycle 4	– Jan. 26th	– Feb. 23rd 1975	Cycle 11	– Aug. 11th	– Sep. 7th 1975
Cycle 5	– Feb. 24th	– Mar. 23rd 1975	Cycle 12	– Sep. 8th	– Oct. 5th 1975
Cycle 6	– Mar. 24th	– Apr. 20th 1975	Cycle 13	– Oct. 6th	– Nov. 2nd 1975
Cycle 7	– Apr. 21st	– May 18th 1975	Cycle 14	– Nov. 3rd	– Nov. 30th 1975
Cycle 8	– May 19th	– Jun. 15th 1975			

Source: Integrated Rural Survey 1974–75 p. 92.

Table 2.5. *Percent of cultivated and used for local and hybrid maize. Small farms and settlement schemes 1969/70.*

Districts	Local maize	Hybrid maize	Total maize
Kisumu	68	2	69
Kisii	35	29	64
South Nyanza	61	1	63
Kakamega	31	36	67
Bungoma	31	39	69
Kericho	51	26	77
Nandi	39	47	86

Source: Calculations of table 2.3.

Table 2.6. *Labour input for local and hybrid maize for Districts within Nyanza, Western and Rift Valley Province (1970/71).*

	No. of observations			Annual labour man-days/acre[1]			Farm size (acres)			Hired labour as % of total on F + H farms
	F[2]	F+H[3]	All	F	F+H	All	F	F+H	All	
Hybrid maize										
Kisii	25	8	33	90	124	98	4.3	7.1	5.0	13
Kakamega	35	10	45	29	54	35	7.7	6.5	7.4	31
Bungoma	67	20	87	72	84	74	13.7	18.1	14.7	33
Nandi	38	23	62	34	56	42	20.8	19.0	20.6	44
Kericho	22	8	30	22	38	27	15.6	19.7	16.7	45
Local maize										
Kisii	38	6	44	146	138	145	4.8	5.0	4.8	12
Kisumu	69	16	85	112	116	112	5.1	5.0	5.1	23
South Nyanza	25	18	44	118	150	128	12.3	16.9	14.0	5
Kakamega	56	11	67	44	57	46	6.3	5.8	6.2	30
Bungoma	56	1	57	84	(34)	83	12.3	(20.0)	12.5	(16)
Nandi	42	22	65	36	43	38	14.9	21.0	17.0	31
Kericho	82	3	85	26	17	24	11.7	18.4	11.9	28

[1] one man-day is 8 man-hours.
[2] F – farms based on family labour only.
[3] F+H – farms based on a combination of family labour and hired labour.

Source: G.D. Gwyer: Labour in small-scale agriculture. An analysis of the 1970/71 farm enterprise cost survey, labour and wage data. IDS W.P. 62, Nbi. Sept. 1972, tables 1 and 2.

with beans tends to have a higher labour input per acre than maize in pure stand. The third factor may be different levels of mechanization, mainly for larger farms where the land is flat. The highest labour input is found in areas where farms are small and the topography is hilly like in Kisii (Gwyer 1972, pp. 9–10). The surprising difference between hybrid maize and local maize, is contrary to instructions and other findings. This may, however, be explained by the higher frequency of two crops per year of local maize than hybrid maize, and that hybrid maize is less likely to be interplanted with other crops. The table also reveals that hired labour is used more often on hybrid maize, possibly because more of this maize is considered as a crop, and due to the short peak seasons of labour demanded in the weeding periods.

Labour input for the cash crops is usually higher than for maize, but the cash crops take up a smaller proportion of the cultivated land. The data are not comprehensive for all the districts, but a few figures are available (table 2.7). Continuously harvested crops like pyrethrum and tea tend to have a more even labour requirement through the year, but show very high needs of labour input. Tea is the highest needing more than 200 man-days per acre. Inter district variations are likely to reflect yield differences (Gwyer 1972, p. 10).

The difference between food crops and cash crops is important in relation to the internal division of labour in the family. Food crops for household consumption are more often cultivated by wife and children alone and without hired labour, whereas the husband and hired labour will more often work on cash crops together with the wife and children.

In a study on women's time allocated in a location of Embu District, Jane Hanger found that on average half of a woman's agricultural work was devoted to the man's crops – coffee and maize – which remained under his control and which were intended for eventual cash sale (Hanger & Moris, 1973, p. 227). This study also revealed that women were working more on the cash crops if the man was present on the farm, irrespective of whether or not the man was working himself on the crops (ibid. p. 227).

In the 1975 study of both women in households, and women traders and shopkeepers the issue of agricultural work and who provided labour for the cultivation was included. The information, however, does not distinguish between men's and women's crops as maize was a cash crop as well as a food crop in several of the areas. Information from the stratum of shopkeepers does not show major differences with the socially differentiated data from the case studies on women.

In order to reveal the social differences in the work pattern the peasant social strata and the rich peasants are separated. Within in peasant strata (table 2.8) the wife is contributing labour in nearly all cases, only in the Kisii

Table 2.7. *Labour input per acre for four cash crops from different small holder surveys.*

Location/District	Coffee	Tea	Pyrethrum	Cotton
Kisii	115	217	177	–
Kitutu (Kisii)	–	368	–	–
Nyanza (Kisii)	–	287	–	–
Gem (South Nyanza)	142	–	–	–
South Nyanza	–	–	–	154
Bunyore (Kakamega)	183	–	–	–
S. Kabras (Kakamega)	73	–	–	–
Bungoma	90	–	–	219
Bokoli-Malakisi (Bungoma)	158	–	–	–
Nandi	–	192	–	–
Buret (Kericho)	–	229	–	–
Komoin (Kericho)	–	182	–	–

Sources: Some aspects of agricultural development in Nyeri District 1964, Report No. 25, Statistics Division, Ministry of Economic Planning and Development 1968, and a report on economic studies of farming in Nyanza Province 1963, Farm Economic Report No. 26, Statistics Division, Ministry of Economic Planning and Development, February 1969. An econometric analysis of smallholder tea production in Kenya, D. Etherington, unpublished Ph.D. thesis, Stanford University, 1970. A. Waters, The Cost Structure of the Kenya Coffee Industry, unpublished Ph.D. thesis, Rico University, Texas, 1969. G.D. Gwyer, Labour in small-scale agriculture. IDS, W.P. 62, p. 22 (quoted by Gwyer).

and Nandi cases is the contribution a little lower, though still important. The contribution of children shows nearly as high and uniform a pattern, though in the lowest contribution areas, only 74–77% of families with children in work age, i.e. over 8 years, worked in agriculture. The husband's work contribution shows major variation – and according to many of the women the contribution was very limited and if the husband worked in agriculture, he only helped in certain periods. The information only registers whether he works at all with agriculture or not. For the cases within Nyanza Province there is little variation, ranging only from 65–77% which is limited in relation to the small basis for the figures. Within Western Province the lowest contribution is found in the cases of Kakamega District, where only 26% of husbands staying at the homestead contributed. In the Rift Valley cases the variations are all larger. The highest male participation in agriculture is found within the Nandi area, which was already described as an exception in relation to female and male responsibilities to provide food. Less than half of the husbands in the cases of Trans Nzoia helped in agriculture and the very few cases from Kericho do not show any with male participation in agriculture. But the 5 cases are certainly too limited a basis for an evaluation.

Table 2.8. *Registration of who works on the land among peasant families (percent).* *

Who contributes labour:	Kitutu (Kisii)	Kabondo (South Nyanza)	Muhoroni (Kisumu)	Areas of Nyanza Province	Isukha, Idakho & Bunyore (Kakamega)	Bokoli (Bungoma)	Areas of Western Province	Kabiyet & Kaptumo (Nandi)	Saboti & Nzoia (Trans Nzoia)	Buret (Kericho)	Areas of Rift Valley Province
Wife	88	100	100	95	97	93	96	81	100	(100)	85
Husband	77	65	71	71	26	73	43	81	42	–	61
Children	94	100	86	96	74	86	77	75	100	(100)	85
Relatives	8	10	–	8	27	71	40	3	11	–	6
Hired labour	40	17	43	30	33	14	28	81	28	–	58
Workgroups	–	–	–	–	18	–	13	3	–	–	2
No information	4	–	–	2	–	–	–	–	–	–	–
Total cases	25	29	13	67	33	16	49	32	18	5	55
Total with land for cultivation[1]	25	29	7	61	33	14	47	32	16	5	53
No. with land and husband present[2]	22	23	7	52	19	11	30	27	12	5	44
No. with land and children of work age present[3]	17	22	7	46	23	7	30	24	11	5	40

[1] N, basis for percentages on work of wife, relatives, hired labour, workgroups and "no information".
[2] basis for percentage of husbands who work in agriculture.
[3] basis for percentage of children who work in agriculture.
* information from women ( ) if basis for figure is 5 or less.

Table 2.9. *Registration of who works on the land among rich peasant families (percent).* *

Who contributes labour	Kitutu (Kisii)	Kabondo (South Nyanza)	Muhoroni (Kisumu)	Areas of Nyanza Province	Isukha, Idakho & Bunyore (Kakamega)	Bokoli (Bungoma)	Areas of Western Province	Kabiyet & Kaptumo (Nandi)	Saboti & Nzoia (Trans Nzoia)	Buret (Kericho)	Areas of Rift Valley Province
Wife	100	100	(50)	93	67	(80)	71	(100)	88	76	85
Husband	45	(−)	(50)	39	−	(33)	7	(75)	24	22	27
Children	100	86	(100)	95	75	(100)	83	(100)	76	95	84
Relatives	−	−	(25)	4	33	(60)	41	(25)	17	4	13
Hired labour	82	100	(100)	89	100	(60)	88	(100)	90	76	86
Workgroups	−	−	(−)	−	8	−	6	(−)	−	−	−
Total cases	17	7	4	28	12	5	17	4	43	26	73
Total with land for cultivation[1]	17	7	4	28	12	5	17	4	42	25	71
No. with land and husband present[2]	11	3	3	18	12	3	15	4	33	23	60
No. with land and children of work age present[3]	9	7	4	19	8	4	12	2	34	19	55

[1] N, basis for percentages on work of wife, relatives, hired labour, workgroups and 'no information'.
[2] basis for percentages of husbands who work in agriculture.
[3] basis for percentage of children who work in agriculture.
* information from women.
( ) if basis for figure is 5 or less.

Table 2.10. *Registration of who works on the land, data distributed by Provinces and social strata. (percent).* *

	Peasant				Rich Peasant				Total
Cases from	Ny-anza Prov.	West-ern Prov.	Rift Valley Prov.	Peas-ant total	Ny-anza Prov.	West-ern Prov.	Rift Valley Prov.	Rich Peas-ant total	
Percent working in agriculture									
Wife	95	96	85	93	93	71	85	84	90
Husband	71	43	61	61	39	7	27	26	46
Children	96	77	85	87	95	83	84	86	87
Relatives	8	40	6	17	4	41	13	15	16
Hired labour	30	28	58	39	89	88	86	87	59
Workgroups	–	13	2	4	–	6	–	1	3
No information	2	–	–	1	–	–	–	–	0
Total cases	67	49	55	171	28	17	73	118	289
Total with land for cultivation[1]	61	47	53	161	28	17	71	116	277
No. with land and husband present[2]	52	30	44	126	18	15	60	93	219
No. with land and children of work age present[3]	46	30	40	116	19	12	55	86	202

* information from women-based cases.
[1] Basis for percentages on work of wife, relatives, hired labour and 'no information'.
[2] Basis for percentage of husband's work in agriculture.
[3] Basis for percentage of children's work in agriculture.

The role of relatives is limited in both Nyanza and Rift Valley Provinces whereas the cases in Western Province seem to rely to some extent on assistance from relatives, especially in the Bokoli cases.

The use of hired labour varies to a great extent, the highest use being clearly the Nandi area. The lowest use of hired labour is found in Kabondo and in Bokoli. But the very low input of hired labour in Nyanza province relative to Western and Rift Valley as indicated in the Integrated Rural Survey graphs 2.1–2.6 cannot be confirmed. The use of hired labour does not indicate how much hired labour is used throughout the year, therefore the work of casual labour in short peak seasons is overestimated and this may be the reason for the discrepancy. Work groups of women only play a role in the areas of Kakamega.

Within the rich peasant families the differences are larger (table 2.9), but uniformly they are less dependent on family labour and more on hired labour. Only children's work contribution seems to show the same uniform pattern; even if it is very high in most areas, it is lower in the sugar scheme of Muhoroni, the Kakamega and Kericho cases.

The husband generally contributes less labour than in the poorer social classes, only in Nandi is he participating in the majority of cases. In most of the areas he contributes to the work in less than half the cases, with as little as zero participation in the Kakamega study.

The role of relatives seems to be more important for the more commercial farming areas such as Muhoroni, Trans Nzoia and even Nandi, but less important in the traditional peasant farming areas. But the cases of rich peasant families from the peasant farming areas of the earlier "Reserves" are very limited. The tendency to rely on relatives in the commercial farming may be the contribution of young girls from poorer relatives mentioned earlier.

The use of hired labour is uniformly high for all the rich peasant farms, the lowest being in the Bokoli cases with 60%, the area apparently most traditional and dependent on assistance from relatives. But the percentage in the Buret cases is also surprisingly low.

Table 2.10 tries to summarize the two tables and compare the social differences for the accumulated data for the Provinces.

Table 2.11, based on interviews with male shopkeepers, seems to confirm the main traits already provided by the women, except that the men reporting, who are all in non-farm self-employment, work less in agriculture within both social strata. The social classes of these businessmen are usually higher than for those in the women-based survey who are classified as peasant families, but still with the effort to classify the shopkeepers the criteria seems to leave them comparable to the medium and top of the peasant families.

The use of hired labour in agriculture in both social strata seems to be higher for shopkeepers in Nyanza Province in relation to the women-based data. But the high emphasis and dependency on family labour from wife and children is still confirmed in this table. The other more qualitative information derived from the shop-keeper cases is the important evidence that women and children can reproduce themselves from the allocated land in agriculture, and the unwillingness to support the family with means for the household from the shop. On the other hand the shopkeepers underline the heavy burden of school fees, which they claim to be totally responsible for.

In relation to the evaluation of the size of the work input the survey, undertaken at one point in time and without time-budgeting does not give much indication. However, through several questions designed to probe the

Table 2.11. Registration of who works on the land in different social strata of the shopkeeper sample (percent).

Who contributes labour in agriculture	Kitutu (Kisii)	Kabondo (South Nyanza)	Muhoroni (Kisumu)	Shopkeepers from Nyanza Prov.	Isukha (Kakamega)	Bokoli (Bungoma)	Shopkeepers from Western Prov.	Kabiyet and Kaptumo (Nandi)	Saboti and Kaptumo (Trans Nzoia)	Londiani and Kericho (Kericho)	Metkei (Elgeyo Marakwet)	Shopkeepers from Rift Valley Prov.
Poor and Medium social strata[1]												
Husband	45	37	8	34	–	28	20	25	25	–	20	21
Other family labour[2]	45	37	8	34	–	28	20	25	25	–	20	21
Hired labour	95	84	75	87	100	94	96	64	89	100	100	83
	68	53	42	57	29	33	32	89	57	36	60	66
Total cases with land to cultivate	22	19	12	53	7	18	25	28	28	11	10	77
Medium to rich social strata[3]												
Husband	–	–	–	–	–	–	–	14	13	–	11	11
Other family labour	(100)	92	67	85	86	(75)	82	57	94	75	89	79
Hired labour	(100)	58	67	65	86	(25)	64	100	94	50	89	87
Total cases with land to cultivate	2	12	6	20	7	4	11	14	16	8	9	47

[1] shopkeepers with less than 20 acres of land and small turnover in shop.
[2] Includes mostly wife/wives' and children's work, but emphasis on wife's work contribution, which is considered most important.
[3] Shopkeepers with 20 acres of land or more and medium or high turnover in shop.
( ) If basis for figure is 5 or less.

Table 2.12. *The average number of days per week that the women report to work in agriculture. (Distribution by area and social strata).*

	Peasant slack season	Peasant busy season	Rich Peasant slack season	Rich Peasant busy season
Kitutu	4.1	5.2	4.4	5.4
Kabondo	3.9	4.3	4.0	4.4
Muhoroni	3.5	3.6	(3.0)	(3.0)
Cases from Nyanza	3.9	4.6	4.1	4.8
Idakho, Isukha & Bunyore	2.7	5.6	2.4	3.9
Bokoli	1.3	4.7	(0.8)	(4.7)
Cases from Western	2.2	5.3	1.9	4.2
Kabiyet & Kaptumo	0.6	3.5	(1.5)	(4.0)
Saboti & Nzoia	1.3	4.5	1.8	3.6
Buret	(1.9)	(4.0)	2.0	3.7
Cases from Rift Valley	1.0	3.8	1.8	3.7
Total cases	2.6	4.6	2.4	4.0

( ) if basis is 5 or less households.

amount of work done by women in slack versus busy agricultural seasons, there is some indication of the amount of work the women provide and the labour profile (table 2.12). Similarly there is an indication of the importance of the work of children by recording whether they are regularly involved or only in vacations and week-ends (table 2.13). The amount of work which men do in agriculture is only, in the women-based cases, reported as work or as assistance and help in shorter periods. The latter being more often mentioned, which is more in line with the traditional role of men in agriculture. Also the amount of hired labour input seems to be difficult to evaluate. Except for the very large farms in Rift Valley, all the hired labour is always casual labour in the pek season and not permanent labour.

Table 2.12 provides some indication of the labour profile for agriculture and for the amount of work women provide for agriculture in the different extreme seasons. It is important to note that there seems to be practically no difference between the two social strata. The other important notion is the relatively stable and high labour input by women in Nyanza especially in the Kitutu cases. The largest seasonal variations are found in Bokoli and the Rift Valley cases. Especially in the Nandi cases the slack season labour input is low. The dependency on women's labour in agriculture becomes obvious in this table and seems to be valid in all the areas studied.

Table 2.13. *Children's work in agriculture by Province and social strata (percent)*

Children's work	Peasant Families				Rich Peasant Families				Total
	Nyanza Prov.	Western Prov.	Rift Valley Prov.	Total Peasant	Nyanza Prov.	Western Prov.	Rift Valley Prov.	Total Rich Peasant	
Work daily/ after school	27	59	65	48	32	25	40	36	43
Work week-ends or vacations	51	21	23	33	58	42	35	41	37
Work – but amount not specified	20	–	8	11	5	17	9	9	10
Do not work	2	21	5	8	5	17	16	14	11
N = families with land and children of work age at home	45	29	40	114	19	12	55	86	200
Families with children too young to work or not home	15	18	13	46	9	5	16	30	76

In relation to children's work in agriculture, it is clear that children's work input has declined seriously with the high school-enrollment. But it is also important to note that even with long school hours and long walking distances, the children are not relieved of the obligations to work, even if in reality many will have to work in agriculture only during weekends and vacations. However, the shortage of secondary schools in the rural areas imply that many of the children in secondary schools have to go to boarding schools and thus stay away from obligations in the home, at the same time as the costs are very high for the family.

The table only includes families with land to cultivate and who have children in working age, i.e. 8 years and over staying in the home. It provides crude data accumulated for the areas within the provinces, as between one-fourth and one-third of the families have only too young children or have no children staying at home.

There is relatively little difference between the social strata with respect to whether children work or not. But there are more children of peasant families who work daily. The emphasis on work only at week-ends and during vacation is dominant among rich peasant families, reflecting the higher proportion going to school also beyond the primary education.

There is a bit of a difference within the provinces, as the cases from Kitutu,

Table 2.14. Children's help with different domestic and farm duties. Distribution by sex, age group and Province (percent).

Area, age	Females Agri- culture	Herd- ing	House- hold	Fetch water	Collect fire- wood	Child- care	Trade	Fe- male N	Males Agri- culture	Herd- ing	House- hold	Fetch water	Collect fire- wood	Child- care	Trade	Male N
Nyanza Province																
4–6 yrs.	4	8	21	17	8	21	–	24	–	15	10	15	15	10	–	20
7–8 yrs.	32	–	47	47	47	53	5	19	31	46	8	31	15	15	8	13
9–11 yrs.	59	23	68	64	68	45	5	22	68	64	24	44	32	16	16	25
12–15 yrs.	82	11	68	61	61	39	4	28	86	55	9	14	14	–	5	22
16 and over	78	–	61	50	39	6	11	18	91	27	9	9	5	–	14	22
Western Province																
4–6 yrs.	–	–	10	20	20	30	–	10	8	25	8	8	–	17	–	12
7–8 yrs.	–	(20)	(80)	(80)	(80)	(60)	–	5	44	33	33	22	33	–	–	9
9–11 yrs.	38	–	50	63	50	63	–	8	42	33	–	17	17	25	–	12
12–15 yrs.	82	9	64	82	82	45	9	11	44	56	–	28	33	6	6	18
16 and over	31	–	38	38	38	8	8	13	63	38	–	–	–	–	13	16
Rift Valley Province																
4–6 yrs.	4	–	30	9	13	70	–	23	9	36	18	18	9	27	–	11
7–8 yrs.	9	9	73	18	36	45	–	11	36	64	14	14	14	7	–	14
9–11 yrs.	29	13	79	42	50	50	–	24	13	60	20	13	13	7	7	15
12–15 yrs.	53	–	93	40	40	33	–	15	50	67	17	6	17	–	6	18
16 and over	67	–	92	50	58	8	8	24	71	52	–	10	5	–	14	21
All Areas																
4–6 yrs.	2	4	23	14	12	42	–	57	2	23	12	14	9	16	–	43
7–8 yrs.	20	6	60	43	49	51	3	35	36	50	17	22	19	8	3	36
9–11 yrs.	43	15	70	54	57	50	2	54	46	56	17	29	23	15	10	52
12–15 yrs.	74	7	74	59	59	39	4	54	62	59	9	16	21	5	5	58
16 and over	62	–	69	47	47	7	9	55	76	39	3	7	3	2	14	59

Young girl fetching water. (Gunvor Jørgsholm)

Bokoli and Buret in both social strata show a majority of children working daily. In Trans Nzoia this is also clearly the case for the peasant families. For the rest of the cases, there is a clear tendency for most of the children to work on the farm only at week-ends and during vacations.

Even if school children tend to be of less value in proper agricultural work and of course in time consuming activities such as herding, they have other important functions in the household. In order to get an idea about the age and sex pattern of the tasks done by children, table 2.14 reflects the percentage of children in each age group and sex, who do the different tasks mentioned – there are multiple answers as children may help with several of the domestic and farm duties.

Generally the pattern reflects what was traditionally male and female duties, showing more female involvement in household duties, fetching water, collecting firewood and child care. Likewise males are more involved in herding. Agricultural work – supervised by the mother – seems to be a duty of boys as well as girls.

With respect to age the heavy duties such as farm work increase with age, whereas most other duties are heaviest for the group of 9–15 year old children.

Already in the age group of 4–6 year old children, many are involved in the necessary duties at home, the most extreme cases are in the Rift Valley where 70% of girls at this age are taking care of younger siblings. Around half of the girls in ages up to 15 years are involved in child care, whereas this work is much less burdensome for boys. The regional differences in this task is limited except for the case of the 4–6 year old girls.

Fetching water and collecting firewood is another typical work task of women, which is shared with their children as soon as possible. Even if some boys and girls do this before 7 years of age, it is only a characteristic job for more than half of the girls from the age of 9.

The burden of fetching water and wood for girls seems to be most heavy in the Nyanza and Western Province cases, where the boys also share these tasks to a higher extent than in the Rift Valley cases. The accumulated data for the provinces cover the local differences, where the assistance with these tasks is higher in the Kitutu cases and more shared by the boys, who in nearly as many cases do this job, compared to the other areas of Nyanza Province. This job is more burdensome also for the Buret male and female cases than for those of the Trans Nzoia.

Household duties consisting of cooking, cleaning, preparing the grains etc. are clearly the work of girls, and most help from the age of 7. One-third or less of the boys assist with this work only in the cases where sisters are not home to do this work.

With respect to herding, this is one of the traditional male duties, and for boys it plays a major role compared to other duties. Herding is the work for over half of the boys of 7–15 years in the cases for Nyanza and Rift Valley Province. Within the latter Province more than 75% of boys from 4–15 herd in the Buret cases. Herding plays a much smaller role in Western Province, especially in the Kakamega cases with the small land plots and no common land for grazing. Girls are only herding to a very limited extent, mostly when no brothers are available for the job.

Very few assist their mothers with trading activities, and only older children, both boys and girls, are involved in this.

Another job not mentioned here is the role of especially the young children to run errands. This is the duty of both boys and girls and considered an important help in the household.

The work tasks of the children reflect the responsibilities and duties of the mother, thus many children are clearly a burden and expensive, given the demand of school fees and costs of buying food in periods of the year, but they are contributing and helping in the household for their own support.

The data are supplemented by more recent research on the work of children in rural areas of Embu, South Nyanza and Tana River Districts. The survey of these districts shows that the 11–14 year age group appears to be the most important to relieve the parents of work. Also in the Nyanza and Tana River cases, female children were perceived to be more important with respect to work input than the male. The work of children which is most valued by the mother is agricultural work and herding (Kayongo-Male & Walji 1978, pp. 6–8). The reported work contribution on agricultural duties, i.e., shamba work and harvesting cash crops, was on average between 21 and 28 hours per week. Approx. half the work was in the cash crops. Herding took between 2 and nearly 12 hours per week, but with 7–12 hours where livestock played any substantial role in the rural economy. The South Nyanza cases showed an input of approx. 23 hours per week in agriculture and nearly 12 hours of herding.

This recent study is unique in the focus on the variety of children's work tasks. There are few studies taking up the work input of children and the sexual division of labour of children. Therefore the importance of child labour is also under heavy debate. The debate on children's labour only considers the work in agriculture and herding, but rarely involves other duties which are not directly economically valued. These other tasks may release the mother for productive agricultural work when the household duties are carried out by the children. The necessity of the work input of children is expressed in the study by Kayongo-Male and Walji: "in all areas over three-fourths of the mothers feel that they would find it difficult to

Cooking porridge at the fireplace. (Gunvor Jørgsholm)

complete the various tasks, since the burden of the work would fall on them." (Kayongo-Male & Walji 1978, p. 10).

The only data from official statistics are from a farm survey in Kenya 1963/64 giving information on the average man-days worked on the farm in Districts of Central, Western and Nyanza Provinces. The data are

The daily meal in a well equipped rural household. (Gunvor Jørgsholm)

unfortunately difficult to compare as the data from the Central Province includes a wider group of farmers and small-holders, and the Western and Nyanza cases have a strong bias to progressive large scale farmers and with very heavy impact of hired labour (mostly males) in relation to the farms in Central Province. Work with livestock is very much work of males and mostly of children. This explains the large input of work of children on the farms of Nyanza and Western Province, where livestock plays a major role in the farm production (table 2.15). If labour for livestock is deducted, the pattern is much more like the Central Province, even if the labour input of males is larger, including the work of hired labour, and the labour intensity is less than in Central Province, given the much larger farms of the progressive farmers selected in the provinces.

The tables seem to have a higher input of labour by males, except in the Bungoma sample, than could be expected from later information. There are, however, major regional differences. In relation to the discrepancy with later data there may be several explanations which may all influence this pattern. First of all more traditional shifting cultivation was done in 1963/64 than now, where much of the heavy work with preparation of the soil is replaced by need for manure or fertilizer, and where ploughing one time per year is gaining momentum, replacing the time consuming and heavy digging, which was mainly the work of men. But the interviews were also

Table 2.15. *Average number of man-days worked on farms in the sample in Central Province 1963/64 (absolute and percentages).*

District	Men	Women	Children	Total
Kiambu	78 (15%)	165 (31%)	285 (54%)	528
Fort Hall (Murang'a)	147 (40%)	179 (49%)	37 (10%)	363
Embu	208 (45%)	227 (49%)	25 (5%)	460
Nyeri	225 (47%)	205 (43%)	45 (9%)	475
Meru	136 (41%)	185 (56%)	8 (2%)	329
Total	714 (37%)	961 (45%)	400 (19%)	2,155

Source: Farm Economic Survey of Central Province. Table 20 p. 16. Quoted from Winans (1972) and calculations.

Table 2.16. *Average number of man-days worked on farms in the sample of Nyanza and Western Provinces 1963 (absolute and percentages).*

Location	Men	Women	Children	Total
Gem (South Nyanza)	314 (61%)	96 (19%)	102 (20%)	512
Bunyore (Kakamega)	173 (34%)	160 (31%)	181 (35%)	514
South Kabras (Kakamega)	448 (41%)	256 (23%)	390 (36%)	1,094
Bokoli-Malakisi (Bungoma)	212 (30%)	237 (33%)	263 (37%)	712
Total	935 (36%)	749 (29%)	936 (36%)	2,620

Source: Farm Economic Report No. 26 table 7.4 p. 74. Quoted from Winans (1972) and calculations.

Table 2.17. *Average number of man-days worked on the farms in the sample of Nyanza and Western Provinces 1963, less the man-days expended on livestock (absolute and percentages).*

Location	Men	Women	Children	Total
Gem (South Nyanza)	202 (62%)	92 (28%)	30 (9%)	324
Bunyore (Kakamega)	140 (39%)	145 (40%)	75 (21%)	360
South Kabras (Kakamega)	220 (50%)	186 (42%)	32 (7%)	438
Bokoli-Malakisi (Bungoma)	49 (17%)	186 (64%)	55 (19%)	290
Total	611 (43%)	609 (43%)	192 (14%)	1,412

Source: Farm Economic Report No. 26, table 7.4 p. 74 quoted by Winans (1972) and calculations.

with the males, who may have strengthened their role in the work and included the supervision work. Also the hired labour of males as casual labourers is included in the men's work contribution. This is the only official survey in Kenya including child labour in agriculture and herding. In 1963 the school enrollment of children was not that high, and the children could use time and energy for the agricultural production. Especially in relation to herding, the labour (time) input of children was very high, as reflected in table 2.16 and the difference between tables 2.16 and 2.17.

The sexual division of labour and child labour is rarely evaluated in relation to the different crop-patterns. Only in more general terms is child labour expected to be more important in subsistence agriculture than in cash-crop production (Caldwell 1967, p. 229). This may be true for areas considered mainly subsistence in relation to areas with a monocultural export crop production. For instance, among sugar out-growers in the sugar belt, family labour and especially children's labour plays only a minimal role. On the other hand, it appears as if children's work is important even on export crops, if they are cultivated in a smallholder area. With respect to rice schemes with a monoculture the perception of the role of children's labour is disputed.

The role of family labour, both according to sex and adult vs. child labour, is studied in relation to the crop-pattern in two Tanzanian studies. In one survey from Westlake Region in Tanzania the details on the four main crops allow for an analysis of both the relationship between family labour, hired labour and relatives/visitors and for a sexual division of labour (table 2.18).

The highest input of family labour was for cattle and for coffee (over 99%), while the lowest was for tea (82.8%). The traditional food crops of banana mixtures and sweet potatoes had a high family labour input (89%), but also higher participation of hired labour than the coffee. It should however be stressed that family labour contribution is by far the dominant part of the labour, and that hired labour is approx. half male, half female. Work of relatives and visitors is mainly female labour.

The men's labour contribution is primarily high in tea cultivation, where it accounts for nearly half of the labour input. Approx. one-third of the labour on coffee and bananas is done by men, and one-fourth of the work with cattle. Women do more than half of the work on sweet potatoes and half on coffee and banana mixtures.

Women are responsible for around one-fourth to one-third of the tea cultivation, and rarely take part in cattle-tending.

The children's work is clearly dominated by the work days spent on herding, where the children are responsible for three-quarters of the work with cattle. They contribute a little less than one-fifth of the labour in tea,

Table 2.18. *Annual labour input (man-days) in four main crops per hectare and cattle tending in a farm survey in Bukoba District, Tanzania. Distribution by sex, adult vs. child labour, family vs. hired labour.*

	Tea	Coffee	Banana mixture	Sweet potatoes	Cattle tending
Family labour					
Men	145.3 (41.8%)	120.7 (32.3%)	90.4 (26.9%)	4.1 (9.0%)	30.2 (26.6%)
Women	86.3 (24.8%)	187.0 (50.1%)	151.3 (45.0%)	24.8 (54.5%)	0.7 (0.6%)
Children	55.9 (16.1%)	63.6 (17.0%)	58.2 (17.3%)	11.6 (25.5%)	81.9 (72.0%)
Hired labour					
Men	18.2 (5.2%)	1.0 (0.3%)	15.4 (4.6%)	1.0 (2.2%)	— —
Women	14.5 (4.2%)	—	6.0 (1.8%)	0.7 (1.5%)	— —
Children	9.0 (2.6%)	1.0 (0.3%)	1.0 (0.3%)	—	— —
Visitors					
Men	3.0 (0.9%)	— —	2.8 (0.8%)	1.8 (4.0%)	0.9 (0.8%)
Women	14.4 (4.1%)	— —	9.6 (2.9%)	1.2 (2.6%)	— —
Children	1.0 (0.3%)	— —	1.0 (0.3%)	—	— —
Male total	166.5 (47.9%)	121.7 (32.6%)	108.5 (32.3%)	6.9 (15.2%)	31.1 (27.4%)
Female total	115.2 (33.2%)	187.0 (50.1%)	166.9 (49.6%)	26.7 (58.7%)	0.7 (0.6%)
Children total	65.6 (18.9%)	64.7 (17.3%)	60.9 (18.1%)	11.9 (26.2%)	81.9 (72.0%)
Family labour total	287.6 (82.8%)	371.3 (99.4%)	299.9 (89.2%)	40.5 (89.0%)	112.8 (99.2%)
Hired labour total	41.7 (12.0%)	2.1 (0.6%)	22.6 (6.7%)	1.7 (3.7%)	—
Visitors total	18.0 (5.2%)	—	13.8 (4.1%)	3.3 (7.3%)	0.9 (0.8%)
Grand Total	347.3	373.4	336.3	45.5	113.7

Source: A.A. Moody, A Report on Farm Economic Survey of Tea Smallholders in Bukoba District. E.R.B. Paper 70.8. Dar es Salaam 1970, pp. 18–19, and calculations.

coffee and bananas, but more than one-fourth in sweet potatoes. This pattern seems to indicate, of course, that they are more important in traditional crops, but the differences are small between traditional food crops and export crops.

The role of children's labour in this analysis seems to be relatively large, at least larger than any other sources of labour apart from the parents. Thus it is more important than hired labour in all these crops.

In the other Tanzanian study of a rice producing area in Mbeya, the children did 11% of the work in the paddy. Most was done during May and June, when they were on vacation from school (Dines 1977). The study revealed that men performed 39%, women 28%, children 8%, relatives 8% and hired labour 17% of the total labour input in hours per hectare. Thus the labour of children was much less than in the previous study, and less important than hired labour. Rice is predominantly considered a male crop. The male tasks in the area are mainly soil preparation for paddy, maize and other crops. This is a time-consuming job, and the man does the bulk of it, even if women do a share of it for the maize and vegetable areas. The men are also engaged in most of the processes for the paddy, but only slightly with the other crops. Women's work is mainly related to their responsibility for the maize production, where they do more than half of the total work, and most of the work after the soil preparation. Women help in preparing the soil and they are involved in transplanting the rice, weeding, keeping birds and animals away, threshing/winnowing and transporting the rice. The women's heaviest workwith the paddy is transplanting in January–February and in June with harvesting, threshing and transporting.

The children mainly assist during school vacations with keeping animals away and harvesting, but also in transplanting, where all labour is needed, and when most hired labour is recruited. Children contribute very little work to the subsistence crops, which is untypical in relation to other studies, which emphasized that the work of children only plays a role in subsistence agriculture.

The importance of child labour, which in this study of a rice scheme seems to be of some importance, is in the Kenyan Mwea rice scheme evaluated in quite different ways. Jane Hanger (Hanger & Moris 1973) perceive child labour as relatively unimportant both in agriculture and in other work, because children go to school and young children are cared for in a daycare centre.

On the other hand the child labour seems to be considered important in the transplanting period, which is in August and during school vacation for children. At the same time the tenants complain of labour shortage as hired labourers are in short supply, and they do not get enough from the rice

Table 2.19. *Expenses to wage of farm labour according to size of farms.*

	Size of farm (hectares)							
	<0.5	0.5–0.9	1.0–1.9	2.0–2.9	3.0–3.9	4.0–4.9	5.0 or more	Total
Wages paid (K.shs.)								
Regular labour	25	76	45	73	83	86	130	67
Casual labour	35	57	75	92	126	147	225	93
Total wages	60	133	120	165	209	233	355	160
Percent of farm costs for								
Regular labour	8.5	20.8	8.6	13.3	10.5	10.5	11.2	11.6
Casual labour	11.9	15.6	14.4	16.8	16.0	17.9	19.3	16.1
Wage in % of farm costs	20.4	36.4	23.0	30.1	26.5	28.4	30.5	27.6
Total farm costs (K.shs.)	295	365	522	548	788	820	1,163	579

Source: Integrated Rural Survey, p. 74 and calculations.

production to be able to pay much hired labour. This leaves them with a high dependency on family labour (Mutugi & Gitau 1975).

The conclusion on the importance of children's labour may be that it is still an important contribution in many areas, but the increasing school enrollment has left less time for agricultural work, and made hired labour or increased female or male labour input necessary to substitute some of this work. In relation to family labour, it seems for to be a salient feature that women are the main cultivators and do most of the work in agriculture, but that with some special crop patterns there may be a higher male labour input.

4. Hired labour within agriculture

The tables in the section on family labour reveal that even if the main emphasis in small and medium-scale farming is on family labour, the use of hired labour at least in short seasons is quite widespread, and ranges between around 10 % to 40 % for the smallholder areas, and up to 80 % for the settlement scheme areas (own data and Gwyer 1972). There seems to be a limited regional variation though, with less use of hired labour in the studied areas of South Nyanza and Bungoma, and according to Gwyer also a relatively low dependency on hired labour in Kisii.

The discrepancy concerning Kisii District in relation to the other Districts of Nyanza Province may reflect the fact that the lowest cost of hired labour

Table 2.20. *The relationship between output, land utilization, employment and farm size on settlement schemes, 1967/68.*

Farm Size Group	Average Farm Size	Gross Output	Land use — Proportion of Land Under Crops	Stocking Rate	Labour Inputs — No. of Family Labourers	No. of Regular Labourers	Total No. of Labourers	Expenditure on Machinery Cultivation*
Acres	Acres	Sh per Acre	Per cent	Grazing Acres per Stock Unit	(Men Equivalents per 1,000 Acres)			Sh per Crop Acre
Less than 10	7.3	635	45	0.9	781	27	808	6
10–19.9	13.8	250	30	2.6	370	29	399	11
20–29.9	23.5	156	24	3.0	211	23	234	9
30–39.9	34.7	161	16	3.8	135	24	159	28
40–49.9	44.4	113	14	4.1	103	21	124	21
50–59.9	52.3	98	13	5.1	93	18	111	19
60–69.9	64.5	98	19	5.3	77	32	109	12
70 or more	124.8	111	14	3.6	42	28	70	10
All farms	30.5	156	19	3.5	164	26	190	14

* These figures do not reflect the charge per acre for machinery services, but indicate the average expenditure over all crop acres.

Source: Kenya Statistical Digest, March 1972, p. 7.

is found in Kisumu District and the highest in Kisii District (50 versus 118 K.Shs.)(Nyanza Household Survey 1970/71). However in relation to the total farm cost, the wage paid for hired labour is less than 50 % of the farm inputs in Kisii and thus less than the other Districts of Nyanza Province (between 50–60 % in Kisumu and South Nyanza and 80 % in Siaya) (Rural Household Survey, Nyanza Province 1970/71, 1977, p. 32).

The data from the Integrated Rural Survey 1974–75 reveal less use of hired labour in Nyanza Province (figures 2.2–2.3). The same survey, however, has difficulties in proving that larger farms use more hired labour. There is a tendency that the larger the farm the higher the absolute expenses used on hired labour, but the wage expenses relative to total farm costs do not show the expected variation (table 2.19).

The use of hired labour increases per farm with larger farm size, but does not increase per acre. This is probably related to the type of farming, the area cultivated and crop pattern of farms with different farm sizes.

Both on the large farms and the settlement schemes employment declined per acres with increasing farm size (tables 2.20 and 2.21). "On the settlement farms total employment fell from 808 jobs to 70 jobs per 1,000 acres between the smallest and the largest farms, while on the large farms in Trans Nzoia there was a similar decline in the total number of labourers employed per 100 acres from 93 to 14 as farm size increased." (Kenya Statistical Digest, March 1972, p. 5).

The explanation of the decreasing labour input per 1000 acres is related to the lower proportion of land under crops as farm size increases. The larger farms have more grazing land for livestock and more unused land. The level of mechanization, however, does not appear to provide any explanation as the expenditure on machinery cultivation per acre is rather uniform within all settlement schemes and within large farms. The level of mechanization of the settlement schemes is much less (approx. one-tenth) than the level on large farms. Thus it may explain the much lower labour input on large farms for Trans Nzoia relative to settlement schemes.

Over time from 1964–1968 the number of regular workers per acre has declined and casual workers have increased, and in the same period family labour input has increased per acre in the settlement schemes, while employed labour has been relatively stable (Kenya Statistical Digest, March 1972, p. 6–7).

The dependency mostly on family labour, but with some help from relatives, was confirmed for other settlement areas in Central Province where a study of a scheme in Nyeri District revealed that 10.6 % used only family labour, while 37.7 % used a combination of family and hired labour. 75 % of the work on the farms was carried out by family labour (Nguyo 1966).

Table 2.21. *The relationship between output, land utilization, employment and farm size on large farms in Trans Nzoia, 1970/71.*

Farm Size Group	Average Farm Size	Gross Output	Land use: Proportion of Land Under Crops	Land use: Stocking Rate	Employment: No. of Regular Labourers	Employment: No. of Casual Labourers	Employment: Total No. of Labourers	Expenditure on Machinery Cultivation*
Acres	Acres	Sh. per Acre	Per cent	Grazing Acres per Stock Unit	(Men Equivalents per 1,000 Usable Acres)			Sh. per Crop Acre
Less than 250	183	248	46	3.2	38	55	93	135
250–499	326	161	21	3.1	31	31	62	140
500–749	546	133	24	3.8	26	17	43	136
750–999	816	113	19	6.2	29	15	44	146
1,000–1,249	1,012	89	13	4.4	19	15	34	119
1,250–1,499	1,194*	149	18	4.2	28	18	46	167
1,500–1,999	1,502	128	10	4.3	18	10	28	155
2,000 or more	2,979	65	9	7.1	7	7	14	131
All farms	890	117	16	4.8	21	15	36	143

* This is outside the farm size group as the range was calculated on the basis of total acres.

Source: Kenya Statistical Digest, March 1972, p. 8.

Table 2.22. *Average wages in small-scale agriculture by type of employment in 1970/71 and District (K.shs. per day)*

District	Casual wage	Regular wage	Farms hiring regular labour as % of farms hiring labour	No. of observations
Kisumu	1.5	–	38	24
Siaya	–	–	23	17
Kisii	3.1	–	10	31
Kakamega	2.5	–	33	18
Bungoma	2.5	–	28	18
Busia	1.6	–	14	43
Nandi	2.1	–	30	37
Kericho	2.7	2.2	82	72
Kiambu	3.0	–	27	70
Murang'a	2.4	2.3	30	64
Kirinyaga	2.5	–	32	56
Nyeri	3.2	–	52	29
Meru	2.1	2.0	66	64
Machakos	3.9	2.1	60	60
Embu	3.2	2.5	38	45

Source: Farm Enterprise Survey 1970/71. Quoted by Gwyer 1972.

The tendency that hired labour is used mostly on cash-crops seemed to be confirmed from other surveys.

In the Tanzanian studies especially tea and rice had a high hired labour input, whereas the cattle herding and subsistence crops had a much lower input of hired labour. Hired labour in the farms of Westlake region mostly consisted of males, even if some women and a few children also were involved in the work, especially tea plucking. Some cash crops, e.g. coffee and maybe also pyrethrum had a low input of hired labour. Crops such as sugar on the other hand seem to have the highest input of hired labour.

The group of agricultural labourers has in different periods and areas shown different social characteristics mainly depending on the pressure on land. The poor-middle peasants seem to have represented the major class basis for earlier farm labourers, as landless adult males were practically non-existent in the early colonial period due to the open land frontier.

With the increasing pressure on land the landless families play a major role in the farm labour force, and this group has increased rapidly especially after independence.

The conditions for agricultural labourers have shown major variations according to the area and historical period. In the smallholder areas of the "Reserves" the emphasis in most of the colonial period has been on communal labour, family labour and labour contributions of relatives. The conditions for labourers in the large farm areas of the alienated "White Highlands", have had much more emphasis on hired labour and a much more capitalistic labour market.

Historically the wage labour relations in relation to the colonial government and especially the white settlers revealed a labour market dominated by forced labour, target labour in relation to taxes levied on male adults in the reserve areas, and of salaries determined by the living costs of male singles, as the family reproduced their own labour on the family farm. Wages have varied across districts, and types of labour contracts, but the general tendency from 1919 is that the salary for farm labourers on the large farms is less than or just about the minimum salary required for subsistence of a single male. Salaries for women and children were always less. Other emoluments such as food, blankets, education, etc. to supplement the wage varied greatly and were never standardized. In the 1919 to mid 1920's the "purchasing power of wages was less than subsistence in the reserves" (Zwanenberg 1975, pp. 36–37). Also in relation to the value added on the farms the wages were low; generally below 30 % (ibid. p. 37). Most male labourers, around three-quarters of the total, worked only for shorter periods such as 3–4 months (ibid. p. 39), remaining on their farmsteads most of the year.

In periods of the 1920's the labour supply for road work, mining and farm labour was too short and a combination of measures to recruit and keep labourers was used. This was a combination of (1) forced labour, (2) all kinds of pressures on workers, who wanted to terminate a work contract, e.g. use of police force and threats of imprisonment to keep the workers. (3) Finally the squatter system developed as a means to acquire cheap labour for the farmers in the periods, where labour was short and land abundant in the scheduled areas.

The use of forced labour received a lot of criticism especially when used for recruiting children and juveniles- often without consent of parents, and when women were recruited for rough work. For instance, the major work force on road work consisted of women and children up to the early 1930's.

In the squatter system the regular problem of recruiting labour in labour shortage periods was solved for the farmers. Men and sons above 16 years were obliged to work on the settler farm – often labour should be provided for 180 days per year. But the benefit of the system to the farmer was also that women and children could be recruited as casual labourers – often at piece rates – in the peak seasons, such as for coffee picking.

The squatter system was based on the relative pressure on land in the reserves, where mainly grazing land became scarce, and the combination of unused settler land in the alienated areas and the settlers' lack of funds for wages.

In the 1920's, especially the farms in Uasin Gishu and Trans Nzoia were totally dependent on squatters as labourers. The main part of the squatters were of Kikuyu and Nandi origin.

The Kikuyu population was pressed very heavily with a high population density in the Central Province, and land shortage especially for grazing. The Nandi population considered Uasin Gishu as part of their own tribal land for grazing (ibid. pp. 219–230).

During the late 1920's the European farmers changed to mixed farming and therefore needed much more grazing land. Also the expansion of grade cattle on the European farms revealed the problem of the spreading of diseases, especially tick fever, from the local cattle breed. Therefore restrictions were put on African livestock in the area. First the movement of livestock from the reserves was restricted, and then severe limitations upon

Table 2.23. *Average retail prices of certain consumer goods in Nairobi, Dec. 1968–75. K.shs./cts.*

	1 kg maize flour	1 kg potatoes	1 kg cabbage	1 kg mixed beans	2 liter milk	1 kg sugar	1 kg beef low grade
1968	0/77	0/73	0/70	1/10	0/70	1/54	4/56
69	0/55	0/50	0/70	1/14	0/70	1/55	5/27
70	0/55	0/50	0/85	1/37	0/75	1/55	5/34
71	0/55	0/63	1/15	1/61	0/75	1/65	5/87
72	0/70	0/50	1/01	1/62	0/80	1/85	5/84
73	0/70	0/85	1/26	1/60	0/80	1/85	6/40
74	0/95	1/08	1/95	2/47	0/80	2/40	6/40
75	1/19	1/26	1/92	3/10	0/95	3/50	7/40
Index: 1970 = 100							
1968	140	146	82	80	93	99	85
69	100	100	82	83	93	100	99
70	100	100	100	100	100	100	100
71	100	126	135	118	100	106	110
72	127	100	119	118	107	119	109
73	127	170	148	117	107	119	120
74	173	216	229	180	107	155	120
75	216	252	226	226	127	226	139

Source: Central Bureau of Statistics: Statistical Abstract 1976, Nairobi 1976, p. 317 + calculations.

the number of heads of livestock permitted were put to force. African cattle had to be moved out of the area or killed, and many squatter families were evicted from the land, or restricted further on their rights to land. By about 1929 almost all cattle belonging to squatters were gone and plots for cultivation were reduced (Mbithi & Barnes 1975, p. 48).

The farmers in this period tried to change the labour system towards a higher reliance on casual labour rather than the earlier squatter system (Zwanenberg 1975, pp. 265–266). But the squatter system in a more limited form did not disappear. The families who had lived as squatters for a long time and had given up rights to land in the home areas, had to remain as squatter families under poorer conditions, where livestock was totally prohibited and the plot of land for food cultivation was limited. The farmers of Trans Nzoia and Uasin Gishu still had to rely on squatter families for their labour. But the contracts were more like permanent labour, with a wage consisting of partly cash and partly in kind such as housing, a small plot of land for cultivation, some maize flour and milk.

Labour contracts show much more variations than this, depending on the district and the type of work. The general feature, however, remained that the salary could be kept very low based on a combination of force and the fact that women and children reproduced their own labour in the subsistence sector. Throughout the colonial history of the 20th century the salaries of urban workers, and even clearer of plantation/large farm workers, have been less than the minimum required for a family to survive. The value of women's and children's work in subsistence has therefore been obvious to the colonial government and the employers.

The major differences in labour costs on large-scale farms and plantations relative to those of wages for casual labourers in the small-holder areas may be related both to the different supply of labour, and to the different economic conditions for the employers, where peasant farmers had less cash for hired labour. But it may also be related to the expectation that casual labour in the small-holder areas only take jobs to supplement incomes from their own farms, and that they were not totally dependent on these incomes to reproduce their family labour.

The approximate salaries of labourers for regular male labour (for 30 days work) are (Zwanenberg 1975, p. 36):

1919/20	8–10 K.shs.	
1921	5–7 K.shs.	
1922/23	6–8 K.shs.	
1924–29	12–16 K.shs.	(rising slowly over this period)
1930/36	6–10 K.shs.	(falling sharply in 1930)
1937/39	10–12 K.shs.	(rising slowly)

In parts of the White Highlands the salaries were the highest followed by Central Province, where the out-migration of labour for the White Highlands was largest. The salaries were compared closely with the salaries in Naivasha and Nanyuki. For casual labour the rates for males were 1 K.shs. per day from the 1927–41/42, and before that 50 cents per day (Cowen & Murage 1972, p. 42), but these types of jobs were only available at the peak seasons. Later, piece rates both for digging, weeding, tea plucking and coffee picking developed as the most normal type of labour contract in the Central Province.

The pattern of salaries is now quite complex, as some of the high density areas and the areas close to alternative urban employment seem to keep the highest salaries, thus Kisii, Nyeri and Embu have more than 3 shs. per day in 1970/71 in the intensive agricultural production, and Kiambu and Machakos have similar high wages probably because of their closeness to Nairobi where a high proportion of men from these areas work.

The pattern from table 2.22 does not however reveal the whole difference as many other reports give higher figures for Central Province, e.g. in October 1972 casual labourers in tea growing areas of Kiambu were offered 5–6 K.shs. per day plus meals for male workers, and 3 shs. for female workers, and only occasionally 4 shs. and meals. Regular workers in the same area had 65–80 shs. per month plus accomodation, food or a plot for cultivation (Leitner 1976, p. 40). Comparable information from the coffee plantations of Central Province (1975) reveals a minimum salary for permanent labourers of 5.75 shs. for 3 debes (tins) of berries and 1.50 shs. for each debe above this. Casual labourers had 1.50 shs. per debe. The average casual worker picks 4–5 debes, making about 7 shs. per day. A very good worker or a mother helped by her children may pick up to 10 debes making K.shs. 15.00 which is close to three times the statutory minimum (Taha 1975, p. 11). The minimum wages at tea plantations in Kericho is 5.75 K.shs. per day (Taha 1975, p. 7), but this is a much more stable income for most of the year, whereas coffee picking is only a short season. While the coffee plantations are estimated to have approx. 22,500 permanent labourers and 100,000 seasonal workers, the tea plantations have only 5,600 seasonal and 38,000 permanent resident workers including the working wives and juveniles (Taha 1975, pp. 6, 11).

In our survey in 1975 only a few cases of landless farm labourer families were collected to get information on the recent labour conditions. The cases seem to show that the salaries have not increased much in the 1970's for most of the areas, and that other benefits and supplementaries to the pure salary were disappearing both in the small-holder areas and in Trans Nzoia settlement and large farming areas.

The usual salary for permanent farm labourers in Kakamega, Bungoma and South Nyanza varied between 40 and 65 shs. per month, or with a working week of 6 days by an average of 1.50 shs. to 2.50 shs. per working day of 5–7 hours. This is usually without extra benefits, except that a few of those with the lowest pay had housing. In the same areas casual labour was paid 3 shs. per day for men and 2.00–2.50 shs. for women. (These data are similar to the data from 1970/71, table 2.22). In these areas only a few people are residing as landless labourers, and farm labour is supposed to supplement a little subsistence farming.

In the Londiani area of Kericho District the normal salary for farm labourers is higher, namely 60–90 K.shs., with 90 K.shs. as the normal for adult male labourers (comparable to 2.40–3.50 K.shs. per day). Juveniles in farm labour and women get 40–60 K.shs. per month. In the Londiani area there were several examples of fringe benefits for permanent labourers such as 1/4–1/2 acre for subsistence cultivation, housing and 1 pint of milk daily. A few farm labourers also had a supplement of maize every 10th day.

The information from Trans Nzoia on the other hand seems to reveal that salaries have been relatively stable around 60 K.shs. per month, but that all fringe benefits have disappeared. In only a few of the Agricultural Development Corporation's farms did the labourers, even casual labourers, living there have 2 1/2 acres for subsistence. In Saboti location however only the skilled labourers, i.e. tractor drivers, milkmen, mechanics and the watchmen were permanently employed.

On most of the large private farms the salary is 60 K.shs. per month and 45 K.shs. for the shepherds. This does not include food, land or housing, which is not provided. The normal house rent is 10–15 K.shs. per month. In January–February and in June–August there is very little work and casual labourers have a lot of problems to survive on the very low incomes. The incomes do not cover the expenses of feeding a man, let alone a family, and women and children try to supplement incomes in the peak agricultural seasons and by trade. The casual labour is mainly piece rates and better paid per day than the monthly permanent labour payment, but it is only available in a few periods. The insecurity of labour for casual labourers may well still provide better incomes than the permanent labour terms as one of the regular complaints of permanent farm labourers were arrears in wages of up to 5 months. This system tied the labourers to the farm as the only chance of having the income is to stay. The cases also revealed a system of declining real wages and severe problems of survival for even single males.

In order to illustrate the declining real incomes for farm labourers the development in average retail prices is provided together with information on consumption of basic food for peasants.

Table 2.24. *Average value per holding of household consumption by Province 1974–75. Value in K.shs. per annum.*

	Nyanza	Rift Valley	Western	Central	Kenya
Self produced items					
grains	583	685	432	366	446
beans	24	6	70	240	164
other crops	103	15	110	454	267
meat + milk	337	980	283	470	420
Crops produced	710	706	613	1060	877
Total food production	1047	1686	896	1530	1297
Purchased food					
grains + flours + root crops	229	240	354	610	498
fruits + vegetables	67	32	66	126	88
oils + fat	47	20	52	163	83
dairy products + meat + fish	417	197	365	210	282
sugar + sweets	120	193	195	254	172
drinks + beverages	84	172	152	196	140
salt + flavourings	29	24	27	29	35
purchased crops + fat	343	292	472	899	669
Total purchased food	992	878	1212	1588	1297
Value of staple food (grains +root crops)	812	925	786	976	944
Value of basic food (crops + oils + fat)	1053	998	1085	1959	1546
Value of total food consumption	2039	2564	2108	3118	2594

Source: Integrated Rural Survey 1974–75, p. 58.

The average retail prices for some of the basic food have increased to more than the double from 1970–75 in Nairobi. Especially in 1974 and 1975 the price increases have been high on the food purchased by the poor income groups (table 2.23). The food price index for low income groups in Nairobi has increased to nearly the double from December 1971 (Statistical Abstract pp. 316–317). Thus the main increases in food prices have been in the years where farm labour incomes have not increased. The prices for the basic food crops have been relatively stable from 1962 to 1970. As an estimate of the income necessary for purchasing the most basic needs, the incomes of farm labourers could be compared with the value of food used per family in the different provinces in 1974/75. These peasant families

Table 2.25. *Average value per holding of food consumption by Province 1974–75. (K.shs. per annum).*

	Nyanza	Rift Valley	Western	Central	Kenya
Integrated Rural Survey					
Value of staple food					
(grains + root crops)	812	925	786	976	944
Value of basic food					
(crops + oils + fat)	1 053	998	1 085	1 959	1 546
Value of total food					
consumption	2 039	2 564	2 108	3 118	2 594
Average household					
size	6.58	7.51	7.44	6.95	6.97
Adjusted values if average household size = 5					
Value of staple food	615	615	530	700	675
Value of basic food	800	665	730	1 410	1 110
Value of total food					
consumption	1 550	1 705	1 415	2 245	1 860

Source: Integrated Rural Survey 1974/75, pp. 58, 32 and calculations.

produce some of their food themselves, but the value of this is included in the table (table 2.24).

Table 2.24, which is of course including higher income groups, shows that the salary of a farm labourer of 60 K.shs. per month or 720 K.shs. per year cannot cover even the staple food of a family, which supplements with their own animal products and vegetables. The argument could be raised whether it is reasonable to compare the value of food for a peasant family with that of a farm labourer family with one farm labour income. But if this income is not enough to cover the basic needs, there is a clear need for more than one person to sell labour in order for the family to survive with just the simplest food. And if a normal house rent of 120–180 K.shs. is deducted per annum, the living conditions of landless farm labour families seem to be eroded even more.

The cases of farm labourer families reveal several age groups and family sizes, but generally the families appear to be smaller than the peasant farmer group. Table 2.25 adjusts the value of stable food, basic food and total food consumption to a family size of 5, i.e. 2 adults and 3 children.

This revision may be too rough in relation to the staple food as landless labourer families have no possibility of supplementing this with protein-rich animal products or crops, and may have to purchase relatively more staples. But the estimate still provides the argument for the pauperization and poor living conditions of the landless labourer families in Kenya. Together with the information on increasing food prices and erosion of emoluments in kind, the picture of rural social class with a rapidly declining living standard, which can hardly survive at the bare minimum is produced.

CHAPTER III

The Family and Exchange

1. The extension of the market

As we saw in chapter II, labour is increasingly being devoted or allocated to other activities than to the production of use-values for household consumption. The constant search for cash previously described, is the immediate expression of this phenomenon or process. But the search for cash through the sale of agricultural produce, trade or employment again expresses somehow the fact that the extension of the market has become a pressing reality of most rural people's daily life.

Now the idea of this chapter is not so much to discuss the extension of the market as a necessary and logical companion of the development of capitalism in Kenya, the intention is rather to relate its forms to the reproduction cycle of the households we studied.

In this first section of chapter III we shall try to describe how the economic activity of rural households is being related to the various mechanisms of the market. Or to put it in a different way, how the labour of the families in its different forms enters the market or exchange sphere.

In the following section the relationships between the household economy and trade will be analyzed, and especially the development of different roles for men and women as traders as a consequence of the ongoing process of the social division of labour.

The last two sections of the chapter will deal with the conditions of trade. The institutional framework of the market transactions, including the historical role of rural market places and trading centres as well as their present status and characteristics, is discussed first. Finally, however, the more area-specific features of market trade in the areas studied in Western Kenya will be discussed, as an introduction to the subsequent presentation of our case studies of shopkeepers and women traders in chapters IV and V.

The extension of the market, or the process of commercialization, means that the buying and selling of goods and labour becomes the dominant pattern of exchange, upon which rural households are increasingly dependent in their cycle of reproduction.

The Mexican economist Alonso Aguilar sees the market as a complex historical category, which branches off and expands into all facets of social life as capitalism develops, but which is also establishing itself as a forerunner of the capitalist system as a mode of production. Not only does the market seize the products of human labour, it will eventually transform labour power itself into a commodity to be sold and bought in numerous forms as capitalism develops in underdeveloped countries (Aguilar 1973, p. 53 ff.).

Where Aguilar is concerned with the expansion of the internal market as the regulating factor of the socio-economic process of change, Bernstein focuses on the internalization of capitalist commodity circuits in the cycle of reproduction of peasant households, as they have to engage in simple commodity production whether of labour power for periodic exchange or of agricultural commodities or both, and become dependent on the purchase of the necessary consumption in the process of reproducing labour as well as means of production (Bernstein 1976, p. 24).

Where Aguilar stresses the extension of the market as the main agent for undermining, changing and even destroying the domestic production structure, Bernstein tends to see this whole process of subsumption under capital as a terrain for struggle over the conditions of production and exchange, in which the household as an economic unit may prolongate its existence by adaptation to the market. Both of them underline that the process of subsumption under capital of the household economy i.e. the labour of the family, may take numerous forms in which the households are being exposed to the market mechanism at the direct level of confrontation with capital.

In Kenya the process of market extension and that of establishing an internal market, based on capitalist exchange relations, went on throughout the colonial period, and it accelerated from the mid-fifties when reforms were introduced to provide for African participation in cash cropping and trade. From independence in 1963 until now the main efforts of the Kenyan regime have been directed towards monetarization of the economy and Africanization of agriculture, cattle raising and trade. The institutional framework for the extension of the capitalist sphere of circulation included land-tenure reforms, which basically made agricultural land individualized property available for transactions in a land market. The market in Kenya therefore now includes all the essential institutions necessary for the development of capitalism at the circulation level.

The general impact of the extension and intensification of the market on the peasant economy since independence may be illustrated by the increase in quantity of marketed crops, meat and milk, by the magnitude of the consumption of industrial goods in rural areas and by the relative and absolute stagnation of subsistence production.

From 1964 to 1975 the quantity of maize marketed via the Maize Produce

Marketing Board rose from a level of some 150,000 tons a year to some 500,000 tons. Most of this increase came from the inclusion of the small farm or peasant sector in the market. Maize is by far the most important staple in Kenya and the increase of marketed maize therefore also indicates the development of the internal market for food. The production of coffee, the most important export crop, rose from a level of 50,000 tons to about 55,000. This increase is practically exclusively due to the encouragement of coffee growing by African small-holders who were previously excluded from coffee production by colonial restrictions but now grow half of the coffee. Correspondingly, roughly a third of the tea leaf production now originates in this sector.

Measured in value terms the marketed domestic food crops, wheat, maize and sugar cane, increased from a level of 150 mill. K.shs. a year in 1966 to that of 700 mill. in 1975, while those of the export crops of coffee, tea and sisal, went up from 600 mill. K.shs. to some 1200 mill.

From the Integrated Rural Survey (I.R.S.) it may be inferred that the 1.6 mill. peasant households in Kenya produce more than half of the total agricultural and animal produce reaching the official market institutions – against between one-fourth and one-third at the time of independence (I.R.S. 1977). On the other hand, it may also be estimated that the peasant households together purchase about half of all industrial goods marketed at the retail level in Kenya (Kongstad, 1977, p. 59).

Contrasted with these figures is the fact that the subsistence production measured in constant prices has only increased some 30% from 1964 to 1974 according to the national accounts, whereas the corresponding value of commercial agricultural production has almost doubled.

The impact on the production of the extension of the market may be inferred from the Integrated Rural Survey which says that 45% of the reported value of total production of Kenyan agricultural small-holders was being sold through the market (I.R.S. 1977, table 8.29). This figure is probably too small however, as the I.R.S. does not include small-holdings or peasant households of the Rift Valley districts of the former "White Highlands". In these areas, according to our own field data, more than half of the production is being marketed. We may therefore conclude that the small-holding sector of agriculture and livestock production, which includes some 70% of all households in Kenya (all holdings less than 20 hectares) as an average markets at least half of its total production in money terms.

We have estimated the share of marketed production to be about 25% of total production in the mid-fifties, and therefore think that the impact of market extension could be illustrated relatively by the difference of those 25% and the 50% or more now reaching the market channels.

The produce entering the market as commodities include crops, cattle and other stock plus milk. According to the I.R.S. a third of the marketed production is being sold directly to Cooperatives and Marketing Boards representing commercial capital whether state controlled or operating privately, since a part of the remaining two-thirds marketed through local market institutions ends up in the hands of Boards or Cooperatives through the transactions of various middlemen at the local level. We may however estimate that roughly half of the marketed production is being somehow controlled by the capitalist sphere of circulation. The other half remains in the local circuits of exchange, i.e. direct sales by producers to consumers at market places, or buying and selling via middlemen but still for unprocessed consumption in the area of production or in a neighbouring area.

Now turning to the reproduction of labour and the means of production, we have estimated from the I.R.S. tables that of the total average reproduction of small-holders, valued at 3652 K.shs. in 1975, some 60% was purchased and thus the remaining 40% was based on the subsistence production of the households. The 60% purchased represents additional food, and other items for individual consumption plus means of production such as seed, machine contracts, fertilizers, spray, feed and wages.

The 40% produced in the household included food, seeds, and feed.

As an average, this percentage of distribution tells us that nearly two-thirds of the reproduction now comes via the market, whether through the local circuits such as buying food in the open air market places or through the local shops selling or distributing industrially produced commodities. The process of reproduction on an average thus has become far from anything like "self-sufficiency". Selling roughly half of the output and purchasing something like two-thirds of total reproduction means that the integration of the household economy into the market, or for that matter the internalization of the market in this economy has already gone very far in rural Kenya.

We shall later on return to the question of the relationship between market integration and size of holding and geographical location. Here, however, it should be noted that the 59% of holdings smaller than 2 hectares bought more than half of their food, in fact those 32% of holdings with less than 1 hectare of land had to buy nearly 55% of their food. With the increasing size of holding, food purchasing seems to drop to a level of 45% in comparison.

These figures thus indicate that the expansion of the internal market in Kenya may very well be due to an increasing necessity to buy food in order to supplement subsistence production among the majority of small-holders. It may be suspected here that the increase of cash cropping has been made at the expense of food cropping rather than through the development of the productive forces. As argued by Judith Heyer, the small-holder sector of agriculture has been rather neglected in terms of government assistance until recently (Heyer, Senga, Maitha 1974, p. 354) and as the I.R.S. also shows, purchased farm inputs such as seeds and fertilizers have remained at the rather modest level of 32% of total farm costs (I.R.S. 1977, table 8.32). The internalization of the market in the household economy in the double sense shown above (production – reproduction) may well be the form of subsumption under capital, by which it has been possible to transfer surplus products from agriculture to industry and government consumption most effectively. Seen from the small-holder point of view, however, this tendency towards the internalization of commodity circuits first of all represents an increasing compulsion to produce and be reproduced via the market as an irreversible process, without visible improvements of the conditions of production in return.

The integration into the commodity market via the production does not however in itself explain the internalization of the market in the household economy. If the average value of reproduction equalled 3652 K.shs. in 1975 (I.R.S. 1977, table 8.6), then 57% of this total was based on the agricultural production, namely 36% consumed in the household and 21% as the surplus of marketed production. 43% however was based on various non-farm sources of reproduction. 22% thus originated from household member's sale of labour power (regular or casual employment). 10% came from the surplus of non-farm activities (trade, crafts, petty production) and 11% was due to remittances or gifts from relatives.

In other words 32% or about a third of the reproduction was based on market relations outside the production sphere of the households. As the size of the holding increases the non-farm component of total reproduction becomes even more important and reached some 50% in the holdings of 8 hectares or more. The sale of labour power tends to decrease and the surplus of non-farm activity, e.g. trade becomes the more important sub-category. While the 14% of the holdings smaller than 0.5 hectare relied on employment for about a third of their reproduction, this percentage was about 10% in the 3.5% of holdings larger than 8 hectares, and vice versa, trade and other non-farm operating surplus increased from 12% to 31%.

If, as some disputable guideline, it is estimated that the 59% of the holdings with less than 2 hectares of land may not be able to sustain the demands of simple reproduction through the household production, their members will face the necessity to sell labour power or to engage in petty trade which demands little money capital to start with, in order to survive. As we have seen in chapter 2 the near to landless families of our sample in fact do have to rely on these segments of the market. ut the search for cash here as in the other commodity markets is conditioned by the market mechanism. The many who struggle to recover a few shillings a day compete with each other to get access to the market. As regards the sale of labour then some 60% of the small-holding households rely on it for about 25% of their total reproduction or in cash terms some 800 K.shs. a year (in 1975). This represents a total payment of 696 mill K.shs. The total purchase of labour power among the 1.5 mill holdings included in the I.R.S. did not amount to more than 270 mill K.shs however. If the data are correct then some 60% of the labour income among the households with less than 2 hectares of land must be obtained outside the peasant economy. If we assume that those 60% or 870,000 households owning less than 2 hectares of land, should increase their average level of reproduction, from the present level of 3100 K.shs a year (1975) to the average of 3650 K.shs for the total small-holder population by additional sale of labour power, then some 480 K.shs would have had to be earned. The market for labour power in the peasant economy however is mainly restricted to casual farm labour in the peak seasons, and even the largest holdings of 8 hectares and more within this sector, only bought labour for K.shs in 1975. If the average payment for casual farm labour is put at 3–5 a day, this purchase hardly represented more than four man-months.

Therefore, it may be argued that the labour market of the small-holding agricultural sector is probably characterized by fierce competition among the thousands of families who are desperately searching for additional cash to even maintain their present low level of reproduction.

Both men, women and older children are looking for employment as we saw in chapter II, but the opportunities in the rural areas outside their own sector of the economy are few. Women occasionally try to form work groups, especially in Western Province where the pressure on land is mounting, to work on the basis of very low piece-rates. Men increasingly try to find employment as migrant labourers in the large farm sector away from their homes, or in the largest cities. Work away from the home area explains therefore in part the difference between labour power sold and bought within the sector itself.

The sale of labour power tends to decrease somewhat as a source of reproduction with increasing size of the holding, but more important of course is the fact that the kind of employment changes qualitatively. 11% of all the holdings surveyed by the I.R.S. reported employment in teaching, government or other urban employment. In the Western Province this percentage was even 19%.

In our own studies we found correspondingly that 10% of the respondents among shopkeepers had teaching as their main source of reproduction.

Where both women and men from households with too little land work as casual labourers, white collar employment is almost exclusively a male affair. As we have seen in chapter II there is a tendency towards a division of the household economy where the husband has white collar employment. The wife is often left with the burden of reproduction whether from subsistence production, sale of labour power or petty trade, while the husband often engages in trade or other non-farm activities on the top of his employment.

The size of the holding does not, however, influence the level of integration into the market. Table 3.1 below shows that reproduction via the market (cash income) and consumption via the market only differs modestly among the three size groups taken as typical of very small, medium and large scale holdings.

If the figures are correct then they may express a tendency towards less dependency upon direct market relationships in the medium group of holdings. Subsistence here was on the basis of 41% of total consumption as compared with 29% in each of the two other size groups. It may however be

Table 3.1. *Reproduction and consumption via the market*

	Selected size groups of holdings in hectares		
	Below 0.5	3.0–3.9	8.0 or more
Reproduction (Cash income)	59%	47%	63%
Consumption	66%	59%	61%
Percentage of holdings included in I.R.S.	13.9	8.9	3.5

Source: I.R.S. 1977, table 8.6.

Table 3.2. *Levels of income, consumption and "savings" K.shs.*

	Selected size group of holding in hectares			
	Below 0.5	3.0–3.9	8.0 or more	Average
Total income	2908	3952	5755	3652
Total consumption	2498	4070	4362	3450
Income – consumption	410	–118	1393	202
Percentage of holdings included in I.R.S.	13.9	8.9	3.5	100.0

Source: I.R.S. 1977, tables 8.6 and 8.14.

dangerous to interpret this difference from the average level, as more than a temporary or random phenomenon when the survey was undertaken in 1974-75.

That the households' economy now have come to depend on the market for between a half and two-thirds of their reproduction, should not veil the fact that the internalization of market circuits here has been associated with a process of social differentiation as well.

Table 3.2 below indicates the difference of reproduction levels in 1975 between the same size of holding groups and, for comparison, the average of all households surveyed by I.R.S.

Between the near to landless households and the group of households having 8 hectares of land or more, the total income in value terms, but including subsistence production is almost double, and a capacity to save cash seemingly also develops far beyond that of the average holding. These figures may serve as a numerical indication of income inequalities and differences in the levels of reproduction within the landholding rural population, and they may for that matter, be supplemented by the mean values of assets per holding. According to table 7.10 in the I.R.S. the assets increase gradually from 3700 K.shs to some 20,200 with the size of holding.

These figures do not however reveal the qualitative differences in life opportunities between those families who have been gradually "marginalized" through the continuous extension of the market, and those who have somehow benefitted relatively from this process, some even since the early years of colonialism.

The marginalized are those who have been subsumed under capital in various indirect ways via the market mechanism. They are approaching landlessness through subdivision of land and land transactions. They have to purchase their subsistence to a large extent, and they also begin to form a labour-power-selling proletariate without getting permanently into wage-labour relations of capital as we have seen. We cannot decide on the basis of our statistical information whether this group is becoming the majority or shall remain a minority for some time to come.

On the other hand a clear minority has benefitted from the extension of the market and the development of capitalism in Kenya. Equal distribution of wealth was not typical of Western Kenya even in pre-colonial days. Colonialism however accelerated the process of social differentiation in terms of access to land, cash income and education and changed it qualitatively by the establishment of capitalistic market mechanisms for transactions in land, labour power and products (use-values). A small, relatively wealthy, landholding stratum of rural families thus emerged already during the colonial period, even if its further development somehow had to await independence because of the colonial restrictions and repressive policy towards African participation in cash-cropping and trade.

Given the liberalization of access to buy and sell land and the deliberate policy of Africanization of trade by the Kenyan regime, this group has expanded its basis of reproduction both in agriculture and commerce. Some of its members have even passed into a process of extended reproduction in agriculture with production for profits and combine agriculture and trade, such as demonstrated in chapter V.

The majority of peasants in Kenya, as we have seen, are being integrated into the market for their reproduction as well, and have also engaged more and more in non-farm activities, petty production and trade, as the only way to counteract their marginal position in the labour market.

2. Non-farm activities

The survey of non-farm activities carried out by the Central Bureau of Statistics at the end of 1976 reveals that 50.4% of rural households in Kenya are engaged in a broad variety of economic activities in addition to agriculture and stock raising as a source of income. 24.0% are even engaged in more than one of these activities.

In broad terms the survey classifies the non-farm activities into resource-extraction, manufacturing on a small scale and trade and services. Table 3.3 below summarizes the frequencies reported by category. The sum is not 100% because multiple replies have been entered in the tables of the survey.

While resource extraction mainly included hunting, wood cutting and fishing, the category of manufacturing was composed of a wide variety of types of productions. Most important however is food and beverage with 22% reporting production here. Beer or pombe brewing, almost exclusively

Table 3.3. *Non-farm activities in rural households in Kenya and in the Provinces of Western Kenya.*

	Frequencies of activity reported in percent.			
	Kenya	Nyanza	Rift Valley[1]	Western
Resource Extraction	12.1	17.5	10.0	14.0
Manufacturing	56.3	79.2	46.7	52.6
Trade & Services	32.5	37.3	19.3	39.7

[1] Rift Valley here does not include the Districts of the former scheduled areas.

Source: Republic of Kenya, Central Bureau of Statistics, Social Perspectives, Vol. 2, No. 2, 1977, table 4.

done by women, was reported in 13% of the sample at the national level, but came up to as much as 26% in Nyanza compared with 18% in Western and 15% in Rift Valley. Fibre products such as bags, woven or knitted material, tailoring and preparation of leather totalled some 12%. Wood products were reported by 14% with charcoal making and carpentry as the most important subcategories.

Production of metalware did not amount to more than 1.2% while construction was reported by 5%.

Trade, whether wholesale or retail, included 9% of the sample at the national level, but came up to 14% in Nyanza and 12% in Western Province compared with 6% in the Rift Valley. As mentioned in the footnote to table 3.3, Rift Valley here did not include the important agricultural districts of the former "White Highlands", foremost Nakuru, Uasin-Gishu and Trans Nzoia.

The remaining activities cover some 30 different services ranging from bus and taxi operators, cafés, bars, storage and clinics to letter writing, healing and entertainment.

It may be noted here that money lenders do not represent any significant number in Kenya with only 0.6 % reporting this activity.

A total of some 100 different non-farm activities were reported by the 2232 households surveyed in the sample, and together their activities contributed with 9 % of the total income of the households. Compared with 22 % earned by permanent or casual employment this outcome may not seem impressive, but as the authors of the survey report mention, non-farm activities seem to be considered a necessary part-time occupation to supplement the income from agriculture and employment (Social Perspectives, vol. 2, No. 1977). We may add that the general participation in these activities reflects probably more the increasing lack of alternative cash earning opportunities in agriculture and urban industries, than it reflects some national inclination to diversify ones labour into fields where the reward is generally extremely low, at least for the majority of those participating, as we shall illustrate later in this section as well as in chapters IV and V.

As regards table 3.3, it seems that the frequencies of nonfarm activities, especially those reported on trade and services, were lower in the Rift Valley than in the two other provinces of West Kenya, and for that matter than the national average.

We are inclined here to think that the survey published in Social Perspectives (op.cit.), demonstrates some of its shortcomings rather than reflects the state of affairs. If the estimates reported by key-informants on the same activities as reported in the survey are used, trade and services as regards Rift Valley, seem to involve some 46 % of the households, instead of the 19 % reported by the survey, while figures on resource extraction and manufacturing remain more or less the same (Social Perspectives, vol. 2, 1977, table 5). This difference may be due to the fact that the surveys on rural households in Kenya, referred to, were based on holdings, i.e. land owning households, while the key informants also utilized by the Central Bureau of Statistics may have had the total number of households in their areas in mind.

In general the Rift Valley Province has a more polarized structure than the two other Western provinces of Kenya in terms of land tenure, and this is true even for the districts of Nandi and Kericho, included in the surveys of the Central Bureau of Statistics. As a general rule therefore small-holders, with a little more land than in most other areas of Kenya, do exist together with a larger number of landless or near-to-landless families, whether squatters or not, on one side and large-scale farms or plantations on the other side. Landlessness certainly means that both men and women have to sell their labour force to exist, and petty trade has more and more become the only way out for the women. The studies referred to in chapter 4 and our own data thus correspond much better with the key-informant views here, namely that around 30 % of adult women participate somehow in petty trade to earn necessary cash. This percentage is probably increasing however, so that the majority of women do trade from time to time. The difference between polarized areas like the Rift Valley and less polarized areas of the old "reserves" like Nyanza may well be, that the women of the former have to buy and sell since they have no crop of their own to offer, while those of the latter sell only their own produce to a larger extent.

Women, whether "petty traders" or just engaged in the exchange of their own produce for other use values, mostly do their business at market places and trading centres. The market place or trading centre however also provides the institutional framework for the penetration of the market, in its more abstract sense, into the reproduction cycle of rural families.

The internalization of the capitalist sphere of commodity circulation in the household economy has to a large extent been mediated through the "dukas" the general retail shops at market places and trading centres located in the countryside.

Apart from their historical role as the agents of the advancing capitalism in shaping its internal market, marketplaces and rural trading centres have also become foci of the ongoing process of social differentiation in rural areas. The competitive game of the market seems to foster graduated strata of petty traders, craftsmen and merchants to which the shopkeepers of our cases in Western Kenya belong. The following section therefore is an attempt to describe the market places and their activities in this context.

3. Trading centres and markets

At present there may exist a little less than 5,000 trading centres in rural Kenya, i.e. outside Nairobi and the 10 principal towns. According to an unpublished survey by the Central Bureau of Statistics there were 4595 rural trading centres in early 1972. A trading centre may be described as a cluster of shops and workshops established according to the legislation which has regulated internal trade since colonial days. Trading centres are divided into plots on which the shops stand. The plots are subject to a licence arrangement, by which the plot holder is authorized to do a stipulated kind of business, retail trade, bar-keeping, butchery etc., and for which the plot holder pays a yearly fee according to the ongoing activity.

The terms "market" and "market-place" in many cases have been used more or less synonymously with that of "trading centre" in Kenya. However, originally as well as regards the actual functioning, they refer to different aspects of the internal market system.

Trading centres were invented by the colonial regime to "integrate the African subsistence economy into the colonial mercantile network" (Memon, 1975, p. 131), i.e. to stimulate the production of saleable crops in the African reserves – and to improve the efficiency of the revenue or tax system.

Markets however were elements of the pre-colonial social and economic life where people gathered in certain places at various intervals to exchange use-values as grain for tools, etc. In principle therefore the trading centres multiplying from 1910 or so, belong to the "vertical" trade system by which African produce was built up to commercial quantities suitable for commercial transactions, whether to feed the farm labourers on the European farms in the Rift Valley or to reach the world market (Memon, 1975, p. 133). The markets on the other hand served also the "horizontal" exchange of goods between peasants trading surpluses and covering deficits. But as demonstrated by Uzoigwe the markets in precolonial East Africa did also function within more complex socio-political relationships such as the royal markets of the kingdoms bordering Lake Victoria, or the frontier markets established to channel economic exchange between different political regions (Uzoigwe, 1975).

As the capitalist circuits of commodities penetrated the rural economy, the original patterns of exchange became modified in trading centres as well as in markets. In the former, the selling of industrial commodities against cash began to dominate over the collection of African produce against returns in kind. In the latter, trade as commercial transactions between professional traders and final consumers came to coexist with horizontal exchange. The markets also came under the legislative control of the colonial administration, and they were classified according to the principles of a regulated and hierarchal market system favoured by colonial offices. As an illustration, Fearn mentions that the number of markets and relative distances between so-called "A" markets as well as the average number of heads per trader in "A" and "B" markets were stipulated in the forties (Fearn, 1955, p. 4).

The administration of trading centres and markets under "gazetted market rules" (Memon, 1975, p. 130), came under the local native councils from the mid-twenties, and gradually both categories developed on the same physical sites as well, or adjacent to each other. In some cases trading centres were established at old markets, as in Nyanza, in other cases markets developed at trading centres. The prevailing usage of one term as synonymous with the other certainly has to do therefore with this locational coincidence.

Trading centres and markets in rural Kenya have not so far been the "foci" of residential settlements. There is no tradition of nucleated settlements or villages in Kenya, families have settled rather on their own land.

Visitors walk to the trading centres or markets or are taken there by "matatus" (small buses). Those acting as market traders or working in the shops often stay with their families in the countryside as well. Visiting the local centre or market therefore is not a daily event, but takes place mainly on market days. Accordingly the geographical range of a trading centre and market and its number of shops and market traders as well as its volume of trade is somehow related to the number of weekly market days it offers.

The trading centres and markets outside the 10 principal towns and Nairobi may account for as much as two-thirds of the total yearly purchases of rural households in Kenya. Using Kimani & Taylor's figures for Murang'a and our own data from Western Kenya, we have estimated that trading centres and markets had a total turnover of something between 2100 and 3100 mill K.Shs. in 1975 (Kimani & Taylor, 1973). According to the Integrated Rural Survey (I.R.S. op. cit) the 1.5 mill landholding households represented in the survey bought for something like 3150 mill K.Shs. in 1974/75. If the purchases of the Rift Valley households excluded from I.R.S. and the purchases of the landless not either included in I.R.S. are estimated at a level of 960 mill. K.Shs., then total rural purchases could be put at some 3100 mill K.Shs.

Trading centres and markets also account for about half of the total sales of rural households according to the I.R.S., but since women's trade has been drastically underestimated in I.R.S. this proportion may be considerably higher.

In any case the trading centre and market-place does play a decisive economic role in the reproduction cycle of most rural families. Also looking at occupation, the trading centres and markets provide the framework for the daily work of about 160,000 people[1] working in the shops and workshops or as professional traders in the markets. In addition probably a third of all adult rural women trade either occasionally or regularly at the markets. This means that about 950,000 women did so in 1975. The total rural employment in non-farm activities is not known – but since only the central government or the country councils offer any significant employment alternative to the trading centres, these do play a decisive role also as a source of vital income.

4. Markets and market trade in Western Kenya

The geographical distribution of trading centres and markets in Kenya reflects the differences in the agricultural resource basis and the population distribution as well as in the specific social history of the Kenyan regions or provinces. As it may be expected, there are more markets in relation to the rural population in Central Province than elsewhere. It may not be surprising either that the inverse situation is found in the former "White Highlands" where large-scale farms and migrant farm labourers or squatters provided the backbone of the colonial social formation.

It is evident from our own field data on market trade in the Central Province in 1974–75[2] that the early improvement of infrastructure, especially the road network in the Kiambu, Murang'a and Nyeri Districts, in the Central Province has led to an increase of the volume of produce traded between the markets and between these districts and Nairobi. A hierarchal structure of markets seems to have emerged with some markets as nodal points for wholesale transactions in collecting grain, pulses, and vegetables from local markets with a surplus in harvest seasons and distributing this produce to other local markets with a deficit, or forwarding these food items to the retail markets in Nairobi. Therefore in the Central Province a hierarchy of market traders has also developed with both women and men as large-scale traders, who travel between local markets buying and selling anything from bags to truck-load quantities. The variety of different agricultural surpluses produced in the province, the geographical

---

[1] From the Kimani & Taylor figures (Kimani & Taylor, 1973), our own field data and the unpublished data from C.B.S. we have estimated that on an average a trading centre employed 35 people in 1975 C.B.S. figures for the number of trading centres in 1972 were 4595.

[2] Some 25 markets were studied in the Central Province. 1974–75 in advance of our study of markets in Western Kenya.

differences between harvest seasons and the presence of the Nairobi metropolitan market, have certainly also delivered a fertile ground for the emergence of a profit making class of market traders. Our own case studies, previously referred to, seem to indicate that such traders do not only collect, store and resell food items, but also distribute industrially made goods or craft-products bought in Nairobi to market places in the Central Province. Moreover, "wholesale" Kikuyu women traders increasingly trade outside the Central Province, either by selling food crops and vegetables in "deficit" areas of Kenya, or simply by establishing themselves as market traders in Rift Valley, Nyanza or Western Province.

As it may be expected, the markets and trading centres which are making substantial progress are typically located along the main tarmac roads and especially at road junctions. Markets located alongside the railside lines or in the "interior" at a distance from all-weather roads, on the contrary, seem to face increasing difficulties in maintaining their level of activity, or seem even to be dying out.

In Western Kenya markets and market trade seem to follow the same pattern of development in principle: The differences–if observed at all–seem to be a matter of the intensities rather than of the nature of the pattern of development.

This observation naturally does not mean that we hold the view that there are no geographical differences in Kenya in terms of agricultural productivity, surplus production and cash income, but rather that we find the same social and economic forces at work which condition market trade and shape the organization and activity pattern of markets and trading centres.

As we have seen in the preceding sections of this chapter, the necessity to reproduce the household through buying and selling does not differ much between the various size groups of holdings[1] nor between the different provinces. Cash consumption, as a percentage of total consumption fluctuates around 60% in most provinces and food purchases seem to make up between half and two-thirds of total cash consumption in most provinces as well.

In table 3.4 below, selling and buying have been categorized in major items, and for comparison, figures from the three Western provinces are shown together with those of the Central Province and rural Kenya as a whole.

As regards the magnitudes of the average selling and purchasing, table 3.4 reflects the differences in the average levels of reproduction between the provinces referred to earlier. Especially Western Province, but also Nyanza,

---

[1] See for example, table 3.1., page 92.

Table 3.4. *Cash sales and purchases, rural households 1975 by major items and in K.shs. (Averages for selected Provinces and for rural Kenya as a whole).*

	Nyanza	Rift Valley[1]	Western	Central	Kenya
Sales					
Farm sales	1184	1906	550	1491	1192
Non-farm sales	553	768	378	726	633
Total sales	*1737*	*2674*	*928*	*2217*	*1825*
Purchases					
Food for consumption	992	878	1212	1588	1297
Non-food consumption	373	601	439	755	547
Miscellaneous for consumption	134	201	261	600	309
Farm inputs	175	581	182	643	333
Non-farm inputs	188	465	252	400	279
Total purchases	*1862*	*2726*	*2346*	*3986*	*2765*
Sales − Purchases	−125	−52	−1410	−1769	−940

[1] Only includes Nandi, Kericho and El. Marakwet Districts.

Source: Republic of Kenya, Central Bureau of Statistics, Integrated Rural Survey 1974–75, Nairobi 1977.

ranged below Central Province and Rift Valley. The unequal geographical distribution of household or per capita income also becomes manifest in the level of market transactions[1].

Measured by the balance between cash sales and purchases of commodities, the Central Province and Western Province however both had to cover a more substantial part of their average spending by other means of reproduction than selling farm or non-farm items, than Rift Valley and Nyanza. The first two Provinces depend more on the selling of labour force and transfers (gifts, remittances) than the latter provinces do.

The two sets of observations, that on the one hand Central Province and Rift Valley seem to exist on a higher level of reproduction, and on the other hand that the same Central Province and Western Province depend more on external sources of income vis-à-vis household production, probably indicate the complex nature of geographical differences in rural Kenya. More resources have been devoted to the transformation of the Kikuyu dominated provinces, Central and Rift Valley. However class formation in Central Province, and the process of increasing land shortage in Western

[1] While the percentage of households with 3000 K.shs. in income or more is 54 % in Central Province, 50 % in Rift Valley it is 42 % in Nyanza and only 29 % in Western Province.

Table 3.5. *Consumption, purchases, sales and production of cereals in K.shs. (by selected size groups of holding in hectares 1975).*

	Hectares		
	Below 0.5	3.0–3.9	8.0 or more
Cereals consumed	738	1058	1094
Own production consumed	327	552	666
Purchases	411	506	428
Sales	335	798	1018
Gross production[1]	662	1350	1684

[1] Does not include own production used as seeds or given to employed labour force.

Source: Republic of Kenya, Central Bureau of Statistics, Integrated Rural Survey 1974–75. Nairobi 1977, tables 8.18 and 8.26.

Province, and with no substantial increase of productivity, has resulted in similar features in both areas observed at the circulation level, namely a mounting dependency upon household external sources of reproduction and therefore necessarily increasing reliance on markets and trading centres.

Unfortunately the data published in the Integrated Rural Survey do not include information on geographical and social variance nor on the occurrence of selling and buying by the same households or by season of the year.

For rural Kenya as a whole however, the reliance upon markets and trading centres in buying and selling cereals may be estimated by the size of holdings. Cereals, first of all maize and maize flour, represent 36%–40% of the total food consumption measured in money terms. In table 3.5 below, the consumption, purchases and sales as well as gross production of cereals have been compiled for some size categories as used previously in this section of chapter III.

In relation to size groups it seems that consumption exceeds production by some 12 % in the smallest size group of holdings, while the opposite relationship than expected characterizes the medium and large holdings. It may not be surprising either that the smallest size group depends more on purchases than the medium and large groups – respectively 56 %, 48 % and 39 % of the consumption. But it is remarkable that the percentage of cereals produced by the holdings, sold at local markets or to marketing boards, remains at a level of 51 % for the smallest size group and "only" increases to 59 % respectively and 60 % for the medium and large groups. The total relative dependency upon market transactions i.e. buying plus selling, therefore seems to increase as the size of holding decreases. Measured in relation to the production for example, purchases plus sales amount to 86 %, 97 % and 113 %, among the three sample groups.

These observations do seem in fact to correspond with the findings of the Nyanza Rural Household Survey of 1970–71 where the authors conclude that "the proportion of consumption that is self-produced by households generally rises with total factor income. Increasing self-sufficiency with increasing net income may thus be taken to imply a greater ability to produce more and varied food-stuffs among wealthier farmers... greater livestock holdings and grain stores make it possible to reduce the length of periods during the year when basic food-stuffs need to be purchased... the proportion of cereals, pulses and roots that are purchased declines with increasing income" (Rural Household Survey Nyanza, 1970–71, 1977, p. 52).

The weaknesses of the figures compiled in table 3.5 are of course that they do not necessarily relate to the same households, but represent averages for the sample by size groups.

Our own field data from some 50 different market places in Nyanza, Western and Rift Valley Provinces however seem to justify the interpretation indicated above, namely that the necessity to purchase and sell basic food-stuffs, first of all maize, increases with poverty. Women of poor peasant households simply have to sell maize at the local markets just after harvest at relatively low prices to provide the necessary cash for which to buy other daily necessities or to pay school fees for their children. Later in the season, when the price of maize at the local retail markets goes up again, the same families have to purchase food.

Even in the Bungoma area, normally known as one of Kenya's granaries, our women respondents trading at local markets reported that they have to buy maize in 3–5 months every year. To sum up here, we would therefore argue that the conditions of market trade not only reflect different geographical levels of reproduction as indicated in the subtotals of table 3.4, but also, and perhaps increasingly, the expansion of the internal market by the necessity to sell and buy food, especially maize, as one consequence of the increasing inequality of land distribution and the growing land shortage for the majority of rural households[1]. The necessity to sell and buy food is not only related to the magnitude of a net deficit on a yearly basis, but is

---

[1] No data are available to illustrate the changes of landownership; but according to the Integrated Rural Survey, holdings in the three Western provinces were as follows in 1974–75.

	Nyanza	Rift Valley	Western Prov.
Less than 1.0 hectare	41.9 %	35.1 %	39.2 %
Between 1.0–1.9 hectare	22.0 %	17.6 %	17.3 %
Above 2.0 hectare	36.1 %	47.3 %	43.5 %

increasingly determined by the compulsion to provide cash at intervals throughout the year. In this respect market trade in Western Kenya certainly does not differ from that of Central or Eastern Kenya. As regards the composition of commodities traded, we may however argue that table 3.4 indicates some geographical variations, reflecting the different average levels of reproduction on a provincial scale. Where food made up 52 % of purchases in Western Province and Nyanza Province, this category did not amount to more than 32 % in the Rift Valley Districts included in I.R.S. Vice versa inputs, whether farm or non-farm, came up to as much as 38 % in the Rift Valley Districts, but did not count for more than 18%–19% of purchases in Western and Nyanza Provinces.

Larger holdings account for a higher percentage of the total number of holdings in Rift Valley, (see below), which would certainly come out more clearly if the former "White Highlands" had been included in the survey. The average farm surplus is probably the highest in Kenya on a provincial basis, and thus the capacity to "save" and "invest" is probably also much larger than in Nyanza and Western Provinces.

Trade with principal export crops such as coffee, tea, pyrethrum, and maize, (the fundamental food staple), has been regulated since the late thirties. This means that statutory bodies, the Marketing Boards, in principle have been given a monopoly to purchase and redistribute surpluses at the wholesale level for such produce. Minor food crops and vegetables for which no central market institution has been established, may however be traded freely, subject to licencing.

Our final task in this chapter is to indicate how the internal market in Western Kenya lends itself to exploitation by the various agents of commodity circulation. According to the scale of their activities and their affinity to the local economy we may categorize them as markets, shops or local businessmen and non-local agencies such as marketing board agents, contractors and other urban commercial agencies.

Selling as well as buying takes place vis-à-vis all three categories. Households thus sell their produce whether agricultural or non-agricultural, through markets, local businessmen, such as cattle traders and marketing board agents.

From the Integrated Rural Surveys we may infer that roughly 20 % of sales were made at the level markets in 1974/75, i.e. through women traders. About 50 % went through local businessmen, which are also taken to include those selling their own craft products. The remaining 30 % has been estimated to represent the purchases of marketing board agencies or dairies.

The proportions however vary from province to province. In Nyanza

Province and Western Province markets thus seem to have a larger share of total selling than in Rift Valley – which again may reflect the different magnitudes of "surpluses". In Nyanza Province and Western Province more households sell their produce in small quantities than in Rift Valley where export crops like tea, but also milk are typically marketed through commercial channels of the capitalist circuit network.

Buying daily necessities such as additional food, salt, kerosene, cooking fat, clothing etc. also means dealing with all three categories of agents. Some 35 % of all purchases seem to be at the market level while 47 % may be estimated to be shopping at trading centres. The remaining 18 % thus represent those shopping in towns for various services obtained there.

But again markets are much more important as supply points in the Nyanza and Western Provinces tha in Rift Valley with about 40% of all purchases in the former against 20% in the latter. Table 3.6 below is an estimate of the combined index (buying plus selling) of the relative importance of the three categories of circulation based on manipulation of figures extracted from the Integrated Rural Survey.

Not taking the interpretation of the table too far, its figures may indicate however the persistent importance of local trade as a social institution in rural Kenya. Between 75–85% of the total exchange involving the households pass through the hands of local traders. Interpreted in economic terms they may also suggest that there is still a basis for local accumulation of capital. But as we shall see in chapter V this anticipation needs a lot of further qualification.

The table however demonstrates another remarkable feature, namely that market trade i.e. trade in the open air, seems to hold a larger share in

Table 3.6. *The relative importance of markets, shops and non-local agencies in buying and selling. Household averages. (Percentages and K.shs.)*

	Nyanza	Rift Valley	Western	Kenya
Markets	37	19	35	29
Shops etc.	39	56	49	48
Non-local agencies	24	25	16	23
	100	100	100	100
Total average annual Buying + selling K.shs.	3943	5458	3234	4510

Source: Rep. of Kenya. Central Bureau of Statistics, Integrated Rural Survey 1974–75, Nairobi 1977, Tables 8.16 and 8.24 (buying), 8.20 and 8.28 (selling).

Nyanza and Western than in Rift Valley, about one-third as compared with one-fifth of total trade. This difference may again be seen as a reflection of the lower level of reproduction in the two first mentioned provinces, and therefore also as an indication of less favourable conditions of "modern" trade, i.e. shopkeeping. On the other hand the importance of market trade in Western Kenya also tells us that the role of women in trade at local market places remains equally important. The following chapter deals with this aspect of social existence.

CHAPTER IV

Women Traders

1. Introduction

The purpose of making a study of the trade of rural women is closely tied to the involvement of rural households in the market economy, and the necessity for family members to earn incomes in order to supplement agricultural earnings.

In order to study the extent of trade and the characteristics of trade, two groups were selected for the case studies. One group of women traders were selected and interviewed at the open market places, and represented different scales and types of trade (212 cases). The other group of women were selected in the households from the study areas (191 cases). The women represented different age-groups and social groups, and both groups were interviewed on their family, their work situation and incomes. The women traders had a more thorough interview on their trade and trade experience.

It appears to be a dominant feature of most of the settled agricultural and urban areas in East Africa that women trade with foodcrops or prepared food and drinks in the open markets. In the literature the mammy traders of West Africa are very dominant. The studies and literature of women traders in East Africa is scarcer, even if women traditionally have been trading, and women traders are an important aspect of the food distribution system, at least in Kenya.

The female dominated market trade in foodcrops could be experted in East Africa according to generalizations on the basis of findings from different farming systems. Thus Ester Boserup in her pioneer work on women in development argues:

> "those regions where women dominate the food trade of rural and urban markets are usually the regions characterized by female farming traditions. Conversely, in the regions where we find market trade dominated by men, we also find that men do most of the agricultural work, while women give only occasional help." (Boserup 1970, p. 91).

The proportion of women involved in trade shows major regional variations, the most general pattern is that women in pastoral and muslim societies rarely trade, whereas trade is a normal business of women in the more intensively cultivated areas.

107

In Machakos District a study of non-farm activities revealed that 29 % of women were involved in petty trade (Mbithi 1971, p. 13), and a small study on Luo women of South Nyanza confirmed this level, showing that 32 % of women were involved in petty trade (Bookman 1973, p. 57).

Generally the petty trade of women is poorly covered in earlier studies. Jane Wills has analysed a few small-scale enterprises in Embu, mostly beer-brewing, water carting and maize-milling (Wills 1967), but of these activities only brewing is still a woman's activity, the others are done by men, but substitute for tasks previously done by women.

The rural non-farm survey carried out by the Central Bureau of Statistics in December 1976–January 1977 goes into details on all non-farm activities which any members of the household above 15 years had carried out for more than one month during the previous year. This survey ought to have the information on the relative frequency of petty trade, food crops, trade etc., but apparently failed to include very many of the women traders. Only within the manufacturing of food and drinks does there appear to be some reasonable coverage, showing that pombe brewing (local beer) is an activity practised in 26 % of Nyanza households, 15 % of Rift Valley households and 18 % of Western Province households. This is a surprisingly high number as most will be brewing illegally without license. Around 1 % of households seem to be engaged in food kiosks, which will mostly be women's activities. But the category on petty trade, phrased in the questionnaire as hawker and itinerant vendors, is reported in only 1.6 % of Nyanza households, 0.4 % in the Rift Valley and 2.8 % of households in Western Province (Social Perspectives vol. 2 No. 2, 1977).

Apparently women's trade in food has not been emphasized either in the categories of the questionnaire or in the instruction of interviewers, and a valuable chance for estimating the dimensions of women's trade has been wasted.

Only in urban areas is there some literature on women in petty trade and business in Kenya. E. Wachtel analyses female shopkeepers in Nakuru and stresses the cooperation in women's groups and the linkage between urban business and agriculture (Wachtel 1976). Other examples of female entrepreneurship are found among women in some of the spontaneous settlement areas around Nairobi, e.g. the beer-brewing in Mathare Valley (Nelson 1973) or the shopkeepers in Dagoretti (Gathungu 1975).

Many of the urban studies seem to show that many women in business and petty trading activities are more often single with children to support. That is, the group of unmarried and divorced mothers should be relatively over-represented.

This seems only to be partly the case for the rural women traders. In the study of rural women traders in the Western parts of Kenya, the proportion of single women was 20 % for the peasant social class, but only 6 % for the rich strata. The group of single women includes unmarried, divorcees and widows.

There is however a relatively high representation of married women who are the youngest wife in a polygamous union, 26 % of all the women traders or 30 % of all the married traders are from polygamous unions. The corresponding figures for women in household cases, show that only 16 % of the married women are from polygamous unions (table 4.1).

With respect to age, the group of young married women with only small children is clearly under represented. Among young women in the twenties family obligations are usually too demanding, and no older children can assist. The major part of the professional women traders are above 35 years, at the age when the oldest children can take care of the younger, and the demand for incomes to pay school fees is increasing.

However, the approx. 40 % of the peasant women traders who are younger than 35 years are mostly single women or the youngest wife in a polygamous union, a group of women who are forced to get incomes to support themselves outside agriculture.

2. The trade of women

In nearly all trading centres and urban areas there are open market places where the main food trade takes place. Chapter III reveals that the food market is important even in the peasant areas, and that open market trade caters for more than 30 % of all buying and selling in most provinces. In relation to the food market, only processed food, e.g. maize flour (Unga),

Table 4.1. *Marital status of women traders, relative to women in household cases (percent).*

	Women in household				Women traders			
	Land- less	Peasants	Rich peasants	Sub- total	Peasants	Rich peasants	Sub- total	Total
Married:* 1 wife	100	76	78	80	53	71	59	71
Married:* 2 wives	–	13	16	13	24	15	21	16
Married:* 3 wives	–	2	4	3	4	7	5	4
Unmarried	–	2	–	1	6	2	5	3
Divorcee	–	2	–	1	8	2	6	3
Widow	–	4	3	3	6	2	5	4
Total	100	99	101	101	101	99	101	101
N =	21	93	77	191	80	41	121	312

* husband has one wife, two wives ot three wives.

sugar, salt, and cooking fat are sold from shops. All vegetables and other food are provided at the open market at market days by women traders.

Men dominate among the group of business people in the shops of the trading centres, but in the open market trade of market days, women are approx. 90 % of the traders, and thus dominate the food distribution. Within the open markets, only the selling of metal work, leather work, livestock, some clothes trade, and tobacco trade are dominated by men. Metal work and cattle trade are solely the trade and business of men, while clothes and tobacco trading have both male and female hawkers.

In the trading centres the whole business is affected by the intensity of the open market trade. The number of market days vary with the size of the trading centres, varying from three times per week to one or two afternoons per week. Many of the smaller shops are closed when it is not a market day in the smaller trading centres, and business both at the market and in the shops is only active on market days, when many customers are around.

In the open markets women sell a variety of food crops such as maize (green, dry, flour), beans, cassava, sorghum, millet, vegetables (potatoes, peas, cowpeas, tomatoes, arrow roots, onions, carrots, cabbages, sweet potatoes, cabbage leaves), fruits, bananas (green, sweet), and groundnuts. But women also sell other food items in petty trade, especially cooked food, e.g. porridge, roasted or boiled maize, boiled eggs, scones, or margarine in spoonfuls, In certain areas wild fruits, flying ants, and firewood collected in the forests supplement the produce. Women also sell sisal ropes, baskets and pots and are responsible for the selling of chickens and eggs.

Among the group of women traders interviewed at the market places, approx. 40 % were trading full time, i.e., involved in purchasing and selling six to seven days per week. The proportion of full time traders and seasonal traders was higher among the better off social strata. More women from the

Table 4.2. *Number of days trading per week (percent).*

	Peasants	Rich peasants	Total
Seasonal or occasional	4	14	7
1–2 days per week	41	27	38
3–5 days per week	11	7	10
6–7 days per week	36	46	40
no. inf.	8	5	7
Total	100	99	102
N =	80	41	121

Market day in a large open air market. Women traders selling potatoes. In the the background the shops of the Trading Centre (Karatina Central Province). (Gunvor Jørgsholm)

peasant families were involved in part-time trading, which is often on a smaller scale and leaves time for farming. Many more of the peasants' wives would be registered in occasional trade if these women considered themselves traders. Most surveys do not include this group as traders and they have also been excluded to a large extent in this survey, mostly because the survey was conducted during the season when most of the farmwork had to be done, and there were no crops from the farms to sell.

3. Agriculture and trade

Agricultural production and trade are closely linked to each other in several ways. First, women are often trading the food crops from their own fields, and secondly, trade is necessary in certain periods of the year to supplement food crops.

The case studies of women in rural households showed that approx. 70 % of peasant wives were involved in trade in one way or another, but 50 % only marketed their own crops (table 4.3.).

Table 4.3. *Trade of own crops versus purchased crops for women in household and women traders (percent).*

	Women in household				Women traders		
	Land-less	Rich Peasants	Sub-peasants	total	Rich Peasants	Sub-peasants	total
Trade							
only own crops	14	53	29	39	–	–	–
Sell own crop large-scale-KFA*	–	–	38	15	–	–	–
Sell own crops and buy and sell	10	14	5	10	53	63	56
Sell only purchased goods	–	–	–	–	47	37	44
Do not trade	76	27	18	29	–	–	–
No inf.	–	6	10	7	–	–	–
Total	100	100	100	100	100	100	100
N =	21	93	77	191	80	41	121

* Kenya Farmers' Association, who have stores and marketing boards in most Districts.

Of the rich peasants' wives, 67 % sell own crops as traders or on large-scale to the marketing boards (KFA). There is, however, a difference in the perception of this as trade. The typical pattern is that the crops sold to KFA are considered the husbands' crops and income, whereas income from trade at open markets is usually considered the women's own income. A relatively small proportion of the household cases were involved in more professional trade. The 14 % (= 3 women) of the landless farm labour strata, who were selling their own crops, cultivated a rented or borrowed piece of land. Some permanent farm labourers still get access to land for cultivation from the employer.

Among the women traders, approx. half were trading partly their own farm produce and were partly reselling other products. The percentage is higher among the larger scale farmer families. Among the group which never markets their own farm produce there is a higher percentage of landless women, single women and wives from polygamous unions without access to land for cultivation. The women traders often use their own harvest as an input in the trade, usually just after harvesting. That is to say many traders are sometimes in the situation where they have used their total working capital. Then they have to go back to the farm and produce a harvest to use as input in the trade, or they may go out and work as casual labourers, or in some areas they may collect wild fruit, green cabbage leaves, or firewood in the forest to sell. This trading, however, give very poor return on the labour invested.

Relatively few women traders can make the investments and have the storage facilities to purchase crops at harvest time and sell later in periods of scarcity, even if these transactions give very good profits for the wholesale traders. For instance, in Luanda market of Kakamega District the price for 1 debe[1] of beans was 15 K.shs. at harvest time (December–January) and 30 K.shs. in November. Maize varies between 40 K.shs. per bag and 65 K.shs. per bag of 90 kilograms (1974). Usually the same traders do not store the crops for nearly one year, but sell after half a year in an area where there is shortage, to secure the profits.

Some of the wholesale women traders get a profit when they can manage to buy from a larger debe (where the sides are hammered a bit concave) and sell from a smaller debe (where the sides are convex).

Most of the trade of women petty traders consists of purchasing crops in debes or bags and reselling in smaller quantities such as kilodebes[1], Kimbo-tins[2], bowls, baskets, calabashes, piles, pieces or other not standardized measures.

The close relationship between agriculture and trade is underlined in the seasons of trade and agriculture. Trade is intensive just after harvesting of maize and in food deficiency periods when granaries are empty before the harvest. There are however several stages and seasons of trade. In periods and areas where many local vegetables are harvested, the vegetable traders buy and resell in other areas, or they themselves sell from their own crops. Some, however, go back to farming, because of the competition in the harvesting period. Vegetable traders complain about the lack of demand and high competition in these periods.

On the other hand the fish traders also complain in these periods. The trade with small dried fish or smoked fish is best, when vegetables are in short supply, and the protein and taste added to the maize has to come mainly from vegetables and fish, the latter especially within the Luo, Luyia and Gusii areas. Meat is too expensive to be a regular part of the diet for most of the small peasant families.

Most of the women traders dealing with vegetables or fruits change to other items during periods of shortages of these crops. It is normal to include other vegetables, i.e. for cabbage traders to include potatoes or change between beans, fingermillet, and maize in the case of some medium-scale traders.

[1] 1 debe is a foursided tin of approx. 15 kg maize. There are 6 debes per bag of 90 kg.
[1] 1 kilodebe is a little less than a normal debe. There are 6 1/2 kilodebes per bag of 90 kg.
[2] 1 tin from a kilogram margarine or cooking fat tin.

In the periods of maize scarcity, the food trade is carried out by either women traders from other areas, as is the case in relation to the Kano plain of Kisumu District. The supplies for most of the year come from the hills to the North up the Nandi escarpment and from the hills of South Nyanza District. Or women wholesalers may go around and buy from other areas as is the case in Vihiga-Maragoli, where the wholesalers go to Lugari settlement schemes, Busia and Rift Valley to buy maize for the local retail market of Luanda.

In the last few months before a new harvest, the economic situation of the different social classes becomes very distinct, as the landless and poor peasants have long had to buy their basic food, and more often have had to expand other income generating activities such as casual employment, selling of sisal ropes, baskets, clay pots, fire-wood, charcoal, goats, chicken, fish, etc. in order to pay for the food (maize) (Mbithi 1971, pp. 13–15).

There is also another relationship between trade and agriculture, as trade declines during the seasons where a high labour input is needed in agriculture. In these periods the peasant wives have to work on the farms and perhaps also work as casual labourers on other larger farms, when this yields better earnings than their trade, or to get an input for the trade.

The supply of food shows major regional variations reflecting both ecological zones, where some have one and others two maize harvests per year, and reflecting different crop patterns, population density and land distribution. Much of the trade is based on the fact that most of the peasant families are not self-sufficient with respect to food crops.

Among the cases of both the women at the farmsteads and the women traders, most indicated that they buy vegetables and other food for the household, and only 46 % of the peasant households were self-sufficient with maize, in contrast to 72 % of the rich peasant households. On average all the households buy maize three months per year, but 18 % of the peasant families bought maize more than six months per year. This indicates the existence of a large internal food market even in peasant farming areas. The food market, however, is much larger and the whole year around in the mono-cultural export crop areas, like the sugar belt in Kisumu and Kakamega Districts, and in the tea plantations of Kericho District where many landless labourers are working. In such areas the food trade is handled by peasant women from surrounding areas, but there may arise problems of shortages when these areas themselves are short of supplies.

The role of African women as traders has to be related to their situation in the family at marriage. According to the traditions of most of the cultivating peoples in Kenya, the wife gets at marriage the right to cultivate a part of her husband's land to support the family with food. The obligation to supply the food seems to be binding to a great extent, even if the plot allocated is too small to support the family. Women usually control the produce of their own food crops and may use them in trade, or sell them to cover specific expenses e.g., school-fees or medical care. In other seasons trade may be the only source of income to supply additional money to buy food. Though women traders have their own economy, closely linked to their obligations towards the family, this may be perceived as a necessary source of income for family survival, but is also a possibility for the man to maintain the division of responsibilities and obligations even under conditions of land shortage and increasing need for cash incomes for the family survival.

Table 4.4 shows that in families with male head-of-household, the husband's contribution to the household expenses is limited. It gives evidence for the point raised earlier, that husbands do not perceive daily household expenditures to be their obligations or duties to cover. More than 40 % pay no cash for the household, but only occasionally pay some food or children's clothes (table 4.4). Husbands usually have the responsibility for a major share of the school-fees and most of the seasonal farm inputs.

The difference between peasant women traders and peasant women who do not trade regularly, is that 82 % of women traders do not receive regular

Table 4.4 *Husband's cash contribution to the household expenses (percentages only for household with male head-of-household)*.

	Women in household			Women traders		
	Landless	Peasants	Rich peasants	Peasants	Rich peasants	Total
Occasionally or nothing	52	33	19	82	29	41
10–20 K.shs. p. month	5	7	1	3	–	4
21–60 K.shs. p. month	19	21	5	5	13	12
61–100 K.shs. p. month	–	5	12	3	18	9
101 K.shs. or more	–	3	29	–	27	11
Only in kind	5	25	24	3	11	17
No information	19	7	9	3	3	7
Total	100	101	99	99	101	101
N =	21	86	75	64	38	284

support for the family, while 33 % of women in the household cases are in the same situation, but with poorer possibilities to support themselves.

In families with male head-of-household, the husband's regular contribution to the household expenses is limited. It is clear from a question concerning what the husband is using his money for, that he contributes to the farm investments and farm inputs such as seeds, fertilizer, ploughing, casual labourers etc. 60–70 percent of those husbands who contribute to the household at all, pay these expenses.

Among the peasant families the husband in approx. 85 % of the cases contributed to household expenses, whereas in 15 % of the households he only used the money on himself and left the support of the family to the wife alone. In nearly 40 % of the cases where the husband did contribute to household expenses, the women complained of too little support because the husband was drinking and most of his income was used in this way. Drinking as a drain on family resources was only mentioned by 10 % of the women from rich peasant families.

Paying of school-fees is another obligation of the husband and approx. 80–90 % contribute to this, even if the wife contributes in nearly as many cases among peasant families (tables 4.5 and 4.6), still this is the obligation of the husband alone in approx. 40 percent of the poorer families. The husband is alone responsible for these expenses in more than 60 percent of the total rich peasant households.

The expenses of school-fees are more often carried by the woman alone if she is trading, and if she is from the poorer families. The interpretation of these findings are open for discussion as it may look reasonable that women who earn an income share the costs and more often have to support themselves. But the trading cannot be used as an explanatory factor, as the reason for starting trading may be that the women are left with these obligations, and that the husband after she started trading argues that she has to contribute and may as well support the family once she has an income.

The other problem of interpreting these economic obligations is that when the wife is contributing cash to school-fees or other expenses, she is trading or selling from her own agricultural crops, which she and her children have produced. But in many of the cases where the husband is contributing money for these expenses it is derived from his cash crops, where the wife, and often the children, have worked and where he may or may not have worked himself, but usually he has not put any labour in this production himself. The surplus belongs to him due to his control of the land and the produce. In some cases the husband's contribution comes mostly from an appropriation of the surplus made by the wife and perhaps the children. Hanger found that in Embu half of women's agricultural labour

Table 4.5. *Responsibility for paying school-fees within a household (percent of familie, paying school-fees women traders and women in households).*

	Women in household				Women traders			
	Landless	Rich Peasants	Sub-peasants	total	Rich Peasants	Sub-peasants	total	Total
Who pays?								
Wife alone	40	18	3	14	32	9	24	18
Husband alone	40	54	71	60	18	41	26	47
Wife + husband	13	22	13	17	38	41	39	25
Adult children assisting one or both parents	7	4	14	7	6	3	4	7
Adult children alone	–	2	–	1	7	3	6	3
No information	–	2	–	1	–	3	1	1
Total	100	102	101	100	101	100	100	101
N =	15	65	62	142	56	32	88	230

Table 4.6. *School-fees contribution of wife and husband (percent of families with male head-of-household and paying school-fees).*

	Women in household				Women traders			
	Landless	Rich Peasants	Sub-peasants	total	Rich Peasants	Sub-peasants	total	Total
Wife contributes alone or with others	64	41	27	37	71	53	65	55
Husband contributes alone or with others	60	87	98	89	87	90	88	89
N =	15	57	60	132	39	30	69	201

was used in the husband's cashcrops, e.g., tea or coffee (Hanger & Moris 1973, p. 227). But the problem is the same when the wife is caring for the husband's cows, milking them and selling the milk for him. In the case of some businesses some similar patterns are found, when the wife is working in the husband's butchery or bar most of the time and gets a small "salary" from which she is supposed to maintain the family. The surplus derived, however, belongs to the husband and may be kept for business investments or consumption.

The actual proportion of men's and women's work and money contribution to the household expenses will therefore be difficult to estimate. Though the findings presented in terms of cash input overestimate the husband's contribution and underestimate the wives' input.

4. Regional variations

The trade of women shows major regional variations mostly based on the differences in agricultural structure, but also based on different traditions of trade in the different regions.

Most of the trade of women is carried out by women from some of the small-holder peasant areas with a combination of their own crops and purchased crops. Within the areas of monocultural cashcrops such as in the sugar belt of Kisumu District and Mumias estate in Kakamega as well as the tea plantations of Kericho District, the supply of foodcrops is usually provided by women traders from farmsteads in the surrounding areas. These women sell from their own products, but also bring many supplies from other maize and vegetable producing areas. The cheapest supplies of maize are usually found in small peasant areas at Bungoma, Busia, Kakamega and South Nyanza around harvest time. The settlement schemes and medium and large-scale farms in the Rift Valley sell directly to the marketing boards in large quantities and the prices never go much below the standard prices of the KFA. In only a few of the settlement schemes, where loan repayment is directly deducted by the KFA, do the farms divert a surplus of maize to wholesale traders instead of selling through the marketing boards in order to avoid the deductions.

On the other hand, potatoes, cabbages, tomatoes and onions are not marketed at any standard price to a marketing board, and in the areas of Rift Valley, where these are grown in large-scale, e.g. in Timboroa, they are sold at very low prices to the wholesale traders. These crops especially give a basis for a very profitable trade between the new settlements and the surrounding small peasant areas.

At any given time there are considerable price differentials reflecting these structures and the ecological zones i.e. especially at the harvest time. Within women's trade these differences in supplies and prices are exploited and the trade is characterized by being very flexible and dependent on good transport. In most of the areas, access to transport is good, either by bus or matatu (a long-distance minibus-taxi with space for approx. 12 people and luggage). But in certain areas transport is very difficult. Especially during the rainy periods, the unpaved roads become impassable, and food trade is hindered for long periods. A large proportion of the petty traders and medium-scale traders, however, live close to the main market from which they sell, and transport their goods by foot or in special cases by donkey.

The transport system and access to it determines the women's possibilities to use the different markets. One example is the railway. Luanda market is relatively close to the railway to Nairobi, and the small special market of Mwibona has developed just beside the railway station, as a market for fruits for the Nairobi market. The outlet for some crops in Luanda, especially bananas, would have been very difficult if the access to the urban market in Nairobi had not been so easy.

Supplies to areas such as the sugar belt of Kisumu District are dependent on good transport, and in periods there are serious problems because of the shortage of buses and matatus (long-distance minibus-taxi), which are overcrowded, and too expensive for the women traders. Most of the supply of maize, beans and vegetables come from Nakuru area, where a group of Kikuyu women traders arrange transport and a variety of crops for the trade in order not to overlap each other. They stay in Muhoroni or Koru until the crops are sold, and then return for a period to their homes in the Rift Valley.

The long-distance trade of women is a relatively recent phenomenon, even if a barter trade between tribes was carried on by women traders also over some distance.

The long-distance trade has been mostly a male trade exchanging ivory, salt, and iron between the tribal areas, by means of special trade caravans.

However it has been a characteristic feature of most of the tribal communities, living relatively close, that food was exchanged in a barter trade, especially between the pastoral and agricultural communities. Within the Western parts of Kenya, the Luo exchanged meat and skins for grain from the Gusii people, and a similar trade developed between the Kikuyu and the Masai (Zwanenberg & King,1975, p. 149 ff).

Even in periods of warfare between the Kikuyu of Central Province and the Masai of the Rift Valley, women could traditionally penetrate enemy land and exchange foodcrops for milk and skins. In Western and Nyanza Province there is evidence of the active barter trade of Luo women.

In the late 19th. and in the first part of the 20th. Century, the women of Kowe (in Northern part of Kisumu District) expanded trade to the North with the Luyias and to the South with the Luo's at the lakeside. (Hay 1976, p. 92). 5'In the years of good harvests, or in seasons of famine or shortage the women of Kowe were active in this local trade in foodstuff" (Hay 1976, p. 92). The trade was rather a seasonal than a regular activity, and was mainly a local barter trade. Some women traders however accumulated wealth in livestock from this trade. In the 1920's the trade declined in a long period of stable harvests. The increasing importance of cash implied that the local barter markets of Kondik, Luanda and Kipasi were stagnating in favour of the larger trading centres, where imported consumer goods were sold from the shops. But with the gold rush to the gold mining in several small mines of Kakamega District in the 1930's, the women's trade increased. Women were selling foodcrops and cooked food for the labourers (Hay 1976, pp. 100–104).

In the Kericho area, women became involved in the production and selling of maize and other foodcrops, first for the railway workers around 1900. Around 1907 the Colonial Government tried to expand the maize production and involved the Kipsigis in this food supply programme. Women in this area were not traditionally involved in trade (Pilgrim 1959).

Women traders from areas, where women traditionally went into trade and also long-distance trade are still dominating open-air markets also outside their home areas. It appears as if the trade in clothes, tobacco and much of the wholesale grain and vegetable trade in Rift Valley and Western Province is dominated by Kikuyu women from Central Province or from the new settlements in the Rift Valley. The Luo women also expand trade to the sugar schemes and Kericho tea plantations, as well as dominate the fish trade of the Western parts of Kenya, including the trade of fish from Lake Turkana.

Women from Kakamega and Bungoma are also expanding trade, but only a few are engaged in large-scale trade with high investments. On the other hand they are responsible for most of the vegetable trade in Nandi District and are a relatively large group among medium and small scale vegetable traders in Trans Nzoia and Uasin Gishu.

In relation to Kenya as a whole, the Kikuyu women are very dominating in trade. Kamba women from Eastern Province are active in trade to supplement the very meagre farming in the marginal agricultural areas.

The Gusii women appear to be an exception as regards trade activities. There are Gusii women traders, but only relatively few, and Luo women are dominating the foodcrop trade in the Kisii area. Gusii women concentrate more on agriculture, and seem to be able to maintain control over the sales of pyrethrum to a higher extent, thus making an income more directly from agricultural production and foodcrops as well as from cash-crops. In the Kisii area, there appears to be a higher proportion of unmarried women traders.

Kipsigis women resemble the Gusii as regards trading, however, they can be seen more as an agricultural community with many features from a domination of a traditional livestock based economy. The sexual division of labour and the responsibility for supplying the daily food is therefore different, and women are not to the same extent as in other areas considered the daily supporters of the family. Women in this area usually concentrate more on agriculture and peasant wives will be less involved in trade. In those cases where women are involved in trade in the same way as in other areas they are more often wives of landless farm labourers who have only the right to cultivate a small plot of the employer's land.

Among the Nandi women, trade is much less frequent than in any of the other mentioned tribal groups. Nandi women have limited access to money, and they concentrate on expanding farming beyond the small vegetable garden which earlier was the only supplement to animal produce. In the cases of Nandi women from both North Nandi and South Nandi, women rarely involved themselves in trade, and seldom had money from their husband to support their family. The general pattern was that the husband supplied household necessities, meat and other items, provided in kind and not in money. The only trade which Nandi women took up in the district was that of brewing busaa (local beer made of millet). In some of the areas busaa was sold at home, and in Southern Nandi, the busaa clubs made contracts with women, who provided busaa on commission to the club on certain days. In South Nandi, near the escarpment, some women brought guavas (wild fruits) and bags of maize by donkey down to the wholesalers in the sugar belt. They were only to a very limited extent involved in other trade ventures. At the time of the maize harvest the trade in maize from the escarpment increased, as this was the season of short maize supply in the Kano plain.

Busaa brewing is not a special phenomenon for the Nandi area. In the non-farm activity survey for rural areas in Kenya (1976) approx. 18 % of the households in Western, Nyanza and Rift Valley Provinces admitted brewing more than one month per year (Social Perspectives, vol. 2, No. 2, 1977). This is exceptionally high for an activity which is mainly carried out as an illegal activity as only the busaa clubs with licenses are legal. Brewing as a women's activity showed the least regional variation of all trades.

5. The scale of women's trade

The question on the incomes of women traders does not directly provide a basis for the estimation of profits from trade. Many, especially the petty traders, gave figures on the sales, rather than incomes, and have difficulties in separating working capital from incomes to be used for immediate purchase of goods.

In petty trade, where only one's own farm produce is traded, the total sales price can be used and disposed of. Some kind of evaluation of the scales of trade may be based on several indicators such as the incomes provided, the amount bought at one time, whether or not the women use the incomes only for subsistence or if they save for other business ventures, and the distance of trade operations. The petty traders usually limit their activities to one or two local markets, they have no investments to go to other areas to purchase bags of crops at a lower price, and no knowledge of where to go at the different seasons. The petty traders buy mostly in debes and only occasionally in bags and resell in piles or other very small quantities. This is a time-consuming and usually not very profitable trade, though the most frequent type at the open market places.

The food-crop market is a market of free competition with no standard or regulated prices. The Maize Marketing Boards, which buy maize in larger quantities from farmers, have standard prices, which influence the market price. The price of maize flour sold from the shops is also fixed. In the open market however the prices of maize may vary to a great extent, both according to the season and the region. The great variations may be explained by local surplus or shortages. Bags of maize at harvest time are usually sold under the price offered by the marketing boards, because there is a local surplus and the boards do not buy single bags. Consumer prices for unsifted maize meal at the open market rarely or never exceed that of the standardized sifted Unga Flour in the shops in rural areas. Whereas the prices of the goods in the shops are regulated, and have a clear profit squeeze, the women traders may operate under totally open competition. Under these conditions the very qualified and the economically powerful may exploit the arbitrage possibilities for big profits. But the typical women traders have found their own pocket in the local market.

The differences in the scale of trade may be revealed in a few profiles of women traders. A few very successful women traders not only trade on a large scale but also invest in other economic activities and may be seen as proper capitalists, who with or without their husband's consent and involvement develop their business. In order to give a better picture of this group of traders, three summarized profiles are provided:

> Rose is 26 years old. She came with her family from Nyeri in 1956–57 to an estate in the Rift Valley. The father was working in the estate and had 4 acres of land to cultivate. The father was given 21 acres of land after independence, but at his death in 1970 the two sons sold the land, without their mother's consent. Rose then married an Abaluyia businessman as his fourth wife, and her mother stayed with her near Turbo after she was thrown off her former land. Her husband's land in Bunyore (40 acres) was cultivated by his other wives and Rose was working in his shop. She started her own bean and onion trade in the Turbo market. From her first profit she rented 5–10 acres of land to grow maize and beans. Together with her mother and her brothers she works on the land. The bean trade is very profitable before the harvest, but just after harvest business is poor and she expands the trade with millet and maize, which she buys in Kakamega, Bungoma and from Uganda. Usually she buys millet for 15 K.shs. per debe and retails at 20–22 K.shs., but when she buys from Uganda, just before the harvest, she may get millet at 10 K.shs. per debe and retail it at 26 shs. per debe. In June (at the time of the interview) she

> bought beans from the local producers for 25 shs. per debe and retailed them at 40 shs. per debe. Rose is trading at a scale where she has managed to get profits to rent more land, buy shares in land-purchasing-societies to get her own land (3,700 shs. are invested in these), and she has invested, together with her mother, in building houses for rent. They have 8 houses and are getting an income of 200 shs. per month from these. She is also paying the school-fees for her youngest brother on the condition that he works on the rented land. To diversify the business she has invested in a car operating as a matatu (long-distance taxi), she and her brothers have each invested 4,500 shs. in this, and it provides an income of 200 shs. per day when it is running. Rose is conducting this entire business by herself with her own relatives. Her husband is living in his shop some distance away and Rose, who has four children from 8 years and younger, want to secure for herself her own land and to be able to support her family.

The long distance trade, especially the smuggling across the Uganda border, has contributed to the high profits and made it possible to expand and direct the business beyond the narrow subsistence level. Also her ability to exploit the work of her mother and her brothers in farming has increased her economic potential.

In another case a Kikuyu woman carried out a prosperous trade in the Kapsabet area, but with her husband as a partner and companion from a certain stage in the trade:

> Wanjiru is 32 years old and was born in Murang'a District. She had 4 years of school education. She married in 1960, and her husband who was with the Ministry of Works was transferred to Kapsabet in Nandi District in 1964. Wanjiru, who had no land, wanted to start trading and her husband gave her 250 shs. to start her business. She went to Eldoret to buy 2 bags of potatoes and 2 boxes of tomatoes at 30 shs. per bag and 12/50 per box respectively. She retailed these in small piles at Seremi market on four market days and had a profit of 60 shs. from tomatoes and 130 shs. from the potatoes. She then bought more potatoes in Timboroa and opened a small stall at Kapsabet market. From 1964–68 she saved 5,000 shs. from the business and opened a busaa club (local beer made of finger-millet). Her husband retired from his job to run the bar, which has a turnover of 4,000 shs. per month and gives a good profit. From this profit they have bought a car, which she uses for transporting crops, and which runs as a matatu five days per week earning 250 shs. per day. Wanjiru continued her vegetable trade buying on a large-scale several bags of potatoes and beans from Eldoret and Timboroa. She rented a store for these crops in Kapsabet. During the whole period she has been renting land to cultivate. She rented 10 acres in 1970, and sold the surplus to buy their own land. In 1973 they bought 7 1/2 acres near Kapsabet for 9,000 shs. and she began cultivating maize and cabbages. They are now renting a small shop and hotel apart from the busaa club. Wanjiru is continuing her trade and provides money for school-fees for 4 of her children in secondary school, and for 3 in primary school. The two youngest are not in school.

This case shows a rather extreme example of how a bright woman from an area with trading traditions who has capital to invest can find profits in the trade of an area like this. She has little competition, as the Nandi women only rarely do any trading, and the few Luyia women are petty traders in vegetables, do not have enough capital to invest in expanding the trade.

Her investments in buying large quantities and paying for transport, enabled her to expand profits and exploit the market. The exceptional factor in this case was that her husband's permanent job made the initial investment possible, but once her trade provided a possibility for higher profits, he left his job to run the new business of the busaa club, and continued investing together with her in their business. It is also exceptional that she can manage these trade arrangements with small children and a child-birth every one and a half years.

These two cases are extremes in their scale and in their reinvestment and constant expansion of their business, while they still carry on vegetable trade in the open market. Other women traders, who in certain periods accumulate and invest their capital are often restricted by family expenditures or problems. One example of this is provided in the following case, which also illustrates the legal problems of women in the rural areas in relation to divorce and to ownership of land:

Priscilla is approx. 38 years old, and has no school education. She is engaged in the maize, millet and bean wholesale trade at Luanda market. She started in business to support her family, with only 3 K.shs. in capital. She baked scones to sell or in exchange for maize cobs. When she had 30/= from selling scones, she bought one bag of maize and sold it as flour in Kisumu. She continued this trade, and after a year she had 800/=. Then she bought 40 bags of maize at harvest and sold them later in the year in Kisumu bringing back fish from Kisumu to resell in Luanda. With this trade for more than a year she had saved 16,000 K.shs. She gave part of the money to her husband, who went to a trade union course in Israel for 3 months. He was employed by COTU, and had no land, so she used 2,000 K.shs. to buy one acre of land for the family and covered all household expenditures for the household with the eight children. Then she went bankrupt and went back to farming. At harvest time she used the maize and beans for input in the trade and for school-fees. Her husband came back and decided to divorce her and marry another wife. He took the land she had bought and stopped helping with any contribution to school-fees. She went into the fish trade again and rented a shop at Luanda market, where she and the children could stay. She expanded the fish trade and bought fish in large quantities in Tanzania along the lake. Together with other women she hired a boat for transport. This trade took her away from the children for long periods, and she went back to grain trade at wholesale level. She buys in debes and bags from brokers or producers at Luanda at harvest time and sells to shopkeepers and stores in Nakuru and Nairobi. Outside the local harvest time she buys from settlement schemes in Western Province, Busia and Bungoma. The trade is improving and she is considering the possibility of buying a lorry for the transport together with some other women traders. She can now manage to pay for the 2 oldest children to go to a secondary boarding school, and to pay school-fees for the other. But the problem is that she is travelling too much from her children.

This last case demonstrates more of the general features of the trade of women in foodcrops, even if the trade is still on a large-scale and characterized by frequent travelling across districts and borders to get good profits for investments and survival.

The trade is characterized by great seasonal fluctuations in the scale over time. In some periods the working capital is exhausted, making it necessary to return to farming, to wait for the harvest, which is used as a new trade input. The family obligations play an important part in draining the working capital and determine the trade conditions.

The more general women traders at medium-level have smaller investments and more limited profits, even if it is possible within this group to find women travelling long distances to buy goods or market their goods, but most use their own crops as at least part of the input in trade. A few cases with different items of trade illustrate some of the more general types of women's trade.

> *Mary is 35 years old and has 5 years of school-education, and is trading 2 days a week at Kiminini market close to Kitale in Trans Nzoia. She started trading in 1972 selling Sukuma Wiki (cabbage leaves) and roasted maize. She has also traded with finger-millet, dried fish and dried maize in certain periods. She is now selling roasted maize, but takes up the fish trade again when there is no green maize for roasting. Her husband has five acres of land which she and her 3 oldest girls cultivate with maize and beans. The surplus of maize is sold to KFA stores, and some of it is used in her trade. She buys only the green maize for roasting. This business, in which her girl of 11 years helps to sell the maize, gives her a profit of 5–12 K.shs. per market day in the slack seasons of trade and 10–18 K.shs. per market day in the best season. She operates with only 2 shs. as working capital. She started trading one day per week to help support the family as the husband's salary was too low. After her husband had an accident and broke his legs, he does not have any income. Therefore she had to expand the trade, which is supplementing farming and makes it possible for the family with 5 children to survive and pay school-fees.*

The case underlines the relationship between agriculture and trade. But it also shows how women are regularly involved in carrying a considerable part of the household expenses, and may have to become the sole bread-winner of the family, when this is suddenly necessary. She manages this expansion of work with the help of her children.

In a case from Mwibona market at Luanda railway station, the potential of the area i.e., abundant bananas, sugarcane and easy transport to Nairobi with the railway, is exploited. Several linkages of trade are involved in this. The producers come with one bunch of bananas early in the morning and sell it for approx. 5–7 K.shs. for sweet bananas and 7–14 K.shs. for green bananas (for cooking). The price depends on the size and quality and there is a lot of bargaining, The buyers are banana brokers, who buy for as much money as they have, usually at least 20 shs. They also buy sugarcane and papaya (paw paw). By around 10 a.m. they have collected bunches of bananas, fruits and sugarcane, and the wholesale women come to offer their prices. At this stage there is hardly any bargaining as it is a "buyers market", dependent on the prices in the urban areas. After the goods are bought by wholesalers, they are loaded onto a railwagon for Nairobi, where the husbands or other relatives of the wholesale women receive them and sell them in the shops.

> Elisabeth is 58 years old and started as a banana middledealer 18 years ago. Her husband had a hotel at the market, but did not support her due to too much drinking. When he died she had 4 children to support, and managed through the banana trade on two days a week to provide enough for the household and for school-fees. She could earn between 2 and 15 shs. on a morning in this trade. She tried at one time to go into the wholesale trade to Nairobi herself, but the contact in Nairobi cheated her of her profit, so she went back to the local trade as a banana broker, where she knows she can get a regular income, and still have time for farming. She is highly dependent on the trade income as the brother of her deceased husband claimed the right to inherit her in a levirate marriage and did so. She has 5 children from this marriage, but not much support neither from her husband nor from her adult children, who do not want to support their half-siblings.

In this generation of women, the refusal of a levirate marriage was considered nearly the same as divorce, in which case the land remained with her husband's family; there were few other alternatives for the woman if the husband's brother claimed his right.

It is a typical feature for most of the medium-scale trade of women, that they trade in more than one crop, and that they change the crops according to the season. A case from Kabondo market in South Nyanza also shows that extensive travelling is necessary to get even small incomes within this group of traders.

> Norah is approx. 50 years old and married to an office messenger in Nairobi. She has no school-education. She started trading in 1963 with 15 shs. she had as a gift from her husband. She bought sweet potatoes, green maize and bananas in Kabondo location and resold in smaller quantities, and she sold also from her own maize and sweet potatoes grown on her husband's land of 10 acres. Now she is going to Kericho market with sweet potatoes, maize and smoked fish. The maize and sweet potatoes are partly her own crops and partly bought from growers for 20 K.shs. per bag for green maize and 10 K.shs. per bag for sweet potatoes. The crops are transported by donkey to Kericho approx. 40–50 km on poor roads and sold 1 shs. for 5. She usually gets around 20 shs. per market day from this trade. Her husband contributes 30 shs. per month and saves money for business. By her trade Norah manages to supplement incomes from farming, to run the household, and to buy household necessities as well as contribute to the school-fees for two of her children. She works on the farm herself 3 days per week together with casual labourers.

In some of the families, where the husband is in urban areas, his contribution is used directly as an input in trade to improve trade especially in periods where most peasant families usually have no incomes to invest in trading.

Many of the women traders are involved in brewing busaa/pombe (local beer made from finger-millet). Many women brew at home and sell from there or they get a contract with a busaa hall to brew occasionally. Women who live close to a market place may carry out this prosperous business without much investments, as the little maize and finger-millet used can often be grown on their own land. Especially in areas with many labourers and large settlements, such as the case of a Kipsigis woman in Kericho tea growing area. This trade is a good source of income for the women.

> Deborah is 35 years old and married to a farm labourer in Kericho District. She has 4 acres to cultivate where she has maize, finger-millet and vegetables plus a few cows. When she married in 1959 she started brewing beer to keep the family, since the husband did not work on the land, and only used his income as a farm labourer on himself—mainly drinking. She is brewing twice a week from her own maize and millet and sells at home to customers. She has between 20 and 80 shs. profit per market day, it is best in the beginning of the month or just after a good harvest. She also sells eggs from her poultry for around 20 shs. per month. From the trade she can support the family with her 7 children between 1 and 12 years, and pay school-fees for the oldest children. Deborah is working on the farm together with her 3 children over 8 years of age to get enough for subsistence and input in the trade.

The income from brewing should be compared with the incomes from occasional brewing of busaa or pombe by women in most rural areas. Each brewing session usually provides an income of 25–30 shs. if all is sold.

The cases may give the impression that it is easy for all women to get a relatively reasonable income from trade and enable them to support their family by supplementing farming with a limited trade. But all the cases still reveal that investment is necessary and also the ability to make a good bargain without being cheated, just as the seasonal variations make some trade very meagre. Some women manage only at a very low level of petty trade by collecting firewood in the forest for selling in bunches, selling wild fruits, flying ants or selling cooked food at very high labour input and low profit.

The most miserable conditions are usually found for the porridge sellers, who have a relatively high labour input, nearly as much as the busaa-brewers, but contrary to the brewers have a very small profit.

> Grace is over 50 years old and has no school-education. Her husband is unemployed, and has 2 acres of land which is very poor for cultivation. They live close to Luanda market, and Grace, helped by her separated daughter who lives with her, prepares porridge and sells it at the two market days per week in Luanda. Grace has tried the maize and bean

trade, but could not manage to learn the art of bargaining quickly enough, she started losing and stopped the trade. She has for 2 years now been in the porridge trade, which she herself describes as a very tedious and hard task. She makes two types of fermented porridge from maize and from sorghum and a small portion of fresh porridge. To get two big pots of porridge she uses one debe of flour from her own land, which she puts in a pot with a little water and stirs 2–3 days before the market day. This is covered and put in the sun or by the fire-place for 2–3 days to ferment and gets a sour taste, which many people like. On the market day, they carry the pots to the market and she cooks the porridge at the open fire in the market-place. They have to fetch water, buy fire-wood, wash calabashes and stay by the fire for many hours. The income from one market day is 5–10 K.shs., and is so little that water is fetched by the river 1–2 miles away rather than bought by the water tap at the market place. The trade helps support the family. Grace has 7 children, and her oldest daughter has brought back 2 children. Only some of the children go to school, supported by relatives, as they cannot afford the school-fees themselves. The trade and farming gives only just enough for food and clothing.

A similar picture is shown of other sellers of cooked food, scones, boiled maize, cooked beans and cooked sweet potatoes. For example, the sellers of cooked beans, and sweet potatoes close to the paper mill in Webuye.

Agnes is approx. 35 years old, her husband is a barber at Webuye and has no land. She buys beans, maize and sweet potatoes in debes and cooks them. She carries the goods nearly 2 miles to the market. From this trade, six days per week, she gets between 5 and 12 shs. per day, and can help support the household. The husband and wife can therefore together pay the building funds for the children in school. They have 4 children.

The trade with "free-goods" such as freely collected firewood from the forests is also time-consuming rather than demanding high investments, and profits are not very high, but depend on the local people's access to firewood.

Rachel is 37 years and lives near Kakamega forest. Her husband has two other wives and 4 acres of land, which they all share. She collects firewood in the forest approx. 6 miles away and carries it on her head to the homestead. Here it dries and is bundled in approx. six thick pieces of 1.5 meter. This is carried to the market and sold for 5 shs. She goes to the market on market days i.e., 2 days per week, and collects wood the other week days. By this trade she gets approx. 10–30 shs. per market day. Sometimes however sales are very poor and she carries several bunches back home. She has been in this trade since 1971, because her husband had no job and could not meet the house hod expenses. She is working on the land every morning before trading, together with her husband, co-wives and children. She has 5 children and pays most of the school-fees of 2,000 shs. per year from her trade.

In this case as the natural resources in the forest are exploited and competition is limited, the trade still provides a relatively good income. But money for investments is totally missing, and she is using her labour as the only input in business to secure the subsistence of her family.

Table 4.7. *Motives for trading indicated by women traders (percent).*

	Peasants	Rich peasants	Total
Support family	89	49	74
Personal income- economic independence	–	39	13
Husband insists or wants it	3	5	3
Other (sacked, too old to farm, always traded)	6	2	5
No information	4	5	4
Total	102	100	99
N =	80	41	121

The three groups of examples give an illustration of the variety in scale and type of business in the areas studied. The large majority of the traders are involved in different types of vegetable and grain trade, which dominate the open markets of all the areas. The cases, however, also demonstrate that some women can make a very good profit from this trade. Most are only getting small amounts to supplement their agriculture and sell at only a little more than if they sell to wholesalers from the shamba (farm). Whether or not it is worth it, depends on the necessary labour input on the land i.e. on the size of the land, crop pattern, the season, and other family labour available for the cultivation.

6. Trade and family subsistence

Women's trade is very closely related to their responsibility in the household. The motivations of women from peasant families are related in 90 percent of the cases to family support. (See table 4.7). The trade is in very many cases narrowly related to the economic pressure on the family and to the allocation of economic responsibility in the family, based upon extension of women's responsibility for and attachment to the children. The husband may detach himself from family responsibilities in period when he is under economic or social pressure, or he may detach himself to use his income for his own consumption or his own business. Women have no chance of detaching themselves from family obligations and all the women's trade will be directed towards reproduction of family labour, except in a very few cases of the more bourgeois women, who argue that they want to be independent of their husband's income. They have secured support for their family without having to fight for it.

Table 4.8. *Utilization of women's income from trade (percent of women. Multiple answers).*

Trade incomes used for	Peasants	Rich Peasants	Total
Expanding trade	34	51	40
Food	81	68	77
Support family	11	5	9
Clothes	65	56	62
Household utensils	50	32	44
Farm input	34	24	31
School-fees	54	34	47
Buy/rent land	15	5	12
Saving	6	24	12
Contribution to husband	10	7	9
Other: pay bridewealth for son or new wife	1	2	2
No information	1	–	1
N =	80	41	121

The element of subsistence in the women's trade is further underlined when the women explain what they use their incomes from trade for (table 4.8). In a few of the interviews the answer "support myself and my children" is not specified as in the other cases, but most likely covers at least food and some of the other items.

The most surprising information in this table is not the high proportion who are using trade incomes for the daily necessities of the family, but rather the high proportion of 34 and 24 percent who are contributing to farm inputs; a responsibility, which ideally, just like the school-fees, is considered to be the husband's alone.

Also 10 percent use part of the trade incomes to provide pocket money for the husband. The differences between the two socio-economic groups are reflected in the higher proportion of women traders from rich peasant families who re-invest in expanding trade and are saving, and the much lower proportion used for covering the daily necessities.

On the basis of the information deducted from the cases, it appears to be a rather consistent feature of women's trade that it is an extension of subsistence agriculture used to support the family. Most of the trade activities of women traders may therefore be considered necessary for the reproduction of family labour, given the increased fragmention of land and structure of the household economy. On the basis of this structure, where women traders appear to be carrying the bulk of the cost of reproduction of labour, the question may be raised whether it is relevant to consider the household as one economic unit or whether the wife and children are to be considered the stable unit for the reproduction of labour.

There are very few women traders who invest in business and diversify their economic activities. But a few of these may be considered as business women at a scale beyond the reproduction of family labour, and a few even as proper capitalists accumulating capital from a variety of sources. The only difference from male businessmen in the same stratum is that these women will *always* be responsible for the reproduction of labour also. None of them can detach their business investments and transactions totally from the family obligations.

In some cases of women's involvement in business, it may be very difficult to distinguish between the wife's and the husband's business, and in these cases the household becomes the economic unit. This is the case for one of the large-scale traders referred to earlier (the profile of Wanjiru), but it is also the case when women are trading goods belonging to their husband, e.g. milk from the husband's grade cattle, or running a bar, butchery, or shop on behalf of the husband. One such case can be summarized in the following case:

> *Wambui is over 40 years old and has 6 children from 22 years to 1 year. Her husband has 8 acres of land and a busaa club. The wife works on the land 1 or 2 days per week and is helped by casual labourers and her children, but is daily in the busaa club to run it. The husband pays her 50 K.shs. for this per month to buy household necessities. She has severe problems with managing both the club and her one year old child as she has a poor health. She wants to stop the work in the club, and start trading or do some other less demanding business instead. But the employees need supervision all the time, and her husband wants her to continue this. All the profits from the farm and the business belong to the husband.*

This is very similar to the women's work with their husbands' cashcrops, only in this case the use of family labour implies that the wife is paid for her work, though she does not have a proper share of the profit. It also implies a much higher labour and time input than is the case with the input in cashcrops, and therefore it directly competes with any alternative activities for the woman, and even with her obligations in agriculture.

Such cases could give a basis for the perception of men exploiting their wives' labour by appropriating a surplus, and may thus open the discussion on exploitative vs. the non-exploitative relations within the family.

The women's trade may be considered an important income for family survival, and an important and efficient food distribution system, but it is hardly an economic potential for accumulation or for providing an economic basis strong enough to make the women totally independent. The close relation to the land is often the basis for the trade and therefore usually dependent on and related to the husband's economic potential.

A few cases exist where women have managed to expand the economic potential of their trade and to go far beyond the subsistence level. In these cases women traders have formed groups which work together or have even formed types of cooperatives. This form of organization gives a basis for controlling storage and transport facilities, which are often some of the major obstacles for expanding trade much beyond the subsistence level. One example of such a group is found in Karatina market of Nyeri District, which is wholesaling potatoes and cabbages, and owns lorries and a store. In Luanda market, groups of women often organize major purchasing tours to buy fish together, using common transport, and even plan to buy a lorry together (case of Priscilla). Also the group of Kikuyu women from the Rift Valley who marketed their crops in the sugar belt of Kisumu District, hired transport together to overcome this obstacle.

CHAPTER V

Shopkeepers

1. Introduction

The following chapter deals with the essential findings of 271 case studies of individual shopkeepers distributed over 84 different market-places in Western Kenya.

In essence the idea of the field-work was to get information on the labour process, surplus extraction and utilization and scale of operations of the various types of trade and production related to the market-places.

The findings presented however do not claim statistical representativity of the market activities. Respondents were selected according to the types and scales of activities represented at the market-places among shops, whether engaged in commodity selling or repair and small-scale production. The so-called "informal sector" i.e., non-licensed activities therefore are not included in our study. Traders in the open market-place present during market days are not included either in this part of the study, since this latter category consists overwhelmingly women traders, which have already been covered in chapter IV.

The purpose of this chapter is mainly to characterize the shopkeepers studied in their social context. How does shop-keeping enter family labour relations? Should it be seen as part of the household economic unit? Secondly, how is market trade related to farming and other economic activities of the respondents?

Thirdly, what are the scales of operation and conditions of reproduction of labour and capital of this stratum? And related to this question, the discussion of whether the shopkeepers studied should, or could be, conceived of as a stratum in an economic and social sense? Here the studies of Kitching (Kitching, 1977) Leys (Leys, 1975) etc., may suggest more diversity within the group than commonly shared features vis-à-vis discriminating variables related to the modes of reproduction.

Fourthly, how should shopkeepers be viewed as agents of economic and social transformation? If they are a stratum in transition, does the process at work fundamentally influence the conditions of circulation and production in Western Kenya? Does simple reproduction give way to capitalist accumulation transforming the stratum in a process of differentiation which leads to the formation of a capitalist fraction and consequently to some form of proletarization as well? If a process of class formation takes place, will it, as a consequence of its particular historical base, lead to the formation of a stratum of "lumpen capitalists" (Gerry 1978) as well? What are the relations of this stratum with the dominant capitalist mode of production in Kenya?

The case studies of shopkeepers do not of course provide a basis for adequate answers to these complicated questions as they are case studies of a particular stratum. They may however serve as illustrations at a more concrete level of the general theme of this book.

2. Shopkeeping and rural economic activity

It is an established fact that rural households in Kenya are engaged in a broad variety of non-farm economic activities in order to provide a basis of material existence.

The survey of non-farm activities (Social Perspectives, Vol. 2.2, table 4) thus reveals that 50.4 % of all holdings (households) in a nationwide sample of some 2000 peasant rural households reported non-farm activities in January 1977. Some 23 % of the households interviewed reported 2 or more such activities. As a consequence of this activity pattern 41 % of the household income in money terms originated from non-farm economic activity. Roughly half of this income was obtained from casual or regular employment and the other half equally from non-farm operating surpluses and various remittances from relatives etc.

Non-farm activities according to the survey, include resource extraction, manufacturing of food, beverages, fibre products, wood products, pottery and metal products, construction, wholesale and retail trading, repair and various other services. Activities located in shops at market-places and trading centres are only part of this broad field of income generating activities.

21 % of the interviewed peasant or small-holding households reported that they were somehow engaged in activities typically located in shops, i.e. retailing, certain crafts such as carpentry, bicycle repair, butchering, posho (maize) milling, tailoring, and black-smithing or tinsmithing, bar keeping and various services.

The majority of non-farm activities surveyed however fall outside the segment of non-farm activities dealt with in our study. Wood-cutting, beer-brewing, manufacturing of bags, baskets etc. charcoal burning, construction, and services like traditional medicine or healing, dancing and entertainment, letter-writing etc., do not often take place in established

Table 5.1. *Shops – types of activity by number.*

	Retail shops	Work shops	Services	Total
General retail	114			
Specialized retail	23			
Eating – drinking	50			
Butchers	14			
Bicycle repair		14		
Carpenters		12		
Other crafts		19		
Posho-mills			12	
Other services			13	
Total	201	45	25	271
Percentages	74 %	17 %	9 %	100 %

shops at market-places but count nevertheless for about 60 % of the non-farm activities reported.

As a source of profit and income, shops at market-places may generate between 10–15 % of total recorded small-holder income. But to this estimate, profits from those shopkeepers not holding agricultural property or being large-scale farmers must be added to arrive at an estimate of the total economic magnitude of this segment of the economy. Such an estimate has been made on certain, but obviously disputable assumptions. If however it is assumed that the total gross product of the market shops amounts to K.shs. 250–300 mill.[1] in 1975, then this segment of the economy is roughly equivalent to 10–13 % of the total gross product of the national retail and wholesale trade sector, according to the national account statistics of 1975. Since the market shops seem to catch 40–50 % of total local retail purchases by rural households, their total yearly sales or turnover could amount to something between 1500 mill. and 2000 mill. shs. a year.

Seen in a national context, shops at rural markets and trading centres do not play any significant role as a basis for capital accumulation or profit making. In relation to the average peasant household they have a fundamental social function as the link between urban industrial, commercial and finance capital and the majority of direct producers in agriculture. The shops at market-places supply daily necessities of which as much as half could be commodities of industrial origin, but shopkeepers also function as buyers of agricultural produce and various crafts for resale to local customers and wholesale agents.

[1] It is assumed that a total of 60,000 shops make a total gross product of 284 mill shs., namely 42,000 making 2000 each, 15,000 medium with 10,000 and 3000 large, making 50,000 each.

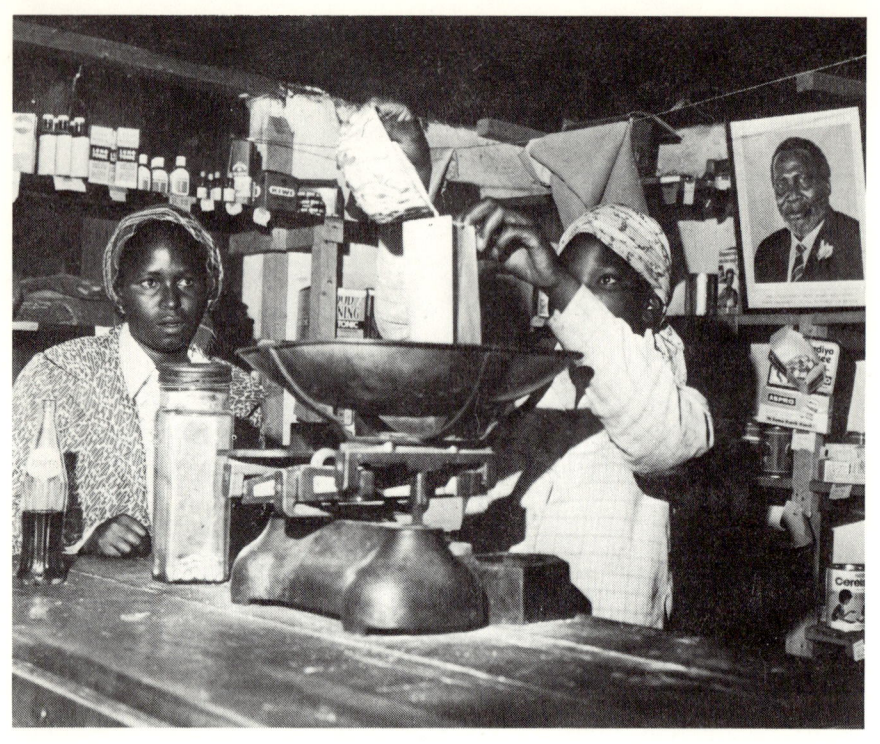

The shop in a trading centre – daily necessities and medicine for sale. (Gunvor Jørgsholm)

The composition of 271 shops at the 84 market-places studied in Western Kenya shows a rather uniform pattern. Table 5.1. below summarizes the distribution based upon types of activity.

The pattern of shop activities does not differ much from what is known from other studies of rural markets in Kenya (Kabwegyere 1976). General retail of the "duka" type accounts for 42 % of all observations. The general retail shops may vary in size, but basically sell the same assortment of commodities such as matches, kerosene, cigarettes, "Kimbo" and other edible fats, soft drinks, sugar, maize-flour, salt, drugs and "tetra-pack" milk. The larger stores in addition sell such commodities as hand-tools, fertilizers and seeds, pesticides and insecticides, lamps and jikos (charcoal burners for cooking), fabrics and various knitwares and other clothing, beer and local produce as eggs and baskets or pottery.

Depending on the size of the market there may be 5, 10 or 25 retail shops of the general type, all f them selling identical commodities at more or less identical prices.

The trading centre lining the open market place. (Gunvor Jørgsholm)

If specialized shops are added to the general retail shops then together these types account for more than half of the shops studied, but specialized shops are normally located at the larger and more important market-places. They typically include trade in grains, (maize) and beans, wholesale as well as retail, clothes, shoes (Bata-outlets), hides and skins buying as well as selling drugs (duka wa dawa), hardware and utensils, tobacco and fish.

The composition of retail shops reflects the general market conditions of the rural agricultural community. Most food items are traded or exchanged in the open air market-place on market days by women traders leaving a relatively narrow line of necessities to be traded in the shops. Since most of these commodities are "branded" goods or commodities distributed by Kenya National Trading Corporation through its agents, retail prices are more or less fixed beyond the control of shopkeepers as standard prices known to most customers visiting the market.

As shops are clustered or lined up in a bazaar-like fashion around the open air market-place, comparisons are easily made by those looking for particular goods. Therefore in many ways one may argue that shop trade in standard industrial goods does approach market conditions similar to those of "perfect competition" at least among the numerous small shops accounting for about 70 % of all shops studied. Profits are mainly proportional to quantities sold since the profit-rate as such in most cases is fixed. Not only because of publicly posted prices, but also because there is not much to gain on the cost side. Most premises or stalls are rented by the shopkeepers with rents beyond their control, licences are fixed by market authorities. Fares to bring the supplies to the market are set by transport agents or wholesale suppliers and discounts on deliveries are not often offered to the small shopkeeper. Family labour is often already exploited without regular pay.

The possibility of expanding sales at the expense of competitors catering for the same and more or less fixed number of customers and purchasing power seems to be far away under these rigid market conditions – at least for the majority of general retailers.

The large general stores operating at the larger market-places or trading centres, on the other hand, have some of the privileges small shopkeepers are deprived of, especially if they have managed to lift themselves out of the competitive trap by obtaining "client" status with Kenya National Trading Corporation., Bata Shoe, Coca Cola etc. as sole agents or as distributors for an area.

But even the medium sized shop will often be able to secure more profits simply because it is better stocked with basic commodities and therefore attracts more customers than the average duka.

The individual shopkeeper's chances of gaining business at the expense of his competitors depend to a large extent on his position vis-à-vis the economic and political institutions controlling the inputs basic to retail trade at market-places. The case studies of medium and large shops reveal that this position is linked to class relations in a broad sense. As we shall see later on, these relationships manifest themselves through landownership, professional status and other class related phenomena.

Bars, hotels, beer halls and busaa clubs account for 18 % of the shops studied and in some market-places there are as many bars and eating places as there are other types of shops. Especially on market days, when food is sold in the open-air market square, the selling of alcoholic beverages seems to be a lucrative business in most places. Consumption of bottled beer in Kenya has more than trebled over the past 10 years and amounts to nearly 50 litres per adult male per year. The number of licences to serve beer and other alcoholic beverages is however being kept within restrictive limits and retail prices are fixed by state decree. Profits from selling bottled beverages therefore mainly increase from the increase of per capita consumption. In addition to bottled beer from large-scale breweries, home brewed beer (pombe) is also being sold or served under licence arrangements in the local busaa clubs. The survey on non-farm activities (Social Perspectives Vol. 2.2 Table 4) in rural areas states that 18 % of the surveyed households report that they are engaged in beer brewing for sale. Part of this brew is delivered to local bars or busaa clubs under special commission arrangements and sold legally by woman brewers. But home-made beer and other alcoholic drinks also find customers at most market-places through various illegal channels.

As it will be seen later in this chapter, bar-keeping seems to be one of the favoured avenues for the expansion of trade activities and profit making by businessmen, but licences to enter this business seem more easily to be obtained by successful individuals who have already established personal liaisons with the establishment than by the mass of small-scale traders unknown to its representatives.

Petty production or crafts represent a little less than 20 % of the case studies. This proportion seems to be fairly well in accordance with most observations made on the position and development of small-scale production at rural market-places (Kabwegyere 1976, Steele 1972). It is the authors' impression that petty production at rural market-places in Kenya as a whole suffers from increasing competition from urban industry or petty production and in certain trades from the impact of industrial goods.

Where the number of operating general retail shops seems to be constant, or slowly increasing, even if many shops tend to change shopkeepers due to an increasing number of personal failures, the numer and variety of craftsmen operating in workshops at market-places seem to decrease. This view is mainly based on statements made by shopkeepers and other people aware of the history of the markets during the field-work in 1975–76. The validity of the viewpoint however is limited to account for the market-places alone. The non-farm activity survey (Social Perspectives Vol. 2.2) reveals that a variety of small-scale non-farm production, much more diversified than that at market-places, does take place among members of the household sample. Altogether as much as 56 % of the responses report some kind of non-farm production for sale, i.e. food processing, wood processing, plant-fibre processing, pottery, metal working and construction. As the replies include households reporting none or more than one non-farm activity the 56 % does not correspond with the actual number of households surveyed. But nevertheless it should be borne in mind that the production recorded at market-places is not representative of the non-farm production undertaken in the scattered homesteads of present households. Many of the goods produced at home such as baskets and pottery, beads and rugs, rope and building poles, charcoal and pombe (beer) and porridge find their way to the market through women traders in the open-air market or through itinerant wholesale buyers whether male or female. In the former case the trade or exchange is normally done by those who actually produced the goods. In the latter case more complicated and commercialized chains of buying and selling may operate to convert the products to commodities to be included in the capitalist sphere of circulation in the large cities, such as "wood carving" for curio shops.

Workshops at market-places typically deal with repair work such as bicycle repair, panel beating and other automobile repairs, while production for the market in a narrow sense mainly includes carpentry, often in the form of furniture making. Shoe-making and tailoring are much less frequent, and also stated to be declining due to the aggressive marketing efforts of large-scale manufacturers represented by hawkers or shopkeepers. Hawkers especially deal with cheap, imported garments or second hand clothing. They move from market-place to market-place according to the market day rotation and sell their goods in the open-air market square. The hawker business has spread rapidly since the government relaxed trade regulations and made it possible to buy a hawker's licence for more than one district. Based on import of cheap "Hongkong" goods or second hand clothing some wholesalers organize their own retail trade while others resell the goods to individual hawkers on various credit arrangements or against cash and discount. Hawkers have cut the market for local tailors and retail shops, many of our respondents claim. In some markets to such an extent that no tailor work except repairs is left.

Metal work, e.g. tin or blacksmithing, tank-making, production of tools and utensils etc. only accunt for 2 % of the 271 case studies and is also rare in the national survey with just 1.2 % of the rural households reporting that they have members engaged in these trades.

Except for bicycle or automobile repairs, metal work also seems to be disappearing almost completely from smaller markets where there was a blacksmith or tinsmith some years back. If it is a general feature, this development certainly has to do with changes of taste and consumption patterns from locally made to industrial goods. For example, that British made hoes or jembes are preferred, simply because they are of a better quality and last longer.

The decrease or stagnation of metalwork in rural areas probably also has to do with the slow technological change in agriculture especially in Western Kenya. Large-scale or medium-scale farming did rely on mechanization to a certain extent already in the colonial days. The Kenyan capitalist farmers who have replaced the colonialists, in principle continue mechanization, but due to low level management and constant liquidity problems the process is slow and often contractors from large towns take over mechanical farmwork instead.

Small-holders, on the other hand, have not changed their agricultural techniques to an extent which would demand more local repair and maintenance work. In household utensils, the local tinsmiths not only face growing competition from industrial products but also from petty producers in large towns making identical products. Since supplies of scrap material often used in production of these articles have been abundant and much cheaper in the large cities, especially Nairobi, petty producers there may have competitive advantages in production.

Moreover, Nairobi wholesalers may bring the products, whether fibres, waterjars, cans or lamps, up-country for sale in competition with local producers, and even make a profit.

Studies of a group of Karatina businessmen may be quoted as a further illustration of this point. Karatina is one of the largest market centres in rural Kenya situated about 50 km from Nairobi. A certain expansion of crafts took place due to increasing demand for household appliances. A group of 3 or 4 traders selling vegetables from the area in the Nairobi markets went into the business of distributing household appliances produced in Nairobi from scrap-material. After a buildup period they worked through standing orders with their Nairobi suppliers on prepaid terms at bargaining prices. In Karatina the appliances were resold to market-traders and wholesalers from other areas of the Central Province. Gross profits of between 50–100 % were realized by the Karatina wholesaling group, who managed to expand their business into road transport as well. The local Karatina tinsmiths, not able to compete with the Nairobi goods, quitted their crafts and went to look for a job in the "open air industries" in Nairobi, producing the same articles.

This example illustrates at the same time that metal working in small-scale or petty production, whether urban or rural, at the present technological level depends on access to cheap scrap as raw material input. If, as planned, a large-scale scrap consuming steel mill is put up in Kenya, the basis of this production will disappear over night.

Petty production in workshops at market-places in many ways seems to reflect the transitional character of the peasant household economy in Kenya. Traditional skills such as basket or rope making etc. are utilized to provide cash income necessary to reproduce the labour of the households with little agricultural land, but the transformation of agriculture in a capitalist direction is moving too slowly to provide a basis for expansion of repair and maintenance of small-scale industries in the countryside otherwise necessary to support the technological transformation of farming.

There are however some exceptions to the general pattern of stagnation of crafts or small-scale production at market-places. Carpentry, especially furniture making and production of window frames and doors, has developed from crafts to something similar to small-scale industry at certain markets. The market for furniture in rural areas has expanded rapidly over the past 10–15 years reflecting the increasing population, change of life-style and increase of cash income among middle peasants. Carpentry thus attracts skilled labour and in itself produces skill formation which is otherwise not a predominant feature of non-farm production in the workshops and market-places.

Looking at the craftsmen or workshop-keepers of the case studies made, it seems that they, as a group or fraction, operate below average conditions. Only 15 % as against 35 % for remaining trades have broken the barriers of simple reproduction and as much as 35 % of them clearly demonstrate signs of decreasing business and profits, where 40 % of shopkeepers in retail and wholesale commodity trade state that they expect their business will expand, only 25 % of the workshop-keepers think that they will move from just reproducing their labour into accumulation of profits.

Shopkeeping at rural markets and trading centres is to a large extent in the hands of local people. 74 % of the 271 shopkeepers studied operate in their own sub-location or district. This observation could be seen as a further evidence of the intimate linking of trade and agriculture dealt with in the following section of this chapter. In most of the areas studied, the percentage is even higher and the only exception here is the Rift Valley district Trans Nzoia where only 10 % of shopkeepers could be termed local. A fact which simply reflects the composite ethnical structure of the Rift Valley farm districts where both Kikuyus and Luyias have moved in and settled in the former "White Highlands".

3. Shopkeeping and agriculture

It is a well established fact that farm and non-farm activities are closely knitted together in the Kenyan rural economy. Historically speaking non-farm activities such as trade grew out of agricultural surplus produce, when peasants were drawn into the market economy of colonial settlers during the first 20 years of their hegemony. The works of Michael Cowen and other I.D.S. scholars[1] as well as that of G. Kitching (Kitching 1977) demonstrate this intimate relationship which is not surprising at all given the rich precolonial traditions of trade and exchange with complementary agricultural and animal produce between the tribes of Kenya.

---

[1] A general reference is made to the papers produced by scholars at IDS, Nairobi.

The reforms of late colonial days aiming at a more systematic exploitation of the peasant household economy in order to increase and extract surplus production for the capitalist market, also led to an expansion of local market trade especially in the Central Province. The subsequent policy of Africanization by the Kenyan government once political independence was gained in 1963, furthermore led to an exodus of Asian traders from all non-urban markets. Retail trade from the shops at markets became exclusively an African affair, and the direct commercial links between producers and the circulation sphere expanded in the hands of a new class or stratum of petty traders or shopkeepers who at the same time were deeply rooted in the sphere of agricultural production.

The relationship between market trade and agriculture personified by the shopkeepers has not been developed exclusively by peasants' or farmers' entering into trading. The opposite way is just as common a phenomenon. Some 29 % of the interviewed originally began their shopkeeping with capital accumulated in agriculture while 31 % came from trade to land-ownership and agriculture. The remaining 40 % mainly entered trade (and agriculture) on the basis of savings from other occupations such as school teachers, other state employees, skilled craftsmen or by selling inherited land or cattle. 89 % of the shopkeepers as a result combine their shopkeeping with agriculture in one or another form, and only 11 % report that they do not possess land property.

Just as 72 % of the shops may be classified as small, according to their yearly sales and stated profits[1], agricultural holdings of the shopkeepers holding land are generally modest in size. 73 % of the interviewed property owners in fact had less than 6 acres but most of the cases in this group fall between 4 and 6 acres. Of the remaining, 24 % reported land property varying from 6 to 20 acres while the last 3 % possessed more than 20 acres.

Agricultural activity or holdings belonging to the shopkeepers is divided into "shamba" cultivation by the wife (or wives) and cash cropping in practically all cases. This distinction is made clear by most respondents by saying: "my wife cultivates her shamba to feed herself and my children and occasionally there is a surplus which she sells at the market, on my land (or farm), I am growing maize etc. for sale".

Now legally the man or husband normally is the owner of all property belonging to the household and the distinction between shamba and farm simply indicates that the farm as part of the property is included in his business. The shamba on the other hand is principally conceived of as a source of reproduction of family labour. Many of the respondents clearly

---

[1] This classification is explained in section 5.5.

indicate that ideally the reproduction of their households should be kept apart from their own business, i.e. shop + farm, even if they claim or admit that in practice things do not come out that simple.

The crop pattern of farming does not seem to diverge from the crop pattern prevailing in the area where the farm of the shopkeeper is located. In this respect farming does not seem to be influenced by trade activity. Only in a few cases did the shopkeeper cum farmer grow products for sale in his shop, for example vegetables or fruits.

In terms of modes of operation, surplus appropriation and objectives of business activity, it is necessary to distinguish between trade and agriculture in small-scale operations and the large-scale fraction of the same combination.

In small-scale combinations of shopkeeping and farming it seems that the distinction between the shamba as the source of reproduction and "business" as a source of surplus extraction for expansion or "luxury" consumption does not really hold. Both sources are necessary to survive and in practice must be considered as one domestic economic unit rather than separate economic entities. Food cultivation and business, whether trade or farming in many of these cases do not reach a scale beyond that of simple reproduction of family labour. 35 % of the 271 shopkeepers do not possess capital except a few acres of land and just manage to reproduce their own and the family's labour, and half of these were experiencing decreasing trade, and profit from trade falling below 1000 shs. a year.

In this type of relationship between trade and agriculture, family expenses are covered by the combined income from both activities, but agriculture is often considered to be the leading or basic source of livelihood by the respondents in this category. Small-scale shopkeeping therefore is seen as a supplement to agriculture, but still a vital part of the subsistence, supplying goods for family consumption and cash to purchase farm inputs in planting and weeding seasons. Vice versa the farm may yield a cash surplus after a good harvest of which a part will finance the restocking of the shop. According to whether the harvest has been good or bad the trade–agriculture–family cycle may be illustrated as shown in diagramme 5.1.

In large-scale combinations of shopkeeping and farming the relationships between the two activities are more complex. 30 % of the respondents reported that they made profit in trade and agriculture above the level of reproducing capital and labour, and that they not only had the intention to expand their business, but actually did so in a rather systematic way.

These 30 % roughly represent "large-scale" operations in agriculture and shopkeeping. Most of the shopkeepers in this group possess more than 6

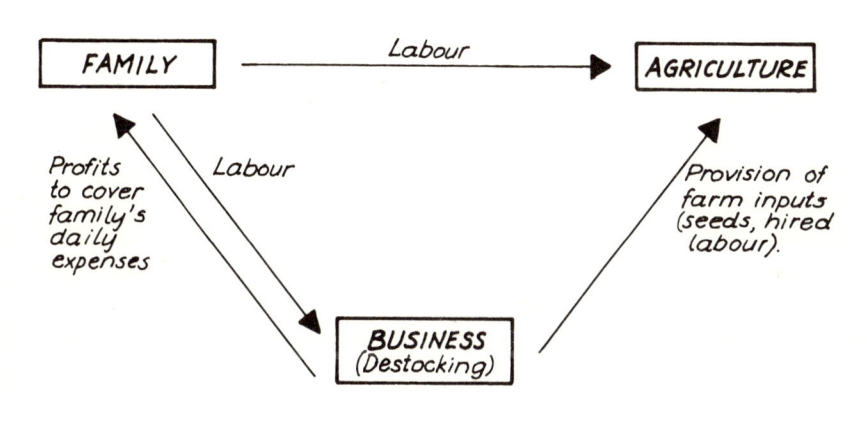

Diagramme 5.1.

Business - Agriculture - Family Cycle. Under Food-shortage Periods.

```
    FAMILY  ────── Labour ──────▶  AGRICULTURE
       ▲  ↖                              ▲
       │    ╲ Labour                     │
  Profits    ╲                     Provision of
  to cover    ╲                    farm inputs
  family's     ▼                   (seeds, hired
  daily       BUSINESS             labour).
  expenses   (Destocking)
```

Business - Agriculture - Family Cycle. Under Periods of Agricultural Surplus.

```
                Farm produce sold
                to supply family with
                basic needs
    FAMILY  ──────── Labour ────────▶  AGRICULTURE
            ◀────────────────────
       ╲                                   ╲
   Labour                              Farm produce
         ╲                             sold to supply
          ╲                            stock for
           ▼                           business.
          BUSINESS
         (Restocking or
          expanding)
```

acres of land and run shops with a yearly turnover of more than 10,000 shs. The group also includes some 7 shopkeepers who at the extreme end of the scale possessed more than 100 acres of land and were engaged in a combination of shopkeeping, transport, bar-keeping and wholesale trade.

In this group, more than half considered business or shopkeeping more important than farming and practically all saw shopkeeping or other non-farm ventures as the principal road to expansion and accumulation of capital, while only half of them would say that farming had possibilities of expansion beyond its present level.

In this group, the relationship between trade and agriculture is certainly more on line with the ideals mentioned a few pages back. The husbands manage their farm and trade as an entity in itself and utilize profits for reinvestments and new investments to expand their activities and for their own consumption. Contribution to the family reproduction is made, for example in the payment of school-fees. But the wives remain in essence responsible for the food, clothes, etc., and the shamba is the main source of this reproduction.

Between the two extreme ends of the scale of operations, the remaining third of the respondents trade and farm in patterns varying from area to area, but in general most similar to those of the large-scale combinations. This means that the separation of the husband's and wife's economy is a more fundamental feature of the sample than the maintenance of the domestic economic unit.

What actually links the two "economies" is family labour. As we shall see in the following section, farming on any scale and shopkeeping to a large extent is physically done by family labour.

There is little difference in scale of operations, mode of appropriation of surplus, etc. between those shopkeepers who own land and the 11 % who reported that they do not possess any land. The latter group however includes slightly more craftsmen than the former. This may have to do with the observation that being a craftsman at a marketplace was often considered the first step towards "business" whether retail, bar keeping etc., or the last station after a long life in other occupations away from the home area.

4. Labour and shopkeeping

As it was demonstrated in chapter II, family labour is fundamentally the basis of reproduction in the domestic economic unit in rural Kenya. In more than 85 % of our cases the family, i.e. the wife or wives and children, work in the shamba or farm, while the husband-shopkeeper only contributes physically to farm work in some 20 % of the cases.

Table 5.2. *Labour relations in trade and farming.*

	N	Percent of cases utilizing: Own labour	Family labour	Hired labour	Percent of cases utilizing the following combinations: Family labour alone	Family labour Hired labour*	Hired labour alone
Farming	233	21	86	64	36	52	12
Trade	262	88	23	45	55*	10	35

* mainly own labour.

Note: N differs from the total of 271 cases. In farming because only those who own land are included, i.e. 86 % and in trade, because of incomplete information, 9 cases.

In trade, as one would expect, labour relations are somewhat different, first of all because the husband-shopkeeper contributes as the main source of labour in his own person.

The differences between labour relations in trade and agriculture may be further depicted from table 5.2 which shows the utilization of own family and hired labour in various combinations.

Apart from the fact that shopkeepers do mainly work physically in their shops and not in the shamba or farm, family labour is much less common in trade than in agriculture where it is the rule more or less irrespective of the size of holdings.

Hired labour is being utilized by a surprising number of shopkeepers given the small-scale of operations in 70 % of the cases. There is however a difference between farming and trade here, apart from the percentage buying labour, namely that hired labour in agriculture tends to be seasonal, i.e. applied in the harvest and weeding seasons only—while it tends to be hired on a permanent basis in shopkeeping according to the information given by respondents.

In shopkeeping, small-scale traders typically run their shop alone with assistance from their wives from time to time, for example on those days when the shopkeeper has to go to town to buy goods from wholesalers. This normally happens once or twice a week and takes from half a day to over a full day. At this end of the scale therefore the division of labour within the family is rather clear-cut. The husband works as "self-employed" in his capacity of a shopkeeper, exploits family labour in the shamba and farm and seasonal hired labour in peak periods.

In large-scale operations, as could be expected, shopkeepers tend to become "managers" both in relation to their shop business and to farming.

147

They supervise the work of wives, farm labourers, and shop assistants and plan the activities in a more systematic and calculated way. In 35 % of the shops hired labour does most of the physical work while only 12 % of the farms are being worked in this way, indicating that the wives of even large-scale farmers do assist in agricultural activities either physically or as supervisors on behalf of their husbands.

Roughly 10 % of the businessmen cum farmers are employed as school teachers or civil servants and in these cases the wife or wives very often supervises both the shop and farmwork done by labourers and shop assistants.

The fact that 64 % of the cases report utilizing hired labour in farming and 45 % employ labour to do shop work may be taken as an expression of the transformation of the rural society in Kenya. The exploitation of hired labour to that extent indicates that the mode of surplus production is changing from the exploitation of family labour to that of appropriation of surplus labour in an emerging social division of labour, between those holding land and capital, and those gradually being forced to reproduce labour force by selling it.

It is however difficult or even impossible to express these changing conditions of reproduction in quantitative terms. The wage rates paid to farm labourers and shop assistants are not standardized by any means, but vary from between 60–70 shs. to 100–150 shs. per month for the same type of work according to the prevailing rates in the particular area and according to the kind of affiliation between those buying and those selling labour force. While family labour from wife and children is normally unpaid, poor relatives, or relatives somehow dependent on the shopkeeper for example for education, may have to work for him at a minimal rate plus food and shelter.

In large-scale business and farming, which is to say in at least 10 % of the cases, it seems that capitalist relations of production are clearly discernible. Not only is surplus labour appropriated to secure extended reproduction of capital, but surplus value is being created in a process of capital accumulation based on mechanization of farm work and transfer of profits in both directions between farm and non-farm business.

In small-scale farming and shopkeeping, labour relations are still characterized by the exploitation of family labour. In those cases where no land property is recorded we find a few examples where husbands report that their wives take seasonal work as farm labourers while they themselves just manage to survive as self-employed whether in petty trade or production as craftsmen.

It is however surprising that many of those respondents reporting that their business and farming just manage to keep the household going also report that they buy labour in peak agricultural seasons. This may indicate that the process of class formation has already gone deeply into the Kenyan rural society. The distinction between those who own just a little more land and command a few more resources than necessary for the bare physical survival and those who just survive has probably gained a lot of meaning over the past 10–15 years in Western Kenya. The level of reproduction of the former may still include education, at least of the sons, while the cash necessary to pay school fees cannot be squeezed out of the budget of the former.

The economic and social opportunities of the next generation therefore increasingly seem to diverge from some point within this group of smallscale traders. But moreover, those managing their existence above the bare level of survival may even be able to do so because they buy labour force from the poorest seeking casual employment at nearly any price offered.

5. Scale of business and farming

As it may be seen from the previous sections, our stratum of shopkeepers cum farmers is far from homogeneous in terms of modes of reproduction, scale, and profit making. The majority, or 56 %, were classified as small-scale by applying a number of criteria based on qualitative as well as quantitative information obtained from respondents or observed.

By the same criteria another subgroup including 39 % was identified as medium scale, leaving a small fraction of 5 % to be considered as large scale.

As regards farming, the criteria discriminating "small" from "medium" roughly correspond with the variations for farm size and net profits from farming, but adjusted to the local conditions. Whereas a farm of 2–3 acres may be considered small in any area of Kenya, one of 5–7 acres would be medium in the densely populated areas of Kakamega or Kisii while the same farm size would be small in the settlement areas of Trans Nzoia.

With respect to shopkeeping and other non-farm business, estimated yearly sales and net profits were applied as criteria in much the same way, so that shops with a turnover of less than 10,000 shs. and a profit range of 0–1000 shs. were termed "small" those selling between 10,000–100,000 shs. and with profits ranging from 1,000–10,000 as "medium" and those above these thresholds as "large". But also with respect to the business classification, qualitative information obtained from the respondents was applied as modifiers to the rather mechanical approach.

In fact, the classification of cases in size groups has mainly secured us an organizing principle in order to be able to examine the variations of other and more fundamental phenomena, which could lead to an understanding of the modes of reproduction characterizing our cases. Variations in labour relations, surplus appropriation and the objectives and prospects of economic activity were taken as important elements in this respect. But also a number of social variables such as educational and professional background, inheritance of land and support from family and access to the state bureaucracy, loans etc. were considered important to reach the said end.

One thing is to get an idea of how the cases vary according to the criteria utilized, another but much more important thing is how the variations should be interpreted as an expression of the social processes of transformation characterizing contemporary rural Kenya. The authors here hold the view that even if some phenomena such as the buying and selling of labour, the breaking down of the domestic economic unit, increasing differences in the modes of operation and scale of business, etc., are becoming more or less general and widespread, local social formations or subsocieties respond in different ways to these phenomena, not only in a quantitative sense, but also qualitatively. In the last section of this chapter an attempt is made to illustrate how they respond. Here the relationship between size of operations and the mode of reproduction, expressed as the total evaluation of the case is summarized in table 5.3. below. The evaluation of the individual cases has been based upon the history of the business, its recorded or stated results, the scale and diversity of operations in agriculture, shopkeeping and other activities. On the basis of "scores" in each of the variables an attempt is made to classify the cases in each size category into those which seem just able to manage to reproduce the labour of the family, those able to reproduce family labour and invested capital and those which

Table 5.3. *Modes of reproduction and size groups. (Number of cases and percentages).*

Mode of reproduction	Small	Medium	Large	N	Percent of N
Reproduction of labour	74	17	1	92	35 %
Reproduction of labour + invested cap.	60	37	0	97	37 %
Extended reproduction	11	40	0	51	20 %
Cap. accumulation	1	8	13	22	8 %
N	146	102	14	262	100 %
Percent of N	56 %	39 %	5 %	100 %	

have moved from simple reproduction to expanded or extended reproduction accumulating profits for further expansion of their agricultural or business activities. This group has been further divided, as those cases have been singled out where seemingly not only expansion of the shopping cum farming takes place, but where there is also an ongoing process of accumulation through technological change such as a mechanization in farming and investments in transport equipment, storage capacity etc. or vertical integration from retail to wholesale trade etc.

Table 5.3 should not be read as a correlation matrix in a strict sense, in fact its two dimensions are interrelated (not mutually exclusive) to some extent. In essence the figures tell us that 72 % of the shopkeepers have managed to survive so far on a rather narrow margin of profits from their combined agricultural and commercial ventures, and that the majority of these fall in the category "small". 28 % on the other hand have managed to bootstrap themselves above the level of mere survival, or have been given the opportunities to do so through inheritance of land or by education and social positions securing their access to privileges. That these 28 % mainly belong to the "medium" or "large" may not be surprising either.

The table to a certain extent also demonstrates the amount of heterogeneity in our stratum. 92 or 35 % of our cases make no or very little profit and will not be able to invest in fertilizers and tools or to restock the shops except in good or relatively good years. They manage to survive by spending every single cent earned from farming, shopkeeping, and the wife's occasionally selling food at market-places etc. Farming and shopkeeping here certainly must be considered as a part of the subsistence economy of the household whether or not it is connected with the market economy as well. Most of the respondents in this group indicated that they see the small scale of their farming and business as the major obstacle to increase their profits, and also held the view that farming and shopkeeping in their case would not lift them out of their present encapsulation in scarcity or poverty. Roughly a third of them have tried at some time to obtain a loan from the Joint District Board but in vain, since they were not able to reach the relevant officers directly or through other channels.

These 35 % have seemingly little in common with the 28 % who have managed to increase the scale and efficiency of their farming and shopkeeping above the level of simple reproduction. Here the average profits are large enough to increase the capital in either farming or business or in both. More than 80 % of the cases in this group report that they are regularly adding to their investments in either farming or shopkeeping i.e. improving their land or buying more land, adding to the stock of their shops or building better premises. In more than 35 % of these cases net investments are regularly made in both farming and shopkeeping. Besides, profits have also made it possible to consolidate the level of material living. A permanent house constructed on the shamba or school-fees being paid for all children may serve as an illustration.

As the shopkeepers in this group therefore possess fixed assets large enough to provide security this also explains why 30 % of them have obtained loans in commercial banks or from the state operated industrial and commercial development corporation, and therefore have been assisted to expand their commercial activities further.

The group of 97 cases or 37 % in between is more difficult to locate in this pattern or scale of farming, shopkeeping and material security. It is tempting to characterize this group as one in a kind of balance. Farming and shopkeeping makes enough profit to reproduce the scale and quality of the present level of activities and in addition to safeguard the material conditions of living of the household.

It is however a too simplistic view for many obvious reasons. Some of the shopkeepers in this group will certainly manage to expand their commercial activities over time and others will face problems and increasing poverty, depending on individual characteristics such as age, professional qualities and class background and depending on the social conditions under which they operate.

When asked about the objectives of farming and shopkeeping respondents classified as small, and just able to reproduce family labour, practically all of them saw their commercial activities as ways to survive, as subsistence. And not surprisingly those classified as large-scale, and able to expand their farming and shopkeeping, clearly indicated that the objectives were growth and profit maximization.

The groups in between however were much more ambiguous as regards their own future. In fact 65 % of them expressed the idea that they mainly had the maintenance of their present level of activity in mind and that they saw farming and shopkeeping as a way to support their family. This subgroup did not have either any precise ideas about the future direction of their farming and business. The remaining 35 % of this group on the other hand, expressed the idea that they were planning to expand their commercial activity in some or another way. Most of them held the view that shopkeeping rather than farming would be the road to increase profits and the level of activity. Many in this subgroup however also underlined that assistance from relatives, or better the "government", was necessary to make the first and decisive steps in this direction. For example by increasing their stocks in the shop and thus improve the competitive position of it vis-à-vis other shops at the market.

If the respondents classified as "medium" in this in-between group are taken alone, some 70 % however saw their future as one of expanding trade and increasing profits, while only 30 % in this subgroup expressed views of only continued subsistence.

Thorough evaluation of the cases in the in-between group of 37 % led to the conclusion that only some 15–20 % of them seemed to have made any significant progress over the past few years, and considered as a group there were more indications of deteriorating business conditions than indications of improving conditions.

6. Three illustrative cases

The preceding sections of this chapter were used to summarize what has been considered important features characterizing our case studies. There may be good reasons to further illuminate the impressions and differences observed by giving examples of individual case studies as well. This will not only illustrate the different types or scales of farming and shopkeeping in a more imaginative way, but also to let the reader see the kind of information on which the summary was based.

Three cases have been selected for this purpose. All of them combine agriculture and shopkeeping and they therefore represent the main stream of case studies. But they differ in terms of scale and mode of reproduction and should be seen as exemplifications of the process of social differentiation here indicated.

The information contained in the three cases has been rearranged in a more or less standardized schedule to facilitate comparisons.

First the type of business activity is presented, then a brief record of the respondent's personal data and family status follows. Next the "business history" of the case is summarized to be followed by an attempt to present the "economics" of the farming and shopkeeping involved.

Finally the respondent's own views on the objectives of his business activity are reproduced and compared with our own evaluation of the case.

Mr. Michael M., medium retailer and farmer

Mr. Michael M. runs a general retail shop at a trading centre in Saboti Location, Trans Nzoia. He also engages in small-scale farming on a plot of 4 acres.

The centre is small, but expanding. There are some 3 shops, a bar, a butcher and a workshop. There is no electricity, but the market is not far from the tarmac road and thus Mr. Michael M. does not face severely the transport problems which are otherwise a major nuisance for market traders during the rainy seasons where supplies may not reach them for long periods.

The shop is in a semi-permanent building. It is small but well stocked with daily consumer goods such as matches, cigarettes, Kimbo, Unga, soap, etc. and some durables such as blankets. The shop is always open in the morning, during lunch break and in the evening. In between it may be closed at irregular intervals.

Mr. Michael M. is 45 years of age, was born in Meru, Eastern Province in a Meru family. He was kept in school until standard IV and never had any other formal education. His father is a poor small-peasant who shares his insufficient piece of land with his brother.

He married at home in 1955 and is still married to the same wife. They have two children who are now grown up and have moved away from the home.

Mr. Michael M. says he trained himself in business when he left his father's home in 1957. For some years he did retailing at market-places in the Central Province including some "hotelli" business. He saved some earnings in this way, 400 shs. to begin with, later on 700 shs. Some of this money was banked in a savings account and with the additions later on he was able to buy a share of 1000 shs. in a land purchasing society, which means that he became share-holder of it, entitled to 4 acres of land including 1 acre for his own family's subsistence. He gradually saved 3000 shs. more, enough to start a small shop in the new place to which he and his family then moved. Since the early sixties. Mr. Michael M. has then been running his shop now installed in a semi-permanent house, but not registered with a plot number and not acceptable as security for a loan.

His business has not developed a lot, but rather seems to stagnate at the level reached some years ago. He has tried to increase the scale of his business however by obtaining a hawker's licence by which to sell clothes at market days in neighbouring markets. Presumably he has the clothes made in his own shop by a tailor working for him. The hawking business does not bring him enough profit to enlarge his shop or stocks. He finds that the competition between him and hawkers coming from the cities with cheap secondhand clothes has become cut-throat so that this part of his business has also been stagnating or declining.

In his shopkeeping he depends on deliveries and credit from Asian wholesalers in Kitale. The wholesalers have however limited his credit at any time to 1000 shs. and being dependent on the credit he has lost "bargaining" power and is also being charged interest. He finds that only a loan from the government (Joint District Loans Board) will enable him to escape the Asians' overcharging him, and thus make it possible for him to buy cheaper and increase his profits.

His wife has assisted him in the shop for a long time, and she replaces him when he goes to Kitale 1–2 times a week to buy supplies or when hawking at nearby markets. She also cultivates the shamba of 1 acre assisted by casual labour in peak seasons. The remaining 3 acres seem to feed 10 cows bought by him.

The economies of Mr. Michael M. cannot be specified in detail since he does not keep books. As so many other small-retailers he nevertheless knows the approximate figures related to his business and to the household expenses.

His assets and liabilities include the following items:

Goods worth approximately	9000 shs.
1 sewing machine	1000 shs.

Shop premises and house 2000 shs.
Land (1 share = 4 acres) 2000 shs.
Cattle 10 cows (heifers) 3000 shs.
Savings account 1000 shs.

or 18000 shs. from which 1000 shs. of current credit may have to be deducted.

Mr. Michael M.'s business records may be reconstructed on the basis of his own information and the interviewer's estimate. The shop sells for approximately 50 shs. a month. The yearly turnover therefore is about 6000 shs. The operating expenses may be estimated to about 3600 shs. leaving Mr. Michael M. with a gross profit of 2400 including his own and his wife's "salary". The expenses include supplies, labour (tailor), rent of plot and licence and transport.

The farm may yield some 3000 shs. from the sale of milk, while 12 bags of maize produced on the one acre cultivated is consumed in the household. Expenses on the farm may be estimated to some 600 shs. and thus a gross profit of 2400 shs. may be the result.

Expenses here include fertilizers and casual labour. The household expenses may be estimated to some 4900 shs. including assistance to his father and young brothers in school and repayment of bride wealth to his father-in-law.

To these expenses a fine of 1000 shs. was added as Mr. Michael M. was caught by police and charged with overcharging his customers in selling goods for which there are government regulated retail prices. He may have been tempted to overcharge customers because he was the only retailer at the market-place at the time of interviewing, and therefore had a local monopoly, especially as he also extended credits himself to regular customers. If Mr. Michael M. was not hawking as well, his profits would be almost zero. Unfortunately this part of his business was not explored during the field-work in detail, but may yield a net surplus of some 1000–2000 shs. a year.

Mr. Michael M. thinks he is an experienced business man, but he did not see how his shopkeeping would have a chance to expand unless he could have some government assistance. He himself thought that he had done what he could to maintain it. He did not believe in farming as a way out unless again some loan could be obtained to buy grade cattle to replace his cows of local stock. As new shops seem to be opened at the market-place and the hawking business is becoming more and more competitive he would probably have to face decreasing sales and a less than zero net profit.

Mr. S.W., small shopkeeper and peasant

Mr S.W. operates a bicycle repair and spare parts shop at a local market in Bungoma District, Western Province. He also owns a shamba of 3 acres. The market is medium sized with some 20 retail shops located in a maize growing area. The market does not expand and there are empty shops.

Mr S.W. does repair-work such as welding, wiring, mending wheels etc. He also sells spares such as saddles, tyres, bells, nuts, grease etc. The shop is stocked for about 2000 shs.

Mr. S.W. is 42 of age, born in the neighbouring location and was in school to standard 6. He has been married since 1961, and the family includes 3 children who stay at home.

Mr. S.W. did not have any formal training, but he worked for another bicycle repairer as an apprentice for some years. In 1972 he went on his own and sold 3 bags of maize from his shamba giving him a starting capital of 90 shs. After some time he was able to expand his business and to rent his present premises for which he pays 1140 shs. per year. With stocks worth 2000 shs. a bicycle, some gas welding equipment and two cows, he thinks that things have moved well. In addition he has saved 800 on his savings account.

Mr S.W.'s biggest problem, as he saw it, is that he must pay 1140 shs. in rent for his shop, and he wants to build a house and shop of his own in the future to retain more of his profit this way. He thinks that his profits have been slightly increasing, but says they fluctuate according to fluctuations in people's purchasing power. With good harvests of maize he sells more and vice versa i.e. in good seasons his monthly sales would average 600 shs., in bad 200 shs. He has tried to extend credits but stopped it again after heavy losses, because of customers who never paid back.

He gets spare parts from Webuye urban centre once a month during bad seasons and once a week in good seasons and goes to pick them by matatu (taxi).

The shamba of 3 acres is mainly cultivated by the wife, but he and casual labour also assist. Maize is grown for subsistence, but the wife sells some maize just after harvest. Apparently some 7 bags of maize represent the surplus of the shamba in good years yielding some 400 shs. (1975).

Mr. S.W. owns assets worth about 7000 shs. including his land and the bicycle. His shop has a turnover of about 7000 shs. a year. The operating expenses include goods for sale etc. 3600 shs., rent 1140 shs., transport 720 shs., amounting to 5460 shs., leaving him with a gross profit of about 1500 shs.

Agricultural produce would give the family some 400 shs. a year and as expenses include fertilizers, seeds and ploughing to an amount of 160 shs. the gross profit from land is about 250 shs. Household consumption was reported to be 200 shs. per month or 2400 shs. a year, school-fees for the children another 100 shs., and various donations for example to harambee projects, to an amount of 100 shs. Mr. S.W. will in other words face a loss of some 800–900 shs. on a yearly basis. This may be balanced by gifts from relatives. It is more likely however that the sales have been underestimated.

Mr. S.W. does not believe in farming as a business, but says that his shop will make it possible for him to pay for ploughing, seeds and fertilizers so that the necessary food may be grown for subsistence.

His plans are to continue in his shop and to try to save enough to build a house of his own to save rent.

Mr. J.O., large store and farm

Mr. J.O. owns a provision store in a marketplace and trading centre in Kisumu District, Nyanza Province. He is a shareholder in another enterprise and in addition owns a farm of 47 acres. The store is located in a relatively large trading centre which includes some 20 shops and 10 workshops (carpenters, bicycle repair, blacksmith and garage).

Goods sold include groceries, blankets, nails and tools, bicycle spares, farm implements and medicine. Retail as well as wholesale trade. The store is located in an area where industrial crops now dominate, the road system therefore is excellent.

Mr. J.O. is 45 years old and born in the area in a land owning family. He went to school until standard 6 and then into business. He was married in 1951 and now has two wives and 14 children. The wives and the children live on his farm at some distance from the store.

Two years after finishing school in 1946 he went into the cattle trade. The family owned grazing land near Kisumu and he joined a group of three men who bought cattle at local markets and resold them to butchers in more distant markets where livestock was less abundant. In 1950 he went on his own and continued in the livestock trade for about 4 years. Realizing that profitable livestock trade involved frequent and long travel, he began to fish in Lake Victoria and also to trade in fish bought at the shores and resold at inland markets. Too much theft of nets etc. discouraged him and with net savings of 3,000 shs. in 1958, he got a plot in a marketplace of trading centre near Kisumu and built a shop. To increase the scale of business he made a partnership with his brother and some other relatives which made it possible to stock the shop for about 4,000.

By 1967 the shop had expanded its stock to some 45,000 shs. and his own personal savings stood at 8,000. He again decided to go on his own and acquired a shop in his present place. The capital invested in the shop was about 20,000 and he also kept shares in the first shop now run by one of the other partners.

As the Asian shopkeepers were leaving, his business increased. His policy of making friendships with (influential) people in the area made him well-known and he was able to buy a farm in the early seventies on which he started growing sugarcane.

Also because Asian shopkeepers left the area as a consequence of the Africanization policy he could now proceed to move into wholesale trading and became an agent for Kenya National Trading Corporation (K.N.T.C.), East African Industries, Brooke Band and other large-scale enterprises. He also now expanded the staff working for him in the store.

Supplies from these companies are delivered at his store, but he bought a van to transport other commodities from Kisumu and Kericho and to deliver goods to his customers among retailers in the area.

He reported that goods worth 100,000 shs. were normally bought by him every month and his stock would normally stand at some 180,000. He is offered credit terms from his main suppliers with credits to be settled within 30 days on cash terms. He himself offers his regular customers credit up to 3 months.

The farm is divided between the shamba, 1 1/2 acres and his own farm, 45 acres, on which some 20 acres had been planted with sugarcane. The remaining 25 acres still had to be cleared before sugarcane could be planted.

One of his wives cultivates the shamba where maize and beans are grown. It seems that this (elder) wife does the work alone not assisted by casual labourers. The other wife may assist him in the store when he is away or on his farm. The farm is being worked by 4 permanent farm labourers supervised by himself.

Mr. J.O. held the view that profits from the storekeeping has enabled him to acquire land and to finance clearance of it. These profits also financed the cane growing since 1–2 years elapse before the first harvest is ready. In this period planting, weeding etc. represent a layout. This case thus demonstrates the interrelationship between shopkeeping and farming often observed.

The economics of Mr. J.O. were not recorded in detail but may be reconstructed on the bases of his own information and the interviewer's evaluation.

The assets including stocks worth 180,000, equipment on the farm, and shares in previous business probably total 340,000 shs. But liabilities including debts on the farm and on the van, and current credits with suppliers, to an estimated amount of 190,000 must be deducted. Net assets therefore could be about 150,000 shs.

The store sells for about 1,400,000 shs. a year (1975) and operating expenses including supplies, wages, rent, transport, licences and interest may be estimated to 1,300,000 shs. leaving Mr. J.O. with a gross profit of 100,000 shs.

The farm in its building-up phase probably had a net loss of 9000 shs. as sales of 100 tons of cane yielded some 9000 shs., but expenses including labour, other inputs and repayment of loans could have amounted to some 18,000.

Mr. J.O.'s shares of 22,000 in his previous business would yield some profit, say 2000. As he said he was now investing 10,000 in his store, the total gross profit of his undertakings could have been around 83,000 shs.

Household expenses are reported to be some 35,000 shs. including family consumption of 25,000 (2 wives and 14 children), school-fees of 5,000 (3 children in secondary school, 9 in primary) and other expenses including support of less fortunate family members 5,000.

The result of Mr. J.O.'s efforts thus seemed to approximate some 50,000 shs. before tax and own salary. His own estimate was 30,000 shs., but may be influenced by his evaluation of the current years' downward trend of wholesale turnover.

Mr. J.O. sees the future as one of expanding his farm activity by clearance of the remaining land and planting sugarcane on it. For the store his problem was to find a reliable manager so that he could concentrate his own efforts on the farm. According to his philosophy a well-managed business would bring a constant and quicker growth of wealth, but once developed a farm offers lasting security.

CHAPTER VI

The Social Consequences of Transformation
An Interpretation at the Household Level

1. The nature and forms of internal dynamics

In this book we have made an attempt to focus on the reproduction of labour at the level of the individual households. The idea has been not only to describe the labour conditions of the family members and the household as such, but more important to relate these conditions to the expanding and intensifying market relations.

At our level of analysis we have argued from our case studies, that in spite of the increasing necessity to reproduce the households and labour via the market, we find that the logic of production efforts is still that of family reproduction, and not that of capital accumulation, except for a minority of the cases studied. Even among that one-third of our cases, where expansion of "business" was stated as a major objective, a large number did not transcend the limits of the household economy, in their own detailed evaluation of their situation, or in our judgement of it.

This is a main reason for our use of the concept of internalization of the capitalist market circuits in the household economy. This concept of course is of a more abstract nature than our analysis, in fact it is directly related to the mode of reproduction, and in principle to the nature of the Kenyan social formation.

Throughout the accounts of the preceding chapters, we have been more inclined to refer to this concept of internalization than to speak about the destruction of any precapitalistic mode of production, or something resembling the capitalist mode of production.

We are well aware that no taxonomy relates our level of analysis to the more abstract connotations of a "mode". The well known shortcomings of empirical evidence vis-à-vis "theory" certainly also characterize our study. We think however that some "bridging of the gap" has been provided by the evidence given of the extent to which relative autonomy over production by households persists vis-à-vis the direct, individual subsumption of labour under capital.

Relating our data on labour, whether in agricultural production or crafts or trade to the intermediate level of autonomy vis-à-vis subsumption, however does not clear the way for an outright judgement of where the rural communities of Western Kenya are moving. At the end of our study we tend to agree with Bernstein when he says that the household economy is somehow a terrain of struggle between the market (or capital) and the households. As the market is seemingly penetrating deeper and deeper into the social life of people as our study indicates, we may argue that subsumption of labour under capital is the inevitable outcome of this "struggle" (Bernstein 1977).

But on the other hand our data on individual households also tend to show that new defence mechanisms are being developed to solve the contradictions produced by the game of the market – namely by the households acting in a rational manner to preserve their autonomy, which again gives the phrase, "internalization", some of its own dialectic logic or sense and perhaps political dynamics.

Therefore in our opinion it is not so easy to describe the observed patterns of reproduction as being just transitional, as we have done ourselves in some of the chapters. Whether the patterns of reproduction which we have described and analysed are, or will, turn out to be transitional, must somehow be dependent on the potential for capitalist transformation of the Kenyan social formation as such.

As has been stated by many authors dealing with Kenya, the essential preconditions for a capitalist transformation have already emerged. A land market has been established, a labour market is being shaped in the cities, the Central Province, Rift Valley and here and there in Western Kenya. The internal market for food and daily necessities accounts for 60 % of household reproduction, etc.

But so far the extension and intensification of the market has not led to a technological revolution of the labour process itself. We do not deny that technical improvements have been associated with, and have even contributed to the expansion of cash crops, especially export crops. But as seen in chapter II, inputs in the form of seeds, fertilizers, and pesticides, not to speak of farm equipment, are "marginal" in the average household farm budget. Moreover these improvements have not really released labour on the average holding where increased production and productivity, resulting from intensifying the exploitation of family labour (particularly that of women), has been the response to the relaxations of restrictions on market crops.

The role of technology in capitalist transformation, at least in European Marxist literature, is crucial to the dynamics of change. Surplus value is being derived out of an ever expanding technological base, from which human labour will produce relatively more and more in relation to its own value. Technological change becomes a "must" to the demands of the expanding accumulation.

But in Western Kenya, this "must" has not so far appeared as some "invisible hand" in the agricultural reproduction process.

We shall not be able here to relate the European past to the Kenyan situation now, and even if we do not necessarily believe that the basic laws of capitalism do not in essence maintain validity wherever capitalist transformation takes place, we nevertheless tend to argue that the forms in which they appear must be identified from the concrete evidence given us by the events of Kenya's historical record.

In this record however we do not find any simple answer to the question of where the change of the agricultural or rural ensemble in Kenya should be located theoretically. In other words, we do not see any guidance in the European concept of primitive accumulation which cleared the way for the technological revolution in British agriculture, and fundamentally changed the social relations of production in Britain. The forms that Kenyan transformation take do not correspond to those of 17th century Europe. We have no reason to believe that mass expropriation of peasant property is going to be an essential feature in Kenya. On the contrary we are more inclined to think that large farms taken over from the Europeans will be split up, and that small holdings will survive as the basic element of agriculture. The will and right to possess ones own land, even if only a small holding, is the most fundamental element in rural ideology in present Kenya, and it is a more forceful political factor in the country than any other we can think of. Coming large-scale agricultural undertakings in export-crop mixes or industrial crops like sugarcane will not change these fundamentals of the "peasantry" in Kenya.

The concrete forms in which small-holding, as the basic principle in agricultural organization, will survive are somehow not predictable from any "peasant theory" either. We tend to think that it depends upon how the contradictions imposed on households by the "market" are solved at the household level, but we admit that external factors such as developments in the world market and the international division of labour will be decisive for the framework or economic and social space in which this "struggle" will take place.

Confrontation with the expanding capitalist circuits of exchange over the past 80 years has certainly changed the conditions of reproduction in a fundamental way. The responsibility for reproduction has been moved from the "community" or clan to the household and from there in many ways to the individual. Authority or autonomy has moved in the same direction, but only as an exception below the household, which has become the decision-making organizational unit. As we have seen, allocation of labour on family land is decided upon by the head of the household, and moreover the family labour force is subject to allocation by its head. At the level of the market however, the individual is very often responsible, such as is demonstrated by the women's obligations to provide cash.

What we have termed the internalization of capitalist circuits in the household's mode of reproduction, then becomes the basic manner (or strategy) to overcome the contradictions produced by the increasing socialization of the conditions of production (via the market) and the individualization of responsibility. These contradictions are being settled at the household level by, for example reallocation of labour in the family or reallocation of land by preserving and even expanding autonomy on decisions on how to respond to the market mechanism. This is a new feature where a conscious exploitation of the market possibilities is being applied. The nature and magnitude of these contradictions will probably be decisive for the "dynamics" with which the household will defend its autonomy and therefore also for the permanent or transitional character of the present mode of reproduction.

Finally, we think that this whole process goes beyond "economics". Kenyan peasant families and their members act in a quite rational manner within the concept of the "market game", but also tend to preserve their own ideology, for example that of the inseparability of man and land. The ways in which state ideology of the primacy of the market will develop and influence the visions and imagination of the rural masses is therefore a crucial factor here to the examination of which we cannot contribute much.

If internalization of capitalist circuits in the reproduction unit of the household is accepted as a concept of reproduction, then at the concrete level of households we find discrepancies between the concept and the actual degree of "internalization". In our own cases there is a majority however, who maintain that their households in reality produce to reproduce themselves, while some of these maintain that in principle the cash crops grown should be a basis for extended reproduction and profit-making.

At the extreme ends we have respectively, the capitalist farms extracting surplus labour out of poor families, and these poor families who have to sell their labour for wages. The autonomy in the households of the latter approaches that of the proletarized European or British peasants of the 17th century. The position of the farmer is more difficult to determine, since it is not quite obvious that we are here dealing with a capitalist class of landowners. While surplus labour is being appropriated, surplus value is not necessarily produced by that. Many of the large-scale farm owners in fact prefer to invest the surplus, realized as a profit on the long working hours of their labourers, in more land, trade or speculative ventures of the circulation sphere.

But the future of large and medium-scale farming of is course one of the major factors determining the internal dynamics of capitalism in Kenya, and therefore also the intensity of the struggle over the modes of reproduction.

Now in the remaining sectors of this chapter we shall return to the main concern of this book and discuss or sum up what we see as the social consequences of the internalization of capitalist circuits in the household units.

In a narrow and simple sense this is a question of material welfare or standard of living of the typical rural family and its individual members. In the wider, and at the same time more profound, sense these social consequences are related to the prospects for the future quality of life moulded by the past and present socioeconomic changes. In order to be able to reach at least some conclusions as regards the direction of changes, we shall briefly return to the elements of these socio-economic changes at the household level which we have dealt with in the preceding chapters; the labour process, the role of the household as an organizing unit and the market relations. Then finally we shall try to link our findings to the much more intricate and abstract issue of development.

In order to premise our conclusions however ambiguous they will turn out to be, a few remarks should be put forward here to unveil our interpretation of development. One basic premise is that the phrase, "development", is associated with the social consequences of changes, their resulting social structures and relations. As pointed out on the foregoing pages, we do not see our cases, or the household level, studied in some rigid or predetermined theoretical context. We have not found solid reasons for deductions from the level of "capital" here. Whether a capitalist process of accumulation will ultimately lead to the direct subsumption of labour under capital or not, is an unsettled question for us. The question of whether the past changes will produce a class structure based on wage labour relations or not, is therefore also unsettled.

At our level of analysis it seems justified to say that the majority of rural households have experienced an increasing level of reproduction as a direct consequence of the extension of the market. Until the early or even mid-seventies, individual consumption expanded as a tendency. Measured in various material welfare indicators, capitalism did not result in poverty for the majority in this period. Let us not forget here that the late colonial reforms, such as the strategy associated with Swynnerton, and their extension into the post-colonial period, did provide an institutional framework, in which cash-cropping and market relations, which were upheld and restricted by the colonial settler politics, developed almost explosively.

Since the mid-seventies, as pointed out in chapter II.4, the statistical indices of rural material welfare however seem to indicate a stagnation or even decrease. Apart from the world market contribution to this reversal, this may very well reflect the process of social differentiation, which continues as an irreversible consequence of market expansion now itself losing momentum, as the first easily removable obstacles to the expansion of production have been overcome at the exchange level by lifting legal restrictions.

As we have tried to demonstrate throughout the book, social differentiation is part and parcel of our observations on labour relations and exchange. We shall therefore return to this social phenomenon in the concluding section, in an attempt to locate it in its wider social perspective.

2. The social consequences of changing labour processes

We argue that the essential variable for understanding both production and reproduction is labour. At our level of analysis the socio-economic processes and the interpretation of the structure of the transformation cannot be understood without focussing on the labour process. Also the living conditions of the population are preliminarily determined by the labour relations, and the conditions under which the families are associated with the market.

The commercialization of the economy and the domination of the capitalist economy affect many different aspects of life in the rural areas, tending to destroy many traditional social structures and transform others in the internalization of the capitalist market. Only through the analysis of labour relations can we reach an indication of how the capitalist market is internalized in the household economy, and what this means for the living conditions of the population.

Chapter II documents that the purpose of labour in the rural families continues to be the reproduction of the family, more specifically the reproduction of labour rather than reproduction of capital. The changing conditions of production have provided certain possibilities for making of decisions concerning the crop pattern and the allocation of labour, and thus for responding to the economic pressures. Labour is still organized by the household and takes place mainly within the family, as such it may be subject to decisions at a household level. This could of course lead to the conclusion that the family labour relations have been carried over from the precapitalistic society, and that the labour relations of the subsistence production are unchanged. But this is not the case. There are different indicators of change in the relations of production and in the labour relations also involving the family labour relations of the peasant families.

Now let us focus on the indicators of change in the family economy, concerning the labour relations. First, the division of labour between men, women and children has been changing with a separation of the family farm into a subsistence and a cash crop area. The labour force for both types of products is mainly family labour, supplemented with hired labour for the cash crop production. Even with new crops the labour processes tend to remain nearly the same.

Secondly, there is an intensification in the exploitation of family labour, reflecting the increased cash cropping and increased shortage of land and of cash for hiring labour. Thus family labour and hired labour may replace each other depending on the possibilities to further extend the burden of work for family labour and the access to cash. It could be expected that a technological change and mechanization of the agricultural production had been part and parcel of the commercialization of the economy, but this has been the case only to a very limited extent in the peasant production. The intensification of the family labour input is to be analysed in relation to the production for profits by the men, who allocate family labour for the cash crop production. This implies that unpaid family labour is involved in the market economy, with the man as the manager and appropriating the surplus. Thus certain features characterizing the labour market and capitalistic labour relations at the surface seem to have penetrated the family.

Thirdly, the communal labour relations and mutual arrangements between relatives as an exchange between equals are dying out and are being replaced by different kinds of labour force exchange at the market. This reflects how the market is penetrating all aspects of social life, also the social superstructure related to the extended family and relatives. Some of the arrangements between relatives still exist, though more as a social arrangement than one of real economic value. Some communal labour arrangements have also been internalized in the new market conditions, as work parties are formed for farmwork in a combination of mutual arrangements and casual labour. Another form is the self-help projects where local labour and cash is appropriated for infrastructural projects in a decentralization of governmental expenditures.

These changes do not however in themselves demonstrate an increasing social division of labour in the society, or the establishment of capitalist relations of production. The complexity of the social relations implies that even if these changes do give indications of a developing capitalist labour market they also show that for the peasant families:

(1) The household is still the basic organizing and decision-making unit of production and reproduction, and family labour is still the basic nucleus of the labour force.

(2) Increasing productivity is obtained through intensification of the labour input and extension of the labour time, thus representing a quantitative rather than qualitative change of labour input.

(3) Wage labour relations do not "transcend" the basic pattern of household reproduction, i.e. labour for wages has not become the main source of individual reproduction, it has remained supplementary in nature even if it is becoming more and more important vis-à-vis family labour on the land.

Consequently no simple and clearcut conclusions can be drawn regarding the nature of changing labour relations. There is a certain polarization regarding the burden of work and the autonomy within the family at the individual level. At the level of the society we cannot talk however about profound changes in the social relations of production, where the combination of family labour and the buying and selling of farm labour within the same households reveals some of the complexity of the production relations. On the one hand, we may perceive the individual household as directly confronted with capital, as argued by Bernstein, on the other hand, many of the labour relations are not clearly capitalistic, but show different features of social relations specific to the social strata and the local community. There is a certain autonomy, exercised by the man, who may decide on crops and allocation of labour. But the sexual division of labour and the division of responsibilities, also implies that not only the household is tied to the capitalist market, but that the single individuals are directly related to the labour market. Thus the women are not only a labour force disposed of by the man in the household production, but they are also involved in labour relations themselves in direct response to the living conditions and the pressure on land for subsistence. The complexity of the labour market is a persistent feature of the exchange of labour, where the same household is employer at one point in time and selling their labour for the same work at another point in time. The characteristic however is that men are more often employers and women more often only selling labour and contributing unpaid family labour, but not hiring labour.

At our level of analysis we may say that the extension of the market seems to explain the accelerating process of social differentiation. This polarization of the societies we have shown, started already in the 19th century, with differences between the ecological zones and the different histories of the tribal communities. But the process has accelerated and tended to make living conditions or production conditions more uniform. Thus the heterogenity may be smoothened out at some level of analysis, and made more homogeneous for the same social strata with respect to labour and market exchange conditions.

The implications of the changed labour relations as mentioned above lead to an increased physical work input from women and children and a decreasing work input from men. Men are instead more involved in management and decision-making or they are totally alienated from the farmwork, e.g. as migrant workers. In some cases however, there appears to be a surplus capacity of male labour, as a labour reserve, which could be mobilized for productive work, for instance, in cases where men have been made marginal in agricultural production or otherwise, and have not found new productive roles in the household economy. The structure implies that women have more work and less relative autonomy, with the heavy responsibilities they carry, they have no possibilities for withdrawing themselves or making any real decisions for alternative work situations. This pattern is somewhat modified by different ecological zones, tribal groups, and different crop patterns, especially whether it is a mixed farming and maize producing area or a monocultural cash-crop area such as the sugarcane schemes.

The main argument concerning the peasant households is that the household as a cooperating work group is dissolved. The validity of the household is more restricted to a labour allocating and organizing unit. The implications of this is also that the single individuals are increasingly confronted with the labour market. For the men this is clearer for the margins of the social groups such as the rich and the poor. Women on the other hand are directly confronted with the market in the exchange of both labour and produce. Women maintain many of the features of unpaid family labour in the household production, but their responsibilities for the daily food supplies lead to a need for supplementary cash and a necessity to be involved as individuals at the market.

Many of the above processes are valid for the majority of the rural population, namely most peasant families, where the household and family labour relations are so important. However, the evaluation of the changing labour relations also have to include labour relations of the margins of our sample. The increase in the use of hired labour on family farms is not all derived from a mutual "exchange" of labour among equals, but the landless, or nearly landless, social strata is a growing part of the population, and they are totally dependent on reproducing their families through selling their labour. The pauperization of the population with increasing fragmentation of land to minimal plots and landlessness is a phenomenon in all areas. The landless labour families are however mostly found in the large-scale farming areas. Here landless labourers are involved in wage labour without the modifying factors related to the peasant household, and all the individual members of the family are directly confronted with capital at the labour market. This form however is not dominating in rural areas of peasant farming, even if the continued fragmentation of land to minimal plots and increasing landlessness among the younger generations may change the features of the labour market also in these areas.

Indications of capitalistic wage labour relations are also found in large-scale business and farming. Even if the basis is family labour for supervision and some physical work, the exploitation of hired labour is very important, and dominates the labour processes involving hard physical work.

The polarization and increasing differentiation of the living conditions of the social strata does not imply that the labour market should be analyzed in fragments, as it is clearly part of the same structure. The argument is that some of the areas of the Highlands with large-scale farming show features of a clear capitalistic labour market. Most of the areas of peasant farming have labour relations which are changing under the domination of capitalist transformation, but the labour relations are not totally transformed to a capitalist labour market, the internalization of capitalist market relations have changed the labour relations to a form specific for the household mode of reproduction.

3. The social consequences of the changing role of the household

In the first section of this chapter it was argued that in spite of tendencies to dissolve the economic unity of household members, the household must be considered as the basic or fundamental unit of economic and social analysis of rural Kenya.

Though there are many variations of the exact pattern of conduct and function related to geographical differences, the household seems to represent something like a mode of reproduction characterizing agricultural Kenya.

Throughout the book we have however also expressed doubt about the validity of the household "concept", both as a descriptive term and an analytical tool. Especially in chapter II, but also in the preceding section of this chapter, the question has been raised about the relevance of the household as a unit, with the wife responsible for the reproduction of labour. Especially with reference to the unequal work and living conditions of men and women, and the structure of obligations, leaving the women with a major part of the responsibility to reproduce labour and therefore marginalizing men in relation to the same responsibilities.

On the following pages we shall try to clarify these conflicting interpretations in an attempt to review the role of the household in reproduction and the consequences of the changes in the role, which we have observed.

Historically the household as an extended agricultural family did organize the farm work as a unit. As the pre-colonial social system was broken, i.e. the superiority of clans over essential questions such as land "ownership", etc., the household became a decisive economic unit executing allocation of land and labour. With legal reforms introduced to provide institutions in which capitalism could breed, landownership was also connected with the individual household with the (male) head of household as landowner.

There is much therefore which seems to support the view that the household, in both an economic and legal sense, represents the basic or elementary social structure of reproduction. This view is strengthened if it is also accepted that the "rationale" of the household is exactly its own reproduction and not in essence reproduction of capital.

If we focus on the labour process and on relations within the household and their change over the past 10–20 years, we will have to modify this simple view however. As shown in chapter II, the sexual division of labour is an important variable in understanding the present day living conditions of women, children and men within the household. The existing pattern is to a large extent based on the traditional division of labour, where women and children were responsible for the daily work in agriculture. The development has changed or made the husband's contributions superfluous, and left him with more options in relation to the family.

The traditional allocation of work and responsibilities according to sex did, however, link the man to obligations for the family, and had clearly defined work for women and children to supply food for their consumption. The problem arose in the household economy when it engaged in the market economy with labour and production of exchange values, rather than production for the purpose of subsistence.

In this process the fact that men became the owners of land and could dispose of the surplus of production was crucial. Women work on the cash crops, besides the work for subsistence, and often on top of that, work for others or in trade to earn cash to buy food and household necessities. The surplus of labour in cash crops is disposed of by the man. This does not only leave the man with more options, but also leaves the possibility for the husbands to extract a surplus from their wives.

As regards the contribution of resources in the reproduction of labour, those of women are important both with respect to labour and cash. Those of the men are much more limited, and difficult to determine, as women and children provide labour for the cash crops, but the income is for the disposition of the husband. The husband often has also other incomes, but only a small part of his incomes are provided for the family as an input to cover daily needs. Some is provided for the school-fees and some for agricultural inputs. A part of the husband's input is derived from the surplus of the labour of women and children. The bulk of the costs of reproduction of labour is thus clearly produced by women and children themselves.

In the analysis we have emphasized the work of women and children and the sexual division of labour as important variables for determining the living conditions. From this analysis, it appears as if women and children form the main stable unit for the reproduction of labour, and that men are only marginally attached to this unit, by providing some land for cultivation and a few inputs in agriculture and school-fees. His economy is largely independent and a fundamental part of this is freed from the obligation of supporting the family, and geared towards his own economic ventures or personal consumption.

In some discussions this has led to the conclusion that men are exploiting the work of women, and that they form a different social stratum. We do not carry the argument that far. Even if there is a male exploitation of female labour, there is also a flow of resources, though limited, from the men, which in a life-time is difficult to evaluate in relation to the labour input of family labour.

The appropriation of a surplus from family labour is not seen as a necessary criteria in order to speak about "class relations". The husband is the owner of the means of production, and may dispose of the surplus also from the work of women and children. But the women are not totally alienated from the produce of their own effort. Women dispose of the food crops from the land allocated for subsistence production, and may use this also for inputs in trade or whatever they find most necessary.

This description of the responsibilities and the work relations, however, leads us to the conclusion that an analysis of the living conditions and the labour relations of the rural population, has to be based on a study involving the unpaid family labour and the internal economic relations in the household. An analysis of labour relations, based only on the study of men overemphasizes the "formal economy" and leaves out the complexity of the main part of labour relations in the household economy. It is only by including this factor in the analysis, that the underpayment of labourers can be explained. The analysis of the internal labour relations in the family raises a question on the relevance of determining the social structure alone on the basis of the man and his assets and work conditions. Even if women are dependent on men for land and to a certain extent controlled by men, they are not just dependents and housewives in the western sense of the concept. Women in rural Kenya have a long tradition for having a separate economy and economic activity outside the home. Men have no traditional role as supporters and sole bread winners for the family, and an analysis of social classes would have to include women as producers and traders. The perception of women as dependents in an analysis of the polygamous households becomes grotesque, where the wives may not even have any land, and may rely totally on themselves for their own and their family's survival.

In relation to an analysis of the social structure of rural areas of Kenya this great difference in living conditions for men and wives adds to the complex structure of the multiplicity of sources of incomes. It also adds to the complexity of incomes of independent business persons, "tenants" and labourers. When the same family provides a whole variation of labour relations, and records on the same persons also show a great variation through the year, a clearcut classification of something like social classes becomes nearly impossible, and would leave out a lot of dubious marginal cases.

In many ways our observations therefore have produced more questions than answers. At our level of analysis, we may however argue, that even if still the most useful unit of analysis, the household of today, displays some fundamental fractioning as a consequence of the legal and economic changes over the past 50 years. Women and children seem to form the stable unit of reproduction, and men have become marginalized in relation to it. The social consequences of this process reflect themselves in an increasing discrepancy of living conditions with women and children as the poorest stratum. This polarization from inside must of course be related to the process of social differentiation between the different strata of households which we have tried to describe and analyse in the preceding chapters. Women and children of "rich households" have not been faced with the same hardships as those of poor. After all, there are flows of resources from husbands to the reproduction unit of the household, the magnitude of them depends to some extent on the wealth of the husband. Since the independence between the fractions of the household also persists in terms of land and labour allocation, and since it seems to us that the rationale of household production in the majority of cases is that of family reproduction, we tend to conclude that the household is still the most appropriate unit of social analysis in rural areas of Kenya.

The household as the organizing unit of reproduction may not only decide to allocate different proportions of land and family labour to food and cash cropping, but the (male) head of household may decide as well to buy labour from outside or sell family labour including his (her) own or both, according to his – and the family's – subjective considerations. We have enough evidence in our data to argue here that such considerations leading to decision-making take place in a rather planned way based on certain objectives of the production and experience.

As an example to illustrate this point, in one year, depending on last years' experience, the crop composition may be somehow different from that of last year, and according to a decision and the "economy", the allocation of labour may also differ. Hired seasonal labour may be utilized to boost food cropping while the family labour assists in cash cropping, and the husband may try to sell his own labour to provide cash for wages and inputs. In another season the pattern may change again with changing roles of men, women and children as a result.

What seems to be a more and more consistent feature of this "relative autonomy" is that the buying and selling of labour has developed a multitude of forms and has become an instrument subject to the objectives of production and of course to the social and economic situation of the household or its male head and the technology it or he commands.

4. The expansion of the internal market and its social consequences

In section 2 of this chapter an attempt was made to identify the position of wage labour relations in agricultural production and its rather complex and unsettled interpretation vis-à-vis the changing patterns of social division of labour in rural Western Kenya.

To understand how labour relations contribute to the social transformation of the rural ensemble we studied, the level of exchange, or the market in a general sense, however has to be drawn into our analysis as well.

As almost no corner of social life has been untouched by buying or selling, i.e. the market mechanism, it could be tempting to see the exchange level as the dominant factor or moment of the social process of change. The extension of the internal market and its subsequent intensification certainly has changed rural life a lot more so far, than have changes of the labour process itself. However whereas the so-called commercialization has already replaced most non-commercial exchange mechanisms of the past, the other and more fundamental transformation of labour relations, and of the very labour process, has just begun to gain momentum. Whereas the market principle dominates all levels of exchange relations, the forms and intensity of social (capitalist ?) relations of production and technological change remain an unsettled question.

The question of whether the market or the exchange level is dominant may not therefore lead us anywhere at this moment. However, what seems to be rather clear is that the subsumption of labour in its many forms under capital goes on and becomes visible in the market at the exchange level. Furthermore the extension of the market and its intensification in itself seems to produce social differentiation, which in the end may be decisive for the forms of social relations of production to develop together with technology.

As was underlined in the introduction, this book has not intended to deal with the global extension of the market or the emerging international division of labour. We have deliberately decided to work with the local dynamics of change resulting from this larger process but also developing its own, so to say, logics and forms within the market framework and its modification through national class struggle.

As we have seen in chapters III, IV and V, the market, in a broad sense of the word, has a double function, exchange of use values through different market mechanisms and at the same time the establishment of exchange relations as a basis for profit making.

The bare fact that 60 % of the average household reproduction takes place via the market, and that food purchases amount to something between half and two-thirds of it, indicates the necessity of exchange use values whether in the form of simple transactions such as purchasing food in the market-place against cash obtained from the sale of own produce or from just labouring or through the involvement in the capitalist circuit of commodities extended to the village level.

As it was shown in chapter III, the extension of market relations has to a large extent been absorbed in the pre-colonial and colonial market system. Trade in the open market-place on market days represents about a third of the combined purchasing and selling, measured in cash, and there is no reason to think that the social function of market-places as the principal mechanism for the exchange of food based on local production will diminish. The profit making element of market trade by women also seems to be little more than payment of the labour involved in the trade. The character of horizontal exchange, i.e. exchange of use values through simple transactions between direct producers, describes therefore in essence the logics of market trade.

Nevertheless, trade in the open market-places as the necessary and increasing exchange of use values, especially food, cannot be seen isolated from its other function as an agent of the market in the more general and social sense of the term. Even if the individual profits of the majority selling their produce at the market-place are small and sometimes insignificant, the total aggregate of profits somehow is being made at the expense of the increasing number of households, who must sell their produce just after harvest to provide cash for the payment of other necessities and have to buy food later in the season at higher prices when they are short of own supplies, as well as at the expense of landless families, who always have to buy the bulk of their food for cash obtained by seasonal labour.

The extent to which trade in the open market-place reproduces and deepens social differentiation through such unequal exchange relations, does in fact depend on the relationships between market prices through the different seasons, and of course on the relationships between those prices and the wage rates paid through the same seasons.

We suspect that these price differentials do account for quite substantial differences in living conditions between those families who on an average can manage their basic food supply from their own production, and those who for various reasons cannot. Increasing land shortage of course is one such major reason, but the splitting of the household economy into a woman's sphere of reproduction and subsistence and a husband's sphere of cash cropping constitutes another reason as was shown in chapter II.

Now exchange in the open market-places of course does not take place as a closed circuit of its own either. Horizontal exchange has been integrated into the wider market, the domestic "internal market", and therefore also into the external or international market relations.

Food prices at the local market-place are related to the buying and selling prices of the Marketing Boards controlled by the state, and the price policy of the Kenyan government regulating basic food prices, somehow also reflects movements in the international markets and their impact on exchange conditions at the various levels.

It is obviously one of the limitations of our study that we have not included a more precise analysis of these market relations in it. In principle however the state buys and sells maize, the main staple food, at fixed minimum, respectively maximum prices, through the network of the Maize and Produce Board. In principle therefore a maximum price-span within these limits should be established at any market-place. Accordingly speculation by surplus producers in local shortage late in the season should therefore also be limited to this range. But since the distribution network of the Maize & Produce Marketing Board does not always reach all marketplaces, or even if so, may have turned out to function through corrupt middlemen, the possibility to exploit temporary abundance or shortage beyond the established price range has often been converted into reality, paving the way for the formation of a professional trading class or stratum whose members have engaged in accumulation of wealth whether cash, cattle or land.

The market forces of course do not alone function via the traditional market-places, as shown in chapters III and V, the trading centres including licenced shops have gradually developed through the colonial period, and contrary to the open-air market. The trading centre is well established within the capitalist commodity circuit, and it functions as the lowest or basic point of exchange in the vertical system of exchange levels of the national internal market. According to our estimates in chapter III, trading centres may now account for as much as half of the total buying and selling by rural households. Adding transactions done by households directly with the urban exchange network or with wholesale agencies buying cash crops or milk, the capitalist market system may be estimated to account for roughly 70 % of all buying and selling.

Accordingly the main effects of the market system on the social relations in the areas studied, first of all as an agent of social differentiation, seemingly should be sought in the trading centres or in linkages with outside wholesale agencies. Now again our research has been focussed on the local dynamics of the exchange phenomenon once set into motion by "external" elements of change whether national or international. Our study therefore has nothing really to say about the changing conditions of accumulation caused by world market mechanisms such as price relations between export cash crops and import goods for individual or productive consumption.

What our cases however tend to show or indicate given this limitation, is that shop trading, as the act of selling necessities or luxuries from the vertical market system to final consumers, does not in itself provide its practitioners with any outright basis for private accumulation. As demonstrated in chapter V, the operative conditions of the majority of shopkeepers in trading centres seem to approach those of "perfect competition" described by liberalistic textbooks. The extent to which the average shopkeeper is involved in the appropriation of surplus labour (product ?) extracted from agriculture, therefore remains a point for discussion. As we have shown in chapter V, the average profits from shopkeeping do not exceed a few thousand shs. a year, which includes as well the shopkeeper's own labour pay. We would argue therefore on the basis of our field data, that the majority of shopkeepers do not get more than a pay for physical work with the necessary distribution of commodities of individual or productive consumption. A pay which of course is mainly borne by the rural communities and not by the industrial or commercial capital involved in realizing their commodities in the rural setting, and a pay which is probably double as much as the farm labourers' monthly wage, but nevertheless below 10 shs. a day.

Moreover even when combined with cash cropping, as our research shows is a common phenomenon, shopkeeping tends to be a more and more hazardous affair as the majority of shopkeepers are being squeezed between the rigidity of posted prices applied by industries or the government and increasing operating costs, especially transport.

As we have therefore tried to argue in chapter V, if the majority of small businessmen actually do extract surplus labour from somewhere, it must be from the own family members, i.e., wives employed in the shops, or from the households which deliver hired labour to the shops.

Now as we saw in that same chapter, there is a minority of shopkeepers, between 5–30 % according to different criteria, who actually seem to make substantial profits and furthermore subjectively manage their business towards expansion and accumulation. This minority quite often includes individuals with certain social characteristics, such as being members of wealthy families, owning land, or being educated, e.g. to become school teachers, mainly by the missions. We would therefore tend to argue that already existing social differentiation in the studied areas are being deepened by commercial venture. Members of this minority have been able to establish social relations with commercial, industrial or state capital, which have lifted them out of the squeeze mentioned before. They act as clients of the vertical market system's institutions, whether as sole distributors of Bata shoes or agents for purchasing agencies. A few of them have actually themselves entered the capitalist class as wholesalers, farmers etc.

Members of this minority generally expand their business at the expense of the average shopkeeper, as they are able to obtain discounts from their suppliers not given to the average shopkeeper. But they are also, by means of different privileges, able to command cash flows beyond their own means, which again means that they may improve their farming and stocks at the same time as they buy cheap produce, land, and labour from those not having cash enough to buy daily necessities.

To us the professional market traders (mentioned above) as well as this minority of large scale shopkeepers quite obviously benefit from the extraction of surpluses from agriculture. It may be as "clients" holding various privileges or as traders exploiting their market position to press down purchasing prices, etc. More directly a few of them also exploit labour in capitalist wage labour relations. To us however it is still an open question to what extent the growing social differentiation via the market, will eventually lead to a more regular and lasting process of accumulation.

5. On the social consequences in a wider perspective

Now at the end, how should we see our partial conclusions in a wider perspective? How could the differential and apparently contradicting patterns of change, which we have discussed, be located in a context apt for some generalization about the nature of the changing social structure and relations of the rural ensemble?

As pointed out in the first section of this chapter, we do not see any unambiguous relationships between more abstract concepts of capitalist transformation and our observations. This of course has to do with the empirical nature of the study itself, in the first case, but even if an attempt is made to ascend to the more abstract level of the Kenyan social formation, its position and direction of change in terms of some "mode of production" seems to us to be an unsettled question.

We shall not be able to speak about "class formation" as a logical consequence of past and present trends of socio-economic changes, nor shall we be able to argue that the polarization at the household level we have observed will lead to a "destruction" of the present mode of reproduction in the foreseeable future. Any stage of social development is by nature "transitional", but whether qualitative changes of the social relations of agricultural production in Kenya are imminent also to us appears as an open question. Which are the conclusions then?

Let us first repeat here that the material quality of life of the many has increased over the past 15-20 years. Not only because unused material and human resources have been converted into marketable commodities, realized via the expanding internal market, but also because the social infrastructure has been developed to reach most social strata in the inhabited areas of Kenya.

Leaving the question aside of whether this dynamic of the market has lost momentum and therefore its role as a conveyor of the civilizing effects of capitalism, we would also argue that the spread of formal education and sense of technology has definitely changed the individual prospects of young generations, from colonial hopelessness to some kind of an instrumental platform for individual struggle towards a more articulated and rewarding social existence. Rational cconduct within the logics of the market is practised, and accepted, by the majority and absorbed in the widespread concept of individualism, characterizing the attitudes and opinions held by most adults one can come across within rural areas.

Secondly, to come beneath the surface of statistics and indicators, we find that this pattern of development is contradicted by an increasing social polarization at both the individual and the family levels; at the individual level between men and women of the household, as shown in chapter II and repeated in section 2 of this chapter; at the household level, between those families or households who have to purchase food and those who have a surplus of staples beyond their own needs for consumption.

As regards the polarization between men and women in terms of workload, responsibility and material living conditions, we tend to think that it represents an increasing instability of the household economy. Women more and more become loaded to the physical limits of their capacity, while men often seem to represent an unutilized labour force in relation to household reproduction, sometimes in a life-long floating position from one (small) job or business to another. To the extent this statement gains validity, it characterizes a socio-economic change which will inevitably result in some restructuring of the household as a social unit.

Studies by Michael Cowen (Cowen 1976) in the Central Province seem to point at one possible direction of restructuring which we think is sometimes overlooked. He describes how males have "reentered" agriculture as a physical labour force on their own shambas working along with the wife and children. Even on relatively small holdings this change of the family division of labour has often been associated with technological changes, such as crop combinations, improved livestock, increased use of fertilizers, etc. and application of industrially produced tools and equipment. Now it may be argued that not only should we expect the Kikuyus of the Central Province to be leading in a true technological revolution of agriculture, given their position in the Kenyan social formation, but we may even doubt that the economic opportunities open to the small-holders of Central Province, for example thanks to the presence of the nearby Nairobi market for vegetables, fruits, milk, etc. will come to exist in Western Kenya.

Therefore the question of whether the household economy will gradually destabilize further or be restructured in some overall technological change, should in fact be related to the prospects of the internal market and to the Kenyan economy's further integration into the world market. We do not, however, find ourselves ready to deal with this complex matter here which lies beyond the scope of our study, but must of course point out that the question of the internal market is intimately linked with the average level of reproduction of labour, or more precisely to the social value of labour.

At the other level of polarization, between these households which increasingly have to purchase their staples, and those which produce a surplus beyond their own needs, we are inclined to repeat that the increasing number of landless or near-to-be-landless households contribute to further dislocation of this vital balance. But again to judge the wider social implications of this aspect of polarization, it is necessary to look deeper into the factors which influence or determine this balance.

It may be anticipated that some process of "primitive accumulation" is taking place by "fencing" what was traditionally communal land and by land "consolidation". As we have said earlier these forms of acquisition of land are part of the ways in which a landholding stratum of farmers establish themselves. As demonstrated in chapter V, successful shopkeepers or civil servants are buying land from their poorer neighbours.

It seems to us however, that land fragmentation at generational transfers is a more important tendency in nearly all types of holdings. Rules of inheritance of land by all sons in a family and a large family size inevitably imply a rapid fragmentation of family land. In areas already heavily populated, with average landholdings of less than 2 hectares such as parts of Kakamega (Vihiga) and Kisii Districts, the land fragmentation continues much below the limits of the capacity to reproduce a family. This fragmentation continues in spite of the legal restrictions against subdivision below a minimum for reproducing a family (Keyonzo 1976, p. 33).

The fragmentation of land is not only a process of traditional smallholder areas, but is also becoming part and parcel of the land tenure pattern in the former "White Highlands" of Rift Valley. It is a known, but for political reasons undocumented fact, that large farms, still figuring as entities in the statistics, are being bought by "cooperatives" or land purchasing companies and subdivided into rather large farms of 20–40 acres. Many of these companies are formed by influential Kikuyu, Nandi or Akamba businessmen, who retain the largest shares of the farms, but still a large number of shares are sold to small peasants and is a characteristic feature of the saving pattern in especially the Central Province. The units of 20–40 acres formally made are often subdivided informally by registering several names (brothers) on the same land.

As demonstrated by Waweru (Waweru 1974) the competition for acquisition of land in the high potential areas of Trans Nzoia is fierce between Kikuyu and Kalenjin groups or land purchasing societies, who somehow, through the political agreements at the national level, have managed to keep other ethnic fractions such as the Luyias and Luos away from the land market of the Rift Valley.

The wider perspective of this division of land process may also somehow be overlooked as a factor which may come to counterbalance, in a socio-economic sense, some of the effects of land fragmentation. The large farms taken over by Kenyan African individuals from white settlers represent an unused reserve of high potential land, poorly farmed as estates and even held by some of their owners for speculative purposes, they may become the objective of a second round of rural stabilization policy, following that of the settlement schemes in the early sixties. Divided into medium sized family holdings, the former European farm sector might come to lift the production of staples or to a second phase of expansion, and therefore to contribute to the decrease in the average level of reproduction costs.

Statistics on the landholdings and fragmentation of land in the Rift Valley is limited due to the generally poor statistics from these regions. There are however a few indicators, family labour is increasing and permanent hired labour input is declining. Information from key persons and our case studies indicate that the landholdings of the settlement schemes are earlier unused land or grazing land. That information seems to indicate that subdivided farms, in fact, begin to develop the same pattern of productivity as Cowen emphasized in the Central Province, and moreover show an increasing utilization of previously unused land.

The land question on one side, and the problem of unutilized or underutilized capacity both in terms of physical resources and labour force on the other, however are in our opinion factors decisive for the direction social changes will take in the next few years. The importance of the land question will certainly increase drastically over the coming years, both because of the population growth, which means that sons will start sharing the fathers' already fragmented pieces of land in increasing numbers, and because of the land market and its restrictions. As many studies have pointed out, land resources in Kenya are ample to feed everybody there. But since profit on the ownership or rent of land is inseparable from the capitalistic market, land distribution has come to reflect the emerging social polarization of the population and of course the power of multinational capital. Landlessness necessarily growws out of this situation in a rural society like Kenya. But the access to buy land is not unrestricted by non-economic considerations either.

The potentially high yielding, but poorly utilized, plains of the Rift Valley, will certainly be divided up among small and medium sized farms in the next decades, likely for members of either Kikuyu or Kalenjin societies. Employment on new family farms in Rift Valley may therefore ease the pressure on land in the Central Province, especially if the post Kenyatta administration will continue the disrupted Swynnerton type of reforms.

On the other hand the privileges of Kikuyus and Kalenjins also mean that land-seeking westerners such as Luos and Luyias will have to find their lot in their own "tribal areas", or be landless. Especially in the densely populated

Western and parts of Nyanza Province, the combination of land fragmentation and these geographical restrictions on the land market is bound to increase the pressure on land.

As it is our firm impression that the access to land, or rather the right to possess it, is the main component of the ideology held by a vast majority of adult Kenyans whatever tribe they come from, the question of landlessness therefore also seems to us to be vital as a factor decisive for the nature of socio-political contradictions to emerge from the present social structure.

As Anne Philips argues at the end of her analysis of the concept of development, the most crucial questions here, are not whether capitalism in one or another form may establish itself in Africa and break its alliances with foreign capital; the most crucial questions are those, "which raise issues about the nature of the class forces developing in Africa. Can capitalism destroy precapitalist relations of production? Is the nature and focus of class conflict changing?" (Anne Philips, 1977 p. 20). Our observations at the household level in selected areas of Western Kenya, will of course be insufficient to answer these crucial questions. We would nevertheless say that if the internal contradictions of the present type of reproduction via the households are being eased, as for example in the Central Province, then this mode of reproduction is certainly not likely to be destroyed in the foreseeable future. The family or household holding will probably even retain a certain amount of autonomy, because it is not export crops but food crops, which may be kept, consumed or sold in the local or capitalistic market, which are the basis for allocation of land and family labour and for the reproduction of the family.

As the addition of new small and medium sized holdings characterizes the development of the agricultural structure, rather than concentration of land and centralization of indigenous agricultural capital, the spread of ownership will come to mark the next years, at the same time as the number of landless households will increase considerably, especially in Western Province. Whether a proletariate will emerge as a consequence of more widespread wage labour relations on farms and family holdings may be doubted. As we have shown in chapter II, the tendency is to exploit family labour more and reduce paid labour. If males return to work in agriculture on their own holdings in larger numbers in the coming years, this tendency may be reinforced.

The prospects for those who will come to seek land of their own in vain therefore seem to us to be bleak, as no one really knows how they can seek compensation in urban areas, where industries develop rapidly, but not as in Europe in the 19th century. They are as capital intensive as industries have to be to compete in the world market, and they do not offer employment to the millions of victims from a "primative accumulation". The agony of those who suffer life-long frustration of their basic claims to land may therefore lead to formations based upon the idea of every individual's right to land and promote this as the basic political question in the country.

The anger of the people living as landless tenants in the large "workers camps" along the Nakuru-Eldoret railway is a genuine protest against the social injustice of capitalism, as is the robbing and mobbing by jobless school leavers in Nairobi. But for the next generation to come there will be more landowning households in Kenya, than landless.

The reader will certainly realize that we have not used the phrase "transitional" in these concluding remarks. It is simply because our studies in Kenya seem to justify the point that the social tensions of the polarization have not yet reached a point, where qualitative changes in the social relations of agricultural production can be expected.

Our analysis of the access to land, and of the market and labour relations, lead us to the conclusion that the potentials for survival for some variants of capitalism are strong, based on the ideology of private landownership, which has not yet come to frustrate the majority of the rural population. A political mobilization to change the system therefore is not imminent in our opinion.

References

Aguilar, Alonso 1973	"Bondeklassens opløsning, det interne marked og underudvikling" (The dissolution of the peasant class, the internal market and underdevelopment), In E. Feder et al.: *Latinamerika. Den Kapitalistiske Udviklingsproces i Landbruget. (Latin America. The Capitalistic Development Process in Agriculture)* Institute for Development Research, Copenhagen.
Bernstein, Henry 1976	*Capital and Peasantry in the Epoch of Imperialism.* Dept. of Sociology, Dar es Salaam Univeristy. Dar es Salaam. Mimeo.
Bookman, Ann Edith 1973	*The Changing Economic Role of Luo Women: A Historical and Ethnographic Approach.* M.A. Thesis.
Boserup, Ester 1970	*Woman's Role in Economic Development.* Allen and Unwin. London.
Caldwell, J.C. 1967	"Fertility Attitudes in Three Economically Contrasting Regions of Ghana". *Economic Development and Cultural Change.* Vol. 15 no. 2.
Cowen, M.P. 1976	*Capital and Peasant Households.* Working Paper University of Nairobi. Mimeo.
Cowen, M.P. with Murage, F. April 1972	"Notes on Agricultural Wage Labour in a Kenyan Location", in *"Development Trends in Kenya".* Proceedings of Seminar, Centre of African Studies. Edinburgh. pp. 39–60.
Din, M. El Awad Galal el 1977	"The Economic Value of Children in Rural Sudan", in J.C. Caldwell (ed): *The Persistence of High Fertility. Population Prospects in the Third World.* Changing African Family – Family and Fertility Change Series no. 1. Dept. of Demography, Canberra. Vol. 1 part 2 pp. 617–632.
Dines, Leslie E. with Thuveson, D. 1977	*The Invisible Woman – The Missing Link in Rural Development.* Swedish University of Agricultural Sciences, Uppsala.
Fearn, Hugh 1955	*The Problem of the African Trader.* Paper to the East African Social Science Conference. Kampala.
Fortman, Louise 1976	*Women and Maize Production: Some Tanzanian Observations.* Paper prepared for the Protein Calorie Advisory Group of the United Nations' System. Mimeo.
Galeski, B. 1972	*Basic Concepts of Rural Sociology.* Manchester.
Gathungu, C.M.W. 1974	*Economic Diversification in the Role of Kikuyu Women. A Case Study of Role Conflict among Emerging Business Women in Dagoretti Location.* Dept. of Sociology. Nairobi University. Student vacation research. Mimeo.
Gerry, Chris & Birkbeck, C. 1978	*The Petty Producer in Third World Cities; Petit Bourgeois or Disguised Proletarian?* Paper to Workshop on Small Scale Industry in Urban and Rural Areas in Africa. May-June Kungälv. Scandinavian Institute of African Studies.
Gwyer, G.D. 1972	*Labour in Small Scale Agriculture. An Analysis of the 1970/71 Farm Enterprise Cost Survey. Labour and Wage Data.* Institute of Development Studies W.P. 62. Nairobi.

Hanger, Jane & Moris, Jon 1973	"Women and the Household Economy", in R. Chambers & J. Moris (eds): *MWEA: An Irrigated Rice Settlement in Kenya.* Afrik – Studien 83. IFO München. pp. 209–245.
Hay, Margaret Jean 1976	"Luo Women and Economic Change during the Colonial Period", in N.J. Hafkin & E.G. Bay (eds.): *Women in Africa. Studies in Social and Economic Change.* Stanford.
Integrated Rural Survey 1974–75	See Kenya 1977 a.
Inukai, I & Ikelo, J. 1973	*Problems of Rural Industries: Case Study of Kakamega District, Western Province, Kenya.* Paper no. 65. Annual Social Science Conference of East African Universities. Dar es Salaam.
Kabwegyere, Tarsis B. 1976	*Socio-Economic Transformation in East Africa. The Growth of Trading Centres in Rural Kenya.* Unpublished manuscript. Dept. of Sociology. University of Nairobi. Mimeo.
Kayongo-Male, Diane & Walji, Parveen 1978	*The Value of Children in Rural Areas: Parents' Perceptions and Actual Contributions of Children in Selected Areas of Kenya.* Dept. of Sociology. Univ. of Nairobi. Seminar paper 27. Mimeo.
Kenya 1972 March	*Kenya Statistical Digest.* Vol. X no. 1. Central Bureau of Statistics. Nairobi.
Kenya 1977 a	*Integrated Rural Survey 1974–75. Basic Report.* Central Bureau of Statistics. Nairobi.
Kenya 1977 b	"Non-Farm Activities in Rural Kenyan Households". *Social Perspectives* vol. 2 no. 2. Central Bureau of Statistics, Nairobi.
Kenya 1977 c	*Rural Household Survey, Nyanza Province 1970/71.* Central Bureau of Statistics, Nairobi.
Keyonzo, N.A. 1976	*The Social and Economic Implications of Land Adjudication and Registration as it relates to Rural Development. A Case Study in Maragoli (Vihiga).* B.A. Diss. Dept. of Sociology Univ. of Nairobi. Mimeo.
Kimani, S.M. & Taylor, D.R.F. 1973	*The Role of Growth Centres in Rural Development. II. Conclusions and Recommendations.* Institute of Development Studies, W.P. 117, Univ. of Nairobi.
Kitching, G. 1977	"Modes of Production and Kenyan Dependency". *The Review of African Political Economy.* No. 8 London.
Kitching, Gavin 1975	*The Rise of an African Petit-Bourgeoisie in Kenya 1905–1918.* Nairobi. Mimeo.
Kongstad, Per 1978	"Kenyas Industrialisering.", (Kenya's Industrialization), in *Den Ny Verden* 12. årgang nr. 1, Copenhagen. pp. 41–66.
Leitner, Kerstin 1976	'The Situation of Agricultural Workers in Kenya", *The Review of African Political Economy,* no. 6 May-Aug. London.
Leys, Colin 1975	*Underdevelopment in Kenya. The Political Economy of Neo-Colonialism.* London-Nairobi.
Marris, P & Somerset, A. 1971	*African Businessmen.* Nairobi.
Mbithi, P. 1971	*Non-Farm Occupation and Farm Innovation in Marginal, Medium and High Potential Regions of Eastern Kenya and Buganda.* Institute of Development Studies, Univ. of Nairobi. Staff Paper 114. Nairobi.
Mbithi, P. & Barnes, C. 1975	*Spontaneous Settlement Problem in Kenya.* Nairobi.

Meillassoux, Claude 1975	*Femmes, Greniers et Capitaux.* (Women, Granaries and Capitals) Paris.
Memon, P.A. 1975	"Some Geographical Aspects of the History of Urban Development in Kenya", in B.A. Ogot (ed.): *Economic and Social History of East Africa. Hadith 5.* Nairobi.
Moody, Anthony A. 1970	*A Report on Farm Economic Survey of Tea Small-Holders in Bukoba District.* E.R.B. paper 70.8. Dar es Salaam.
Murdock, G.P. 1960	*Social Structure.* New York.
Mutugi, Petterson K. & Gitau, Francis 1975	*Labour Supply in Mwea Rice Irrigation Settlement.* Undergraduate Vacation Research, Dept. of Sociology. Nairobi. Mimeo.
Nelson, Nici 1973	*Buzaa Brewing in Mathare Valley.* Seminar paper. Dept. of Sociology, Univ. of Nairobi. Mimeo.
Nguyo, N. 1966	*Some Socio-Economic Aspects of Land Settlement in Kenya.* East African Universities Social Science Conference, Kampala Vol. IV.
Phillips, Anne 1977	"The Concept of 'Development' ", *The Review of African Political Economy*, no. 8. London.
Pilgrim, J.W. 1959	*Landownership in the Kipsigis Reserve.* Institute of Social Research. Makerere Univ. Kampala. Mimeo.
Richards, Audrey I., Sturrock, Ford & Fortt, Jean M. (eds.) 1973	*Subsistence to Commercial farming in Present-Day Buganda.* Cambridge.
Rural Household Survey	see Kenya 1977
Skinner, G. William 1964	"Marketing and Social Structure in Rural China. Part I–III". *Journal of Asian Studies* vol. 24 Nov. pp. 3–43 and vol. 25 pp. 195–228 and pp. 363–399.
Social Perspectives	See Kenya 1977 b
Steele, David 1972	*The Theory and Practice of the Intermediate Employment Sector.* Institute of Development Studies. Disc. Paper 7. Sussex.
Storgaard, Birgit, Arnfred, Niels & Mululu, Joseph 1971	*Report on the Kibichori Water Scheme.* Århus 1971.
Taha, Abdel Rahman E. Ali 1975	*Employment Problems in the Kenyan Plantations.* J.A.S.P.A. ILO Addis Abeba.
Uzoigwe, U.N. 1975	"Precolonial Markets in Bunyore-Kitara", in B.A. Ogot (ed.): *Economic and Social History of East Africa. Hadith 5.* Nairobi.
Wachtel, Eleanor 1976	"A Farm of One's Own: The Rural Orientation of Women Group Enterprises in Nakuru, Kenya". *Rural Africana* no. 29 Winter 1975–76.
Waweru, Peter Kuna 1974	*Trans Nzoia District – Politics or Government 1963– .* B.A. Diss. Dept. of Government, Univ. of Nairobi. Mimeo.
Wills, Jane 1967	*A Study of Time Allocation by Rural Women and their Place in Decision-Making. Preliminary Findings from Embu District.* RDR 44 Faculty of Agticulture, Makerere Univ. Kampala.
Wills, Jane 1968	*Small Scale Enterprises in Embu District; Beer making, Maize Milling and Water Carting.* RDR 51. Makerere Univ. Kampala. Mimeo.
Winans, E.V. 1972	*Migration and the Structure of Participation. An Investigation of the Effects of Migration on Small Farms and the Role of Rural Women.* Technical Paper for the ILO Mission, Kenya. Nairobi.

Zwanenberg, R.M.A. van 1975 *Colonial Capitalism and Labour in Kenya 1919–1939.* Nairobi.

Zwanenberg, R.M.A. van with King, Anne 1975 *An Economic History of Kenya and Uganda 1800–1970.* Nairobi.

61,25

The idea of this book is to illustrate how work conditions of rural families in Western Kenya change as the market penetrates the household economy.

The emphasis of analysis is on the reproduction of labour in the peasant household. The conditions of reproduction however are increasingly being determined by the market and the changes in land-ownership. The necessity to increase the productivity in agriculture has resulted in an intensified exploitation of family labour, especially that of women. The analysis of labour relations therefore focuses on family labour and the changing work conditions of women as breadwinners, family labourers, traders and casual labourers.

The analysis of household labour processes and exchange relations shows the overall and increasing necessity to engage in market relations. Sixty percent of the average household reproduction takes place via the market. Two chapters present cases of women traders and shopkeepers, illustrating the conditions of local trade in food and industrial necessities.

The consequences of this social process may be seen at two levels. The household as an economic unit may be questioned, as the stable unit of reproducing labour increasingly includes only women and children, while men become more and more marginalized in this process. With the growing inequality of land distribution a progressively increasing number of landless or near-to-be-landless families are being forced to sell their labour in order to be able to buy food.

Scandinavian Institute of African Studies
P.O. Box 2126
S-750 02 Uppsala, Sweden

ISBN 91-7106-164-9
ISNN 0348-5676

Offsetcenter ab
Uppsala 1980